Public Service Broadcasting Online

Palgrave Global Media Policy and Business

Series Editors: **Professor Petros Iosifidis, Professor Jeanette Steemers** and **Professor Gerald Sussman**

Editorial Board: **Sandra Braman, Peter Dahlgren, Terry Flew, Charles Fombad, Manuel Alejandro Guerrero, Alison Harcourt, Robin Mansell, Richard Maxwell, Toby Miller, Zizi Papacharissi, Stylianos Papathanassopoulos, Caroline Pauwels, Robert Picard, Kiran Prasad, Marc Raboy, Chang Yong Son, Miklos Suksod, Kenton T. Wilkinson, Sugmin Youn**

This innovative series examines the wider social, political, economic and technological changes arising from the globalization of the media and communications industries and assesses their impact on matters of business practice, regulation and policy. Considering media convergence, industry concentration, and new communications practices, the series makes reference to the paradigmatic shift from a system based on national decision-making and the traditions of public service in broadcast and telecommunications delivery to one that is demarcated by commercialization, privatization and monopolization. Bearing in mind this shift, and based on a multi-disciplinary approach, the series tackles three key questions: To what extent do new media developments require changes in regulatory philosophy and objectives? To what extent do new technologies and changing media consumption require changes in business practices and models? And to what extent does privatization alter the creative freedom and public accountability of media enterprises?

Benedetta Brevini
PUBLIC SERVICE BROADCASTING ONLINE
A Comparative European Policy Study of PSB 2.0

Karen Donders, Caroline Pauwels and Jan Loisen (*editors*)
PRIVATE TELEVISION IN WESTERN EUROPE
Content, Markets, Policies

Michael Starks
THE DIGITAL TELEVISION REVOLUTION
Origins to Outcomes

Palgrave Global Media Policy and Business
Series Standing Order ISBN 978-1-137-27329-1 (hardback)
(*outside North America only*)

You can receive future titles in this series as they are published by placing a standing order. Please contact your bookseller or, in case of difficulty, write to us at the address below with your name and address, the title of the series and the ISBN quoted above.

Customer Services Department, Macmillan Distribution Ltd, Houndmills, Basingstoke, Hampshire RG21 6XS, England

---

Public Service Broadcasting Online

A Comparative European Policy Study of PSB 2.0

Benedetta Brevini
University of Sydney, Australia

First published 2013 by
PALGRAVE MACMILLAN

Palgrave Macmillan in the UK is an imprint of Macmillan Publishers Limited, registered in England, company number 785998, of Houndmills, Basingstoke, Hampshire RG21 6XS.

Palgrave Macmillan in the US is a division of St Martin's Press LLC, 175 Fifth Avenue, New York, NY 10010.

Palgrave Macmillan is the global academic imprint of the above companies and has companies and representatives throughout the world.

Palgrave® and Macmillan® are registered trademarks in the United States, the United Kingdom, Europe and other countries.

ISBN 978–1–137–29509–5

This book is printed on paper suitable for recycling and made from fully managed and sustained forest sources. Logging, pulping and manufacturing processes are expected to conform to the environmental regulations of the country of origin.

A catalogue record for this book is available from the British Library.

A catalog record for this book is available from the Library of Congress.

Typeset by MPS Limited, Chennai, India.

A mio padre, il mio unico grande maestro.

Contents

List of Figures and Tables

Preface

This book investigates the extent to which a Public Service Broadcasting (PSB) ethos has been extended to the online world in Europe. It examines the most significant policy initiatives carried out by PSBs in Europe on online platforms, and analyses how the public service philosophy is being reinvented by policy-makers at both the national and European level, by PSB institutions and by their competitors. It examines in detail five different European countries as case studies – Denmark, France, Italy, Spain and the UK – in each of which over the last few years PSB has been the object of landmark reforms that have changed their legal and policy frameworks. Concurrently at the European level, the debate about the redefinition and expansion of PSB in the new media has been vigorous.

In March 2009 the French parliament adopted a law that radically changed the financing and organization of France Télévisions (TV Law, 2009). The reform, strongly advocated by Nicolas Sarkozy – the first *téléprésident* of the French republic – has for the first time banned advertising from French PSBs. This move activated an interesting policy transfer process (Dolowitz and Marsh, 2000) in neighbouring Spain, concerning Spanish PSB (RTVE). In March 2010 a new law was adopted in Spain that progressively abolished commercials on RTVE, radically changing the traditional funding system of Spanish PSB (Spanish Law, 2010). Italy has developed a new PSB Charter, and the UK has also seen the implementation of new policies concerning its online activities, following the adoption of a new Charter and Agreement. Moreover, an intense discussion has taken place at the European Commission regarding the adoption of the new Communication on State Aid to PSB (European Commission, 2009), which is impinging on the online expansion of PSBs in Europe. Denmark was the first country to adapt its framework to the new guidance coming from the EC by introducing in 2011 a 'public value test' for the new services of DR, the Danish PSB.

The book is conceived as a comparative policy analysis that explores how the analytical categories derived from political economy and institutionalist traditions have dictated these policies and practices. In particular it identifies how historical/cultural/national legacies, the European framework and commercial pressure from rival competitors mould these policies. In order to add another critical tool of analysis, it elaborates and discusses a normative framework for PSB online in Europe, identified as PSB 2.0.

The book concludes that the development of institutional and national policies on PSB online in Europe is essentially framed by each national context. However, it also demonstrates that the European policy framework has developed a progressively more restrictive attitude towards PSB online, thus potentially accelerating the process of Europeanization and marketization of online PSB policies. The book argues that if the online world is to be infused with the same public service ethos that characterized traditional broadcasting, European policy-makers and institutions need to be persuaded that a reconfiguration of public service values and principles – in other words, PSB 2.0 – is now becoming essential.

Acknowledgements

This work would not have been possible without the moral and practical support and guidance of many people. I am grateful for the feedback and critique I received from professors and policy experts, including Professor Steven Barnett in the UK, Erik Nordahl Svendsen and Christian Nissen in Denmark, Enrique Bustamante in Spain, Francesca Fanucci in Italy and Jean-Claude Sergeant in France. A special thank you to my friends around the world, to my family and in particular to my dad, who taught me to always fight for justice, equality and solidarity.

Finally, I am first and foremost grateful to Paolo, my love, partner and best friend, for having shared hours of conversations that made the often banal process of writing and editing simply the best time of my life.

1
Introduction

In January 2011, the BBC announced that it was to cut its online budget by 25% by 2013. A total of 360 staff in the corporation's online operation would lose their jobs, editorial policies would be redefined and several news blogs as well as local sites would be ditched. Overall, the BBC promised to close half of its 400 Internet domains.

This announcement illustrates graphically the concerns raised in this book about the extent to which a Public Service Broadcasting (PSB) ethos has been extended to the online world. It also demonstrates how relevant and how vital the issues raised in this study are for the continuing democratic and cultural role of PSB. Not only is this research focused on a relevant European media policy problem of our times – namely supporting PSB on the Internet, or shunning its development – but also it provides a useful framework for explaining the contemporary state of PSB online in Europe, and the forces involved in determining its success or failure. Furthermore, this book develops a framework to explain institutional and structural factors at play when the policies on PSB online are developed in Europe.

This study investigates to what extent the values of PSB have been translated into the online world in Europe. It examines the most significant policy initiatives carried out by PSBs in Europe on the new platforms, and analyses how the public service philosophy is being reinvented by policymakers at both the national and European level, by PSB institutions and by their competitors. It examines in detail five different European countries as case studies – the United Kingdom, France, Spain, Italy and Denmark – in each of which over the last few years PSB has been the object of landmark reforms that have changed their legal and policy frameworks. Concurrently at the European level, the debate about the redefinition and expansion of PSB in the new media has been vigorous.

1

In March 2009 the French parliament adopted a law that radically changed the financing and organization of France Télévisions (TV Law, 2009). The reform, strongly advocated by Nicolas Sarkozy – the first *téléprésident* of the French Republic – has for the first time banned advertising from French PSBs.[1] This move has activated an interesting policy transfer process (Dolowitz and Marsh, 2000) in neighbouring Spain. In fact, the French reform triggered the adoption of a very similar policy in Spain concerning Spanish PSB (RTVE). In March 2010 a new law was adopted in Spain that progressively abolished commercials on RTVE, radically changing the traditional funding system of Spanish PSB (Spanish TV Law, 2010). Italy has developed a new PSB Charter, and the UK has also seen the implementation of new and interesting policies concerning its online activities, following the adoption of a new Charter and Agreement.

Moreover, in recent years an intense discussion has taken place at the European Commission (EC) regarding the adoption of the new Communication on State Aid to PSB (European Commission, 2009a) that is impinging on the online expansion of PSBs in Europe.[2] Denmark is the first country to adapt its framework to the new guidance coming from the EC by introducing in 2011 a 'public value test' for the new services of DR, the Danish PSB.

Hence, this analysis aims to provide a valuable insight into the development of national and institutional policies that has shaped PSB online in Europe. But it also attempts to stimulate a debate around the importance of PSB in the online world and elucidates the extent to which the principles traditionally enshrined in PSB in Europe have in fact translated into the new online environment.

Thus, this book addresses three main questions:

1. Which are the main policies adopted by national governments in Europe to develop PSB online? And what are the institutional policies and practices adopted by the PSBs themselves in respect of their Internet activities?
2. What are the key institutional and structural forces moulding these policies across Europe? More specifically, how important are the historical, political and cultural legacies of each nation, the influence of European Union (EU) policies, and pressure from rival commercial competitors in shaping these policies and practices?
3. To what extent has the ethos traditionally enshrined in PSB in Europe in fact been translated into the new online environment? Having outlined the normative values of PSB online (PSB 2.0), has the potential of PSB 2.0 been realized in Europe?

By adding a normative component to the comparative policy analysis, the study seeks to employ another important tool to interpret PSB online and answer Born's call that 'we need to break down the boundaries between normative theories and the design of democratic institutions including media systems suited to democratic pluralism' (Born, 2006: 119).

A normative democratic theory might in fact stimulate a debate around the importance of PSB in the online world and in turn suggest alternatives for improving it. Surely, the structural and institutional factors that will be considered – the historical, political and cultural legacy, the influence of the EU and the commercial pressures – have a bearing on the actual development of the policies under consideration. Nevertheless, a normative theoretical discussion is of great help to ascertain the appropriateness and usefulness of certain policies and practices.

Public Service Broadcasting: Tradition and challenges

As a starting point, it should be clarified that PSB will be framed here as a media policy arrangement. More precisely, since its origin in Western Europe, PSB as a policy framework has been based on a socio-democratic set of beliefs that recognize the crucial function of the State in providing the conditions for an effective social, cultural and political participation in a democratic society.

According to this approach:

> media pluralism and diversity are not necessarily best served by the expansion of commercial media, and there remains a strong role for national public broadcasters, either as the principal bearers of public sphere issues in the national media and communications system, or as an important countervailing influence to the commercial broadcasting sector. (Flew, 2006: 296)[3]

As Van Cuilenburg and McQuail (2003) explain, public service media policy in Europe has been characterized by the following features:

- It is primarily shaped by normative concerns deriving especially from the needs of democratic (thus representative and participatory) politics;
- It is largely bounded by the limits of the national territory and focuses on 'national interests';
- It legitimates government intervention in communication markets for social purposes;

- It generally requires active and continuous policy-making and revision; (Van Cuilenburg and McQuail, 2003)

Thus, Public Service Broadcasters have played a prominent role in the democratic life of Western European countries for decades. They performed a function that has been recognized and reaffirmed by all European institutions. For example, the Protocol on Public Service Broadcasting annexed to the 1997 Treaty of Amsterdam clearly states that:

> The system of public broadcasting in the Member States is directly related to the democratic, social and cultural needs of each society and to the need to preserve media pluralism. (Protocol on PSB, 1997)

Traditionally, PSBs in Europe have been required to fulfil public interest obligations, such as universal coverage, diversity and quality of programming, an appeal to minority groups, an emphasis on local and national content, and a commitment to impartial standards of journalism. Yet, it is important to highlight that each PSB system is developed according to its nation's particular and unique set of historical, cultural and political traditions. Even so, there has been a common rationale behind European PSBs aimed at developing a 'new kind of access to virtually the whole spectrum of public life' (Scannell, 1989: 140).[4]

Throughout its history, the PSB model has showed a remarkable resilience in Europe; PSB institutions have adjusted to ever-changing social and technological changes (Scannell, 1989). Today, the principles behind PSB are facing new challenges posed by convergence, digitalization and global media market pressures (Humphreys, 2006; Helm, 2005; Barnett, 2006). In fact, the traditional role of PSBs as guardians of the public sphere, their impartiality and the quality of their programming is increasingly being undermined by the proliferation of multi-channel platforms, the progressive fragmentation of audiences and increased competition for revenues. Moreover, the recent economic downturn and a cyclical decline in advertising revenues have put the private media sector under aggravated strain around the world. As a consequence, private media enterprises are increasingly demanding that national authorities reduce regulatory control on private enterprises, while raising regulatory oversight on public initiatives and cutting new initiatives within the public sector. The liberal market arguments that see PSBs only as a policy tool to correct 'market failures'[5] are gaining more and more relevance.

If the new digital scenario could on the one hand constitute a threat to PSB, on the other hand it also offers new opportunities for PSBs to realign their democratic role by fostering online participation and new ways of social interaction, as well as exploiting online delivery mechanisms for distribution of traditional content. As will be amply detailed in the next chapter, a broad consensus exists among European institutions about the importance of PSB in the changed environment. Also, since 1994 the Council of Europe has emphasized the importance of public broadcasters exploiting new technologies and offering new media services (Council of Europe 1996, 2007). As a consequence, in the late 1990s, several PSBs in Europe started expanding into the online world (Brügger, 2010) with different paces and ranges of investments, according to the distinct nature of each nation.

Academic research

When this study began, no research that had investigated the policies of PSB online was available. Several studies had focused on exploring the theoretical justifications for maintaining PBS in the new digital era,[6] but none had investigated the policies concerning PSB on the Internet. The only study published at the time was an institutional account by Bakker (2006) on the webcasting offer of the Dutch Public Service Broadcaster (Bakker, 2006). Furthermore, as far as European policies on PSB were concerned, much research had examined the broader framework of European Community audiovisual policies, rather than specifically addressing Member States' policies on PSB in a comparative perspective.[7] Conversely, the studies that concentrated on Member States' PSB policies in a comparative perspective had not directly explored policies on PSB online (see above all Humphreys, 1994, 1996, 2006, 2007, 2009), although they contained some elaborations on PSB online in Europe (Humphreys, 2009; Michalis, 2007). More recently, the only new study that concentrated specifically on PSB online policies in a comparative perspective has focused on Norway, Germany and the UK as case studies (Moe, 2008). Hence, the present comparative study contributes to relevant literature in the field in numerous ways by shedding light on PSBs' online expansion in the north and the south of Europe. Moreover, the elaboration in this study on normative criteria for PSB online and the establishment of the PSB 2.0 policy framework constitutes an important new critical dimension that might stimulate future investigations of online media developments.

The structure of this book

The book is structured as follows:

- Chapter 2 describes the European and global policy framework of PSB. It considers how EU institutions have reaffirmed the prominent role of PSB in developing democratic life. It also explores the more recent policies developed by European institutions to sustain the development of PSBs into the online world. Furthermore, it elucidates the basis of the European regulatory framework developed by the European Commission with its decisions on State Aid to Public Service Broadcasting. Finally, it catalogues the approach of various international bodies to PSB on the Internet, including the World Summit on the Information Society (WSIS), United Nations Educational, Scientific, and Cultural Organization (UNESCO), World Trade Organization (WTO) and Council of Europe (COE).
- Chapter 3 discusses the different sets of literature derived from policy studies, sociology, political philosophy and political economy that inform this book. It also describes the main concepts of these literatures and elaborates on the analytical categories for explaining and understanding the policies of PSB online in Europe.
- Chapter 4 adds a new dimension to policy critique. It examines democratic theories shaping PSB values on the Internet. It then elaborates normative values inherent in a revised definition of PSB that can be applied to the online world and that has become known as PSB 2.0.
- Chapter 5 describes the histories of PSBs in European Member States. It also compares historical developments in broadcasting and technology in all the countries considered as well as their Internet and technological take-up. The analysis explores the considerable differences between the backgrounds in which each institution matured and examines the political, cultural and historical legacies of the DR, BBC, RTVE, RAI and France Télévisions.
- Chapter 6 analyses the national and institutional policies on PSB online in the European states considered. It specifically examines how historical, political and cultural legacies that characterize the ethos of each PSB have impinged on and influenced their online expansion in each case considered. It concludes by demonstrating the clear parallel between PSBs' online and offline activities, in which a typical broadcasting ethos rooted in historical, cultural, political and institutional factors is replicated online.

- Chapter 7 discusses the influence of the EU on national policies of PSB online. In contrast with Chapter 2, it focuses on the most recent policy-making of the European Commission regarding PSB online activities and assesses its impact on domestic PSB policies. It first reviews the most important decisions on State Aid concerning PSB online, and subsequently discusses the newly adopted Communication on State Aid Rules to Public Service Broadcasting (Communication 2009). Finally, it adds an examination of the national and institutional policies of BBC online to reflect the strong influence of the BBC policy framework on Brussels, and the policy transfer between the UK and Brussels.
- Chapter 8 is concerned with the extent to which the pressure from rival commercial competitors has shaped national and institutional policies and practices on PSB online in European states. It shows a very different state of affairs between the north and the south of Europe. In fact, in Denmark the bulk of complaints against DR concentrated on limiting DR's online expansion, while in the south complaints were specifically directed at limiting the type of funding that both RTVE and France Télévisions received from advertising. Hence, the chapter focuses on the two recent reforms of the PSB frameworks in France and Spain and on the policy debates started in Denmark regarding the new agreement between DR and the Danish government.
- Chapter 9 discusses the main conclusions of the book and critically assesses the extent to which the ethos traditionally enshrined in PSB in Europe in fact has been translated into the new online environment.

2
The European and Global Policy Framework of Public Service Broadcasting

This chapter sets the context of the European and global policy framework of PSB. It describes how the European institutions have recognized and supported the role of PSB in European democracies. It also reviews the most important resolutions that have encouraged PSBs' expansion into the online world. Finally, it focuses on global media governance and on debates on PSB in multilateral policy venues including the WSIS, UNESCO, WTO and Council of Europe.

Europe and Public Service Broadcasting

The question of whether PSB should be supported and maintained in the digital era has animated media policy debates in Europe for over a decade (Prosser, 2005; Tambini and Cowling, 2004; Syvertsen, 2003; Harrison and Wessels, 2005). Although some authors detect a constant tendency towards commercialization of European media (McChesney, 2000) and European policies on television are increasingly market-oriented (Harrison and Woods, 2001: 478), 'a general consensus has been revealed about the core values embodied within PSB' (Harrison and Wessels, 2005: 834). In fact, PSB in Europe has been considered as 'a tool of expression of fundamental European values'.[1]

The role of the public service in general is recognized by the Treaties, in particular Articles 16 and 106(2). The interpretation of these provisions in light of the specific nature of the broadcasting sector is provided by the Protocol on Public Service Broadcasting annexed to the 1997 Treaty of Amsterdam, which reaffirms the democratic and cultural value of PSBs (Protocol on PSB, 1997).[2] Accordingly, all European institutions have underlined on several occasions the prominent role of PSB in developing democratic life. For example, the European Parliament in its 'Resolution on the role of public service television in the multi-media society' reaffirmed that PSBs should make further efforts to carry out their duty, 'which will help to build a European and democratic public sphere' (European Parliament, 1996b). Likewise, the Council has stressed the 'social, cultural and democratic functions' of PSB and its 'vital significance for ensuring democracy, pluralism, social cohesion, cultural and linguistic diversity' (Council, 1999)[3] and states that 'broad public access, without discrimination and on the basis of equal opportunities, to various channels and services is a necessary precondition for fulfilling the special obligation of public service broadcasting' (Council, 1999). Furthermore, following the ratification of the Lisbon Treaty on 1 December 2009, the role of Public Services (known as Services of General Interest or SGI) has been boosted by the European Charter of Fundamental Rights (EU Charter, 2000)[4] and by a series of principles contained in a Protocol on SGI that reiterates the fundamental role of Public Services to fulfil the values of the European Community (Protocol on SGI, 2007).

Europe and Public Service Broadcasting online

On a number of occasions European institutions such as the European Parliament and the Council have reaffirmed the relevance of PSB in the new digital era and the importance for PSB to develop online media services. More specifically, EU institutions have claimed that the development of new media is necessary for the fulfilment of PSB's remit.

Likewise, the European Parliament stressed in July and September 1996 that PSB is crucial 'for the development of an information society for all, ensuring the largest possible number of citizens benefit from the potential offered by new services' (European Parliament, 1996a) and that PSB should take a 'lead in the development of new services' (European Parliament, 1996b). In its 1999 Resolution, the Council backed the Parliament's view, stating that 'Public service broadcasting has an important role in bringing to the public the benefits of the new audiovisual and information services and the new technologies,' emphasizing that the 'fulfilment of the Public Service Broadcasting's mission must continue to benefit from technological progress' (Council, 1999) and that 'it is legitimate for public service broadcasting to seek to reach wide audiences' (ibid.).

The necessity for PSB to develop new media services in order to fulfil its remit has been even more encouraged by the new strategy for the Union adopted in the European Council meeting of 2000 in Lisbon. The so-called 'Lisbon Strategy' considered social cohesion as part of the knowledge-based economy to be built in Europe: 'every citizen must be equipped with the skills needed to live and work in this new information society. Different means must prevent info-exclusion' (Council, 2000). Once again, Europe emphasizes that digitalization and the development of new services on the new platforms available are essential to achieve its objectives.

More importantly, in 2001 the European Commission issued one of the most significant documents regarding PSB: the 2001 Communication on the application of State Aid to Public Service Broadcasters that clarifies the meaning and the principles of the Protocol to the Treaty of 1997. In this document, the Commission reaffirms the need for the PSBs to expand online:

> The public service remit might include certain services that are not 'programmes' in the traditional sense, such as on-line information services, to the extent that while taking into account the development and diversification of activities in the digital age they are addressing the same democratic, social and cultural need of the society in question. (European Commission, 2001)[5]

In 2004 the European Parliament once again underlined that PSB should evolve in the new information society to include new digital and online services that are crucial to achieve its remit, since

> to promote cultural diversity in the digital age, it is important that public service broadcasting content reaches the audiences through as many distribution networks and systems as possible; it is therefore crucial for public service broadcasters to develop new media services. (European Parliament, 2004: 24)

It also stressed that:

> the concept of public-service broadcasting is evolving in the converging information society; in addition to traditional television and radio broadcasting the development of new media services is becoming increasingly important in order to fulfil their remit to provide pluralistic content. (ibid.)

Eventually, not just European organizations but also the Council of Europe has indicated the importance for PSB to make use of new technologies and offer new media services. In 1994, with its Resolution n. 1 on the Future of Public Service Broadcasting, the Council of Europe stressed that 'Public Service Broadcasters should be able to exploit new technologies necessary for the fulfilment of their missions' (Council of Europe, 1994). The importance for PSB to expand in the new media is supported again by the 'Recommendation n. 10 of 1996' according to which 'Public Service Broadcasters should be able to exploit new technologies necessary for the fulfilment of their missions' (Council of Europe, 1996). More recently, the 'Recommendation Rec (2007)3 of the Committee of Ministers to Member States on the remit of public service media in the information society' and the 'Recommendation CM/Rec (2007)16 of the Committee of Ministers to Member States on measures to promote the public service value of the Internet' confirmed this approach. Lastly, Recommendation 1878 (Council of Europe, 2009) of the Parliamentary Assembly on the 'Funding of public service broadcasting' reaffirmed that 'Public service broadcasters should diversify their services through thematic channels, on-demand media, recorded media and Internet-based media services in order to offer a comprehensive and competitive range of media services to the public at large in accordance with their public service mission'. However, these Recommendations (Council of Europe, 2009), while representing important policy guidelines for the signees of the European Convention of Human Rights, constitute non-binding agreements for European Member States.

European law and Public Service Broadcasting: The regulatory framework

Despite the determination that the remit of PSB in Europe is still a prerogative of the Member States (Harrison and Woods, 2001; Levy, 1999; Prosser, 2005), each member of the Union is constrained by European competition policy, and more precisely by State Aid rules contained in Art. 106 and 107 of the Treaty on the functioning of the European Community:[6]

> The provisions of the Treaty establishing the European Community shall be without prejudice to the competence of Member States to provide for the funding of public service broadcasting insofar as such funding is granted to broadcasting organisations for the fulfilment of the public service remit as conferred, defined and organised by each Member State, and insofar as such funding does not affect trading conditions and competition in the Community to an extent which would be contrary to the common interest, while the realisation of the remit of that public service shall be taken into account. (Protocol on PSB, 1997)

Art. 107§1EC defines State Aid as

> any aid granted by a Member State or through State resources in any
> form whatsoever which distorts or threatens to distort competition
> by favouring certain undertakings or the production of certain goods
> shall, in so far as it affects trade between Member States, be incom-
> patible with the internal market.[7]

However, the EC Treaty does not impose a total ban on State Aid but
indicates a number of situations in which national measures are allowed
(Psychogiopoulou, 2006) such as 'aid to promote culture and heritage
conservation where such aid does not affect trading conditions and competition in the Community to an extent that is contrary to the common
interest'[8] or in the case of providers of Services of General Interest (SGIs)
in accordance with Art. 106§2 EC.[9] In current practice, judicial decisions
taken by the European Court of Justice[10] and European Commission
determinations 'reveal that assessment of State Aid takes place mainly
on the basis of Article 86 2 EC rather than 87 3 EC' (Psychogiopoulou,
2006: 14). Moreover, with its 2001 Communication on the application
of State Aid to Public Service Broadcasters,[11] the Commission reaffirmed
authoritatively the principles developed in previous decisions and
clarified the conditions under which State Aid for PSBs is legitimate.[12]
However,

> As regards the definition of the public service in the broadcasting
> sector, the role of the Commission is limited to checking for manifest
> error. ... The definition of the public service remit would, however,
> be in manifest error if it included activities that could not reasonably
> be considered to meet – in the wording of the Protocol – 'the demo-
> cratic, social and cultural needs of each society'. That would normally
> be the position in the case of e-commerce, for example. (European
> Commission, 2001, Para. 36)

In conclusion, as Prosser (2005) put it, the European Commission is
prepared to

> to grant a very considerable degree of latitude to Member States in
> defining the public service remit of broadcasters, so long as the defini-
> tion falls within what appears to be a broad concept of meeting the
> 'democratic, social and cultural needs of each society'. What is crucial
> is that a clear definition and a supervisory authority are provided by

a Member State wishing to take advantage of these provisions. (Prosser, 2005: 222)

This conclusion certainly worked as an interpretative framework developed before the most recent policy-making of the European Commission and certainly prior to the approval of the new Communication 2009 on 2 July 2009 (European Commission, 2009). As Chapter 7 explains, the political climate in Brussels has gradually grown more diffident towards PSBs' new media ventures, and it is arguable that has extended its 'check' beyond manifest errors.

PSB online: The global policy context

Before exploring how national and European policies can shape the evolution of PSB on the Internet, it is important to examine its global context. Increasingly, communication policy is enacted within multilateral systems of governance. Global corporations, multilateral organizations and international treaties are progressively diminishing the role of individual states in dealing with these issues, and new international venues are emerging to debate them (Costanza-Chock, 2005). These include the World Summit on the Information Society (WSIS), World Intellectual Property Organization (WIPO), International Telecommunication Union (ITU), United Nations Educational, Scientific, and Cultural Organization (UNESCO), Internet Corporation for Assigned Names and Numbers (ICANN) and the World Trade Organization (WTO).

The following analysis attempts to shed light on debates concerning PSB at a global governance level, and catalogues the approach of various international bodies to PSB on the Internet.

Multilateral discussions of PSB and the Internet

Of all the global forums for media governance, UNESCO has traditionally been considered the most important because of its commitment to foster economic, social, cultural and human rights. As Puppis (2008) rightly observes, UNESCO is expected to deliver 'an alternative perspective on the media' (Puppis, 2008: 416). By stressing the importance of cultural diversity, its activities and direction have been seen as 'a counter-manoeuvre to the free trade doctrine of the WTO' (ibid.: 416).

The UNESCO Convention on the Protection and Promotion of the Diversity of Cultural Expressions of 2007 came into effect on 18 March 2007. This reaffirms the right of nation states to take measures to secure the diversity of their media, and specifically includes the establishment of public service broadcasters. As Iosifidis (2011) observes: 'The convention is based on the core principles of the right to sovereignty, respect for solidarity, human rights, culture and sustainable development' (Iosifidis, 2011: 130). Burri (2010) goes further:

> The UNESCO Convention can be seen on the one hand as the culmination of some previous, mostly exhortatory acts in the fields of culture and trade [41] and cultural heritage [42,43]. On the other hand, and as we stress in the present context, the Convention is a clear reaction to economic globalisation and to the emergence of enforceable multilateral trade rules through the WTO. In both of the above respects, the UNESCO Convention is often said to be a significant success for those state and non-state actors advocating the 'cultural exception' doctrine. (Burri, 2010: 1064)

Accordingly, the convention allows states to adopt measures aimed not only at 'protecting and promoting the diversity of cultural expressions within its territory' (Art. 6.1) but specifically at enhancing the diversity of the media – 'including through public service broadcasting' (Art. 6.2.h).

What it does not discuss is how these goals can be met by PSBs making use of online technologies. Moreover, it has the recognized weakness of lacking any specific binding obligations on the parties (Burri, 2010). Instead, in stark contrast to (for example) the WTO agreements, it 'merely reaffirms the right of states to protect and promote cultural diversity' (Puppis, 2008: 418).

Public Service Broadcasting and GATS

Another powerful multilateral player in global media governance is the WTO, which aims to supervise and eliminate barriers to international trade. General Agreement on Trade in Services (GATS) became effective on 1 January 1995, supplementing the General Agreement on Tariffs and Trade (GATT), and now affects 157 countries. Because GATS deals with regulation of trade in 'services', it is relevant to all electronic media, including telecommunications, audiovisual and database services (Iosifidis, 2011).[13] The current trade negotiation round of the WTO (Doha Development Agenda) – which commenced in November 2001 – has stalled, partly because of disagreement over the agricultural subsidies of the USA and EU. Some countries claim that these market-distorting measures constitute trade barriers for the purposes of WTO agreements, ind it is easy to see how the provision of public service broadcasting could likewise be claimed to discriminate against the services of other rade partners. This is especially true of PSB online, which can cross nternational boundaries more easily than print or radio.

As Costanza-Chock (2005) observes, the WTO has become

> a symbol of corporate globalization because of its closed door decision-making, massive imbalance in influence between the developing countries and the countries of the north, and its attack on public services based on the professed blind faith, not espoused even by mainstream economists, that markets, left to themselves, will serve the needs of all. (Costanza-Chock, 2005: 17)

For now, although no official 'cultural exception' has been clearly inserted in the GATS, its impact on the audiovisual sector has been less extensive than on the telecommunication sector. Canada, Australia and various European countries have exercised their rights under GATS to request specific and temporary exemptions from the most favoured nation (MFN) principle, and have made no commitments to liberalize the audiovisual market. Nevertheless, the WTO's agenda of progressive liberalization and its mission to shrink public subsidies are considered serious threats to PSB institutions around the world.

The World Summit on the Information Society (WSIS)

The World Summit on the Information Society was a two-phase UN-sponsored forum hosted by the International Telecommunication Union (ITU)[14] where industry representatives, governments and civil society organizations met to debate global media policy issues. The first phase took place in Geneva from 10 to 12 December 2003, and the second in Tunis from 16 to 18 November 2005. As Raboy (2004) recalls, the WSIS opened 'a space in which to explore new ways of dealing with global issues, which bodes well for the democratization of communication and its use as a vehicle for human development' (Raboy, 2004: 231).

The WSIS should be regarded as the first UN-backed forum in which civil society players were critically important. But as Sean O'Siochru and Costanza-Chock (2004) have highlighted, power in policy-making is not equally distributed among stakeholders and the weight of industry lobbying on global media governance often overtakes the demands of civil society actors. Still, the participation of civil society groups in the WSIS represented not only 'a call to social justice' but also 'a reflection of and inspiration for global struggles over the right to communicate' (Calabrese, 2004: 324). Explicitly, the Civil Society declaration confirmed:

> that communication is a fundamental social process, a basic human need, and a foundation of all social organizations. Everyone, every-where, at any time should have the opportunity to participate in communication processes and no one should be excluded from their benefits. (Civil Society Declaration to the WSIS, 2003)

Although the WSIS has no direct normative impact on policies concerning public media, its ethos lies closer to that of UNESCO and the Council of Europe than to the vision of global media governance dominant in the 1990s and still prevailing today – that of the WTO, which considers culture as merely another commodity for international trade.

Council of Europe and Public Service Broadcasting on the Internet

As this sketch of multilateral decision-making and its impact on PSB online has shown, several UN/UNESCO-backed initiatives for media democratization and promotion of culture have considered PSB as a potential vehicle for their goals, but none have specifically examined addressed the expansion of PSB on to the Internet.

The international institution that seems the most concerned with the future of PSB in a digital and networked economy is the Council of Europe (COE). One of the most important initiatives is Recommendation 2007/3c of the Committee of Ministers to Member States on the remit of public service media in the information society.

In this document, the COE assigns to PSB a renewed and substantial role in the new information society. It recommends that Member States enable PSB to 'use new technical means to better fulfil this remit and adapt to rapid changes' (Council of Europe, 2007: Para. i).

Two years later, with its Recommendation 1878 (2009), the Parliamentary Assembly of the COE restated the idea that PSB online can foster universality, both in terms of diversity and 'inclusion'. Thus, the Recommendation recognizes and reaffirms the principles of the 2007 UNESCO convention previously discussed. But it also specifically refers to a new role for PSB; according to the Recommendation, public service broadcasters should

> ... utilise new technologies to increase the accessibility of their services and offer new services including interactive and on-demand

media services on all available platforms so as to reach all audiences, and in particular young people. (Council of Europe, 2009: Para. 17.2)

It further specifies that

> ... public service broadcasters should diversify their services through thematic channels, on-demand media, recorded media and Internet-based media services in order to offer a comprehensive and competitive range of media services to the public at large in accordance with their public service mission. Technological progress in the field of audiovisual media and electronic communications means that public service broadcasters should also make use of new technologies. (ibid.: Para. 9)

The COE thus makes a significant claim: that if the Internet can actually *enhance* and *improve* the ability of PBS to perform its public service functions, then broadcasters have a duty to make the best possible use of it.

Four international mandates on freedom of expression and PSB

There are four special international mandates on freedom of expression: the UN Special Rapporteur on Freedom of Opinion and Expression; the OAS (Organization of American States) Special Rapporteur on Freedom of Expression; the ACHPR (African Commission on Human and Peoples' Rights) Special Rapporteur on Freedom of Expression and Access to Information; and the OSCE (Organization for Security and Co-operation in Europe) Representative on Freedom of the Media. Together, these mandates adopt every year a Joint Declaration that lays out their crucial concerns for freedom of expression worldwide.

In their 2007 Joint Declaration, these mandates stressed the importance of public service broadcasters and specifically added that 'special measures are needed to protect and preserve public service broadcasting in the new broadcasting environment.' (Joint Declaration, 2007). Later, in their 2010 Joint Declaration, they expressed concern that the role of PSB was coming under threat. In a declaration on Ten Key Threats to Freedom of Expression (Joint Declaration, 2010), they refer to 'increasingly frequent challenges to public funding support for public broadcasters' – exacerbated by the global economic crisis.

Conclusion

While numerous international bodies have debated and affirmed the need for a free and plural media – and specifically cited public service broadcasting as a way to achieve this – few have caught up with the impact of the Internet. With projects and discussions taking years to complete, perhaps this should not be surprising. But it is clear that the use of new technologies by PBS is consistent with the function established for it within international frameworks. Moreover, non-binding but influential bodies have specifically addressed the expansion of PBS on to the Internet, and the Council of Europe in particular has resoundingly affirmed the part that new technology has to play in extending PBS to reach, serve and include all corners of society.

That said, agreements of the WTO potentially threaten the provision of public service broadcasting, as do the government pressures outlined by the 2007 Joint Declaration of special rapporteurs. In light of the global financial crisis, public broadcasters make easy targets for politicians seeking cuts to government budgets.

Yet, this chapter has also showed the wide consensus expressed by all European institutions on the importance of PSB in Europe. It has also illustrated the strong support expressed by European bodies towards PSB expansion into the online world within the constraints of the regulatory framework developed by European Commission decisions on State Aid and by the Court of Justice of the European Union.

3
Theorizing Public Service Broadcasting Online

Introduction

The field of media and communication policy research encompasses a variety of theoretical approaches derived from traditional disciplines, such as political science, sociology, economics and law. Hence, each of these fields has contributed to diverse theoretical accounts of how media policies are shaped and developed. This chapter highlights the main concepts of these literatures and sets out the analytical categories for explaining and understanding the policies of PSB online in Europe. Furthermore, the following chapter revisits and explores democratic theories shaping PSBs' values on the internet. It then sets out normative criteria in order to add a new dimension of policy critique.

New institutionalism and the political economy of communication

The underlying hypothesis of this study is drawn from a combination of New Institutionalism and the political economy of the media: in order to explain and understand media policies, a systematic attention to institutions, social actors and structures is needed. New Institutionalism,[1] usually associated with the scholarly work of March and Olsen (1984) or Hall (1986) places a particular emphasis on institutions as the principal factors shaping policy.[2] Moreover, 'whereas the earlier institutionalism militates against cross-national comparisons, this approach utilizes them to identify the most salient institutional determinants of policy' (North: 20).

This approach therefore clearly rejects what has been called the 'interest group approach to policy', which explains policy as the outcome of competing powerful interest groups' preferences (Schlosberg, 1998). According to Galperin:

> The basic unit of analysis is a social aggregation called the interest group, whose preferences are typically determined by its long-term economic interests. [...] In this approach, policy outcomes are typically explicated by the organization and the resources available to interest groups and their support coalitions. (Galperin, 2004: 160)

Moreover, the technological approach to policy is also discarded. This research strand sees technology as the critical determinant of communication policies and has been frequently employed by techno-enthusiasts and official publications issued by international organizations and government agencies (e.g. Bangemann, 1994). By contrast, this research holds that the new scenarios opened by new technologies are moulded by political, economic and cultural factors (Freedman, 2002; Mansell, 1996; Syvertsen, 2003; Williams, 1974, 1985), and that considering technology as the most important variable would mean overlooking the complex system of structures and institutions that affect policy change. As Galperin puts it: institutions and social actors are key mediators between technological innovation and policy reforms, which ultimately makes the outcome more unpredictable than many would like to think, or preach (Galperin, 2004: 162).

The second theoretical account that informs this study is the political economy of communication,[3] which shares with New Institutionalism the same concerns for meta-determinants of policy outcomes, but also stresses a particular emphasis on structural, political and economic factors.

Today, political economy still defines itself as the study of how values of all kinds are produced, exchanged and consumed (economic); how power is produced, distributed, exchanged and exercised (political); and how these aspects of the social world are related at any given place and time in history (Graham, 2005: 2).

The ambitions of a political economy approach are high, as it aims to explore 'the wider totality of capitalist social relations' (Mosco, 1996: 263) and to engage in the basic 'moral question of justice, equality and public good' (Golding and Murdock, 2001: 72). Thanks to its holistic approach and its ambition to explain 'social totality', this tradition has always recognized the crucial importance of the State's action in the formation of media systems. Hence, it can offer useful concepts to frame the policies on the expansion of PSB online.

The following sections describe some fundamental concepts derived from policy studies that shaped the analytical categories of the theoretical framework.

Policy: Decision, output and outcome

At this point, a definition of what should be considered to be 'policy' needs to be provided. Defining policy has never been an easy task in the literature (Colebatch, 2002; Hogwood and Gunn, 1984). For some, policy is 'what governments do, why they do it, and what difference it makes' (Dye, 1976: 1). However, governments are not the only bodies that produce policy, and certainly this approach would not be beneficial to this study. In fact, 'there are policies in which at least one of the major actors is an international organization' (Karagiannis and Radaelli, 2007: 7). But there are also policies developed by independent regulatory bodies, public institutions and trade organizations (Galperin, 2004).

Hogwood and Gunn (1984) identify different uses of the word policy: policy as a label for a field of activity (for example, economic or social policy); policy as an expression of general purpose or desired state of affairs; policy as a specific proposal; policy as a decision of government; policy as a formal authorization; policy as a programme of activity; policy as output, or 'what a government actually delivers as opposed to what it has promised or has authorized through legislation' (Hogwood and Gunn, 1984: 16); and policy as outcome, 'in terms of what is actually achieved' (ibid.: 17).

A common model applied to the study of policy is the 'cycle model' (Colebatch, 2002: 55), which sees policy-making as a sequence of stages: 'agenda setting (problem recognition); policy formulation (proposal of a solution); decision-making (choice of a solution); policy implementation (delivery); and policy evaluation (checking the results)' (Howlett and Ramesh, 2003: 10).

Yet, it should be noted that, in reality, the policy-making process is more articulated than the cycle model assumes. In fact, stages may not follow the predicted order or may be omitted. As Hogwood and Gunn (1984) observe: 'in practice, of course, policy is often a seamless web involving a bewildering mesh of interactions and ramifications' (Hogwood and Gunn, 1984: 26). If we consider, for example, the last two stages of the model, 'policy delivery and impact are rarely a matter of straight-line relationship between a single policy instrument or organization interacting with its environment to produce a clear-cut impact' (ibid.: 17).

Therefore, as Karagiannis and Radaelli (2007) point out, 'to assume perfect implementation is highly unrealistic. Negotiations and adaptation prevail over the goals set by the legislator. Redistribution, distribution and regulation are not perfect contracts. Rules are enforced in real-world settings, where inspectors and firms interact and specify the meanings of what are often abstract and vague norms. Goals have to be clearly defined and understood, resources made available and the system able to communicate effectively to control those individuals and organizations involved in the performance of tasks' (Karagiannis and Radaelli, 2007: 22).

Thus, this study embraces a comprehensive approach that takes into account all the complexities built into policy-making without neglecting the fact that 'much political activity is concerned with maintaining the status quo and resisting challenges to the existing allocation of values' (Ham and Hill, 1993: 12).

Path dependency and political cultures against policy convergence

From the institutionalist and political economy framework that I have established, other important analytical notions need to be defined. I have explained how the fundamental assumption of this study is that PSB online policies are shaped by different structural and institutional forces. Another interesting question that arises is the extent to which these constraints drive PSB online policies towards convergence or whether national differences prevail.

New Institutionalism is particularly fruitful in this regard, because it highlights the persistence of policy: 'The context of modern social policy begins to flesh out one major theme: the considerable impact of policy inheritances upon the substance of policy-making' (Heclo, 1974: 63). This argument is often referred to as *path dependency*, which implies a great resistance of institutions to change and the persistence of certain institutional legacies on policy (ibid.). As Peters and Desmond (2005) explain:

> Apparently small choices in institutional arrangements can have remarkable consequences at a later date (regardless of whether they were adopted purposefully or unthinkingly), and ... some policy choices may prove almost irreversible. (Peters and Desmond, 2005: 1287)

Accordingly, Storsul and Syversten, studying the factors leading to convergence in European television policy, argue that we should look at 'institutional legacies, politics and cultural values' (Storsul and Syversten, 2007: 278) as three factors that can modify and limit the impact of technological change. For them, 'institutional and regulatory arrangements are, as a whole, resilient to change, and ... the forces of stability are often underestimated in media policy research' (ibid.: 278).

The concept of path dependency, therefore, constitutes an important analytical category for this study. It can help frame the question of the extent to which the institutional and structural forces impacting PSBs' online policies are operating as a deterrent to policy convergence. Or are national peculiarities still prevailing?

Like Storsul and Syversten (2007), other authors have stressed the high impact of politics on the field of broadcasting policies. Levy, for example, observes that 'broadcasting's peculiar resistance to policy convergence owes much to its institutional structure and intense politicization' (Levy, 1997: 37).[4] Hence, 'this politicization has led to a strong desire to control the policy process and outcomes in a way that has limited the scope for technocratic decision-making and inhibited cross-national policy convergence and Europeanization' (ibid.: 38).

Therefore, Levy argues that national peculiarities in the specific field of broadcasting will prevail. He concludes that technological change alone – even as dramatic as digitalization – seems unlikely to undermine the belief of politicians that the cultural and political impact of broadcasting dictate that most regulation must be decided according to priorities established within each Member State (Levy, 1997: 38).

Humphreys (1996, 2006) and Hallin and Mancini (2004) have drawn a similar conclusion to Levy (1997, 1999). For Humphreys (2006), because of its more politically and culturally sensitive character, broadcasting regulation has remained much more domestically 'embedded' than telecoms. For Hallin and Mancini (2004), by contrast, 'politics has played a key role in defining the shape of national broadcasting systems' (Hallin and Mancini, 2004: 111).

Policy transfer and the limits of national peculiarities

Besides the institutional and structural forces that constrain policies within their historical and political paths, there are also pressures that strengthen the potential for change. Hence, policy transfer or policy convergence (Dolowitz and Marsh, 2000; Bennett, 1991) refers to a dynamic where 'knowledge about how policies, administrative arrangements, institutions and ideas in one political setting (past or present) is used in the development of policies, administrative arrangements, institutions and ideas in another political setting' (Dolowitz and Marsh, 2000: 5). According to Bennett (1991), four causes of convergence can be identified: emulation; elite networking; harmonization; and penetration. *Emulation* involves 'the utilization of evidence about a programme or programmes from overseas and a drawing of lessons from that experience' (Bennett, 1991: 221). *Elite networking* refers to the 'existence of shared ideas among a relatively coherent and enduring network of elites engaging in regular interaction at the transnational level' (ibid.: 224). *Harmonization* arises 'through the coincident recognition and resolution of a common problem through the pre-existing structures and processes of an international regime' (ibid.: 225). Finally, convergence through *penetration* refers to a situation where national governments 'are forced to conform to actions taken elsewhere by external actors' (ibid.: 229), such as international organizations.

Certainly, policy transfer has received growing attention recently, especially in areas of policies where technological pressures for change are strong. Yet, as highlighted in the first section of the chapter, technology alone cannot explain the policy outcome. As Bennett points out, while 'the technology frames the context of policy choice, authoritative decisions are only made by political actors who develop critical views about that technology' (Bennett, 1988: 427).

Finally, as Galperin explains:

> While new technologies enable some choices and preclude others, policy outcomes ultimately depend on the interaction between the attributes of innovations and the permeability of existing regimes for change. (Galperin, 2004: 162)

The concept of Europeanization

The issue of policy convergence is strictly connected to another important concept that needs to be defined: Europeanization. Yet, as Radaelli (2004) warns

> Europeanisation is not convergence. Even in cases of convergence, the pattern is more one of clustered convergence (Börzel, 2002; Goetz, 2002) than of uniform convergence across Europe. The idea is that countries with the same structural characteristics respond with similar strategies to the opportunities and constraints provided by Europeanisation. (Radaelli, 2004: 14)

There is a vast body of literature in existence on Europeanization and its meanings (e.g. Radaelli, 2000, 2003, 2004; Börzel, 1999; Cowles et al., 2001; Harcourt, 2002). For Börzel (1999), Europeanization is a 'process by which domestic policy areas become increasingly subject to European policy-making' (Börzel, 1999: 574). Yet, Featherstone (2003: 6–12) explains that although the term is often used as an 'adaptation of policies and policy processes', it has also been utilized as a 'historic phenomenon', and as an 'institutional adaptation'.[5]

Radaelli (2004) provides a very thorough explanation of the concept:

> Europeanisation consists of processes of (a) construction, (b) diffusion and (c) institutionalisation of formal and informal rules, procedures, policy paradigms, styles, 'ways of doing things' and shared beliefs and norms which are first defined and consolidated in the EU policy process and then incorporated in the logic of domestic (national and subnational) discourse, political structures and public policies. (Radaelli, 2004: 3)

Harcourt (2002: 737) elucidates that Europeanization can be achieved through two different mechanisms: the first is a 'top-down' mechanism, 'wherein the European institutions mandate the form that national policy choices should take'. She goes on to explain that:

> This mechanism can occur in two ways: either directly, whereby national governments comply with EU mandates, or indirectly, whereby domestic policy-makers – once their frameworks are Europeanized – bring national policy in line with EU options even in the absence of a direct compulsion from Brussels. (Harcourt, 2002: 737)

The second mechanism of Europeanization is defined as 'bottom-up', which occurs when specific policy schemes developed in a Member State are then transferred to the European level. Once again, this mechanism can operate in two ways:

> either formally, whereby a national court refers decision making to the European Court of Justice (ECJ); or informally, whereby domestic policy-makers attempt to influence debates at the EU level in order to steer domestic policy choices at home. (Harcourt, 2002: 737)

The framework of this study focuses on both processes: the process through which national regulatory frameworks are brought into line with EU policy and the process through which Member States seek to export ideas and policy models to the EU.

Despite the 'national political and cultural sensitivities' that – as described in the preceding section – characterize broadcasting policy, both Harcourt (2005) and Humphreys (2006) detect a certain degree of policy convergence in the field of broadcasting in Europe. Harcourt claims that all EU institutions 'have played a decisive role in shaping both the development of national media markets and the direction of national media policies' (Harcourt, 2005: 193). For Humphreys, while the level of convergence in the EU has been stronger in telecoms policy, broadcasting policy has also converged: 'in responding to the challenges of adapting regulation to technological change [...] there was pressure on Member states to adopt a pragmatic, technocratic problem solving rather than a politicized, bargaining approach to negotiations' (Humphreys, 2006: 326).

However, Humphreys makes clear that regulatory harmonization in the EU has progressed at a greater speed in the technocratic sector of telecommunications than in the 'politically sensitive' (Humphreys, 2006: 305) broadcasting sector. This conclusion brings the author in line with Radaelli's (2004) conclusion, which is based on several empirical studies that found that: 'The evidence on the Europeanisation of public policy is more robust than the evidence on the Europeanisation of political competition, state structures, and the polity domain. Some policies are more impermeable than others to "Europe" (Bulmer and Radaelli, 2004: 14), as shown by the difference between competition and environmental policy, on the one hand, and higher education and justice, on the other' (Radaelli, 2004).

Marketization

Since the 1980s, the shift towards a progressive liberalization and marketization of media policy in Europe has been well documented (Humphreys, 1996, 2007; Levy, 1999; Hallin and Mancini, 2004). There is also a broad consensus on the overall 'marketizing' character (Humphreys, 1996: 174) of EU broadcasting policies (Katsirea, 2008; Michalis, 2007; Harcourt, 2005). As Murdock and Golding (1999) put it:

> over the last decade and a half, the terms of the debate about the future of European Communications and the balance of power between the main actors involved in its reconstructions have shifted decisively under the impact of two parallel movements: the ascendancy

of marketization policies within both the European Union and its major member states and accelerating convergence of the computing, telecommunications and audiovisual industries. (Murdock and Golding, 1999: 118)

How can we define the process of marketization of policy? The political economy of the media tradition provides some of the most accomplished accounts. Murdock and Golding (1999) explain that:

> By marketization we mean all those policy interventions designed to increase the freedom of action of private corporations and to institute corporate goals and organizational procedures as the yardstick against which the performances of all forms of cultural enterprise are judged. (Murdock and Golding, 1999: 118)

The two authors thereafter distinguish five dimensions of the process of marketization of policies:

- The first dimension is *privatization*: 'the sale of public communication assets to private investors' (ibid.: 118) that has characterized in particular the telecommunication sector, but also the broadcasting sector. A clear example of this could be the sale in 1986 of the most important PSB in France – TF1 (Kuhn, 1995; Humphreys, 1996; Levy, 1997).
- The second dimension is *liberalization*: 'the introduction of competition into monopoly markets or its extension in markets with limited competition' (Murdock and Golding, 1999: 119). Here, examples can draw on the introduction in all European countries of new commercial channels alongside the existing terrestrial channels.
- The third dimension is *corporatization*: that is, 'encouraging or compelling organizations still within the public sector to pursue market opportunities and institute corporate forms of organization' (ibid.: 119).
- The fourth dimension identified consists of *moving from licensing to auctions* (ibid.: 119).
- Finally, the fifth entails *reorienting the regulatory system* designed at increasing 'corporate access to markets and enhance their freedom of action within them' (ibid.: 119).

As outlined in the Introduction, public service media have been among the institutions that have suffered the most through market pressures in the last decades (Humphreys, 1996; Levy, 1999; Michalis, 2007).

Therefore, the marketization hypothesis provides this study with another important tool to test the impact of the pressure coming from the commercial world on the development of PSB policies on the Internet.

Comparing media systems and PSB policies

In conducting the analysis of the five countries under scrutiny, the framework for classifying media system developed by Hallin and Mancini (2004) can be useful. The three models identified by Hallin and Mancini (2004: 67) are:

- The 'Mediterranean or Polarized Pluralistic model', represented by countries of Southern Europe, with low circulation of print media, high levels of political parallelism, weak professionalization, a strong state intervention and politicized public service broadcasting.
- The 'Northern European or Democratic Corporatist model', corresponding to Scandinavian countries, Germany, the Netherlands, Austria, Belgium and Switzerland. This is characterized by early development of the press, a shift towards a neutral commercial press, strong institutionalized professionalism, strong state intervention and strong public service broadcasting.
- The 'North Atlantic or liberal model' (typical of the USA, the UK, Canada and Ireland) is distinguished by early development of the press, limited political parallelism, non-institutionalized journalistic professionalism and weak state intervention with the exception of public broadcasting in the UK and Ireland.

Although these broad models can be helpful in a selection of cases that move from particular explanations to more general ones, they constitute just the starting point of my analysis. In fact, the cases under examination show subtle and important divergences even within the same cluster that a wide model could certainly not expose. Hence, the five States selected present relevant differences in terms of institutional historical and political legacies. Yet, they are all are Member States of the European Union and therefore are all subject to the EU framework.

Denmark certainly fits within the Northern European or Democratic Corporatist model proposed by Hallin and Mancini (2004), while Spain and France and Italy are assigned to the Mediterranean. By contrast, Britain fits within the North Atlantic or liberal model. However, the significant discrepancies between the PSBs policies of France, Spain or Italy cannot be overlooked. Spain's PSB, Television Española (TVE), was implemented in 1956 during the dictatorship of Francisco Franco (1939–1975), when competition was introduced into the Spanish media system. TVE has been assigned to a secondary place in the market, with a highly commercial orientation and scarce financial resources (Rodriguez-Pardo, 2006). By contrast, France Télévisions and RAI have enjoyed a stronger position in their respective markets, even though from the 1980s, under the pressure of commercial competition, they both developed a more commercial outlook. Denmark, on the other hand, is small Northern European country, with one of the most successful examples of PSB in terms of its political support, independence and quality. Furthermore, Denmark stood in top place in the IT world, according to the *Global Information Technology Report 2008–2009* released by the World Economic Forum in March 2009.

Conclusion

As explained in this chapter, the theoretical framework of the study draws upon different sets of literature from policy studies, sociology, political philosophy and political economy. In particular, the New Institutionalist and political economy traditions offer the essential hypothesis of this study and provide different concepts that will guide the level of analysis. The following chapter reviews normative theories of democracy and constructs a normative framework for PSB online in order add another fruitful dimension of investigation.

4
A Normative Framework for PSB Online: The Idea of PSB 2.0

By adding a normative component to the policy analysis, the theoretical framework has been complemented with another important tool to interpret the empirical findings. In fact this study seeks to take on board and develop Born's (2006) suggestion that:

> From a policy perspective, we need to take political philosophies seriously to realize that they offer tangible bases on which to construct institutional arrangements; but also to acknowledge that our existing institutions embody political philosophies that themselves deserve scrutiny and updating. (Born, 2006: 119)

In taking up this challenge, this book aims to stimulate a debate around the importance of PSB in the online world and enhance a reflection on the extent to which the principles traditionally enshrined in Public Service Broadcasting in Europe have translated into the new online environment. This chapter therefore aims to establish a normative framework for PSB online, which has been named PSB 2.0.

PSB 2.0: The four normative criteria

Defined as a tool of expression of fundamental European values, Public Service Broadcasting has often been investigated from the point of view of the institutions, and more often the corporations that carry the remit (Jacubowicz, 1999; Blumer, 1992).[1] Hence, definitions of PSB have always been focused on delineating their set of obligations and legal and financial arrangements (Baldi and Hasebrink, 2007; Collins, 2007).[2] But, as explained in the Introduction, this study frames PSB as a media policy arrangement. Therefore PSB 2.0 becomes a media policy instrument (Syversten, 2003) based on a set of normative values that aims to fulfil the democratic, social and cultural needs of the society by transferring traditional PSB ethos online.

More precisely, PSB 2.0 is not limited to a technocratic definition that might relate it just to PSB online services boosted by the participation architecture of Web 2.0.[3] Rather, PSB 2.0 involves a set of new policies regarding online media – a phase 2.0 of PSB – inspired by the PSB ethos. Evidently, the idea of PSB 2.0 clashes with dominant liberal market ideologies that see liberalization and deregulation as the logical consequences of new technological development. According to this logic, the Internet – given its intrinsic democratizing potential and its interactive and 'liberating' nature – would be able to perform traditional PSB functions regardless of ownership or economic structure (Gilder, 2000; Negroponte, 1998).

In fact, for many technology enthusiasts, the new communicative opportunities opened by the Internet would lead to a certain expansion of dialogue, to an enhancement of democracy and citizenship and to an improved community exchange (Fukuyama, 1999).[4] Furthermore, by offering more unmediated opportunities for citizens to participate in the public sphere through online, mobile and other interactive technologies, the Internet offers new prospects for information exchange beyond the traditional information gate-keepers of the press and broadcasting. In particular, the growth of non-professionalized news-gathering and reporting – usually known as 'user-generated content' or 'citizen journalism' – has arguably led to a democratization of news and information sources (Beckett, 2008).

However, there have been growing concerns on a number of levels about the efficacy of these claims about the new opportunities offered by the Internet. For some authors, the Internet is progressively dominated by business interests and commercial purposes (Murdock, 2004). A variety of computer-science studies have raised concerns about access to information on the Web (Introna and Nissenbaum, 2000), and, for example, showed that search engine results tend to be biased towards larger, commercial and well-funded websites (Vaughan and Thelwall, 2004; Lawrence and Giles, 1999). More recently, Curran and Witschge (2009) have further challenged the assumption that the Internet is enhancing democracy because it makes available a vast sum of public information. They demonstrate that: '... the internet is used primarily for entertainment rather than for news and political information (Ofcom, 2007b: 90; Hill and Hughes, 1998). The most visited news websites, as in Britain and the USA, are the websites of the dominant national new organizations (Ofcom, 2007a; McChesney, 2008), with national news priorities' (Curran and Witschge, 2009: 103).

The same authors conclude their study of the open Democracy website – an example of a collaborative online platform for political and cultural debates – with the pessimistic analysis that:

> the international space between commercial and state-linked media – between CNN and BBC World News, the Economist and Al Jazeera – is not sustained by an online revenue stream that will enable new ventures to grow and flourish. (Curran and Witschge, 2009: 117)

Hence, it can be argued that the advocates for deregulation in the field of new media, on the basis of the Internet's allegedly democratizing nature, base their argument on a conception of a media marred by market forces that are disguised as technological determinism (Williams, 1974, 1985). By contrast, the political economy tradition has demonstrated that the scenarios opened by new technologies are always moulded by political, economic and cultural factors (Freedman, 2002; Mansell, 1996; Syvertsen, 2003; Williams, 1974, 1985). In fact, technology is not autonomous from society; hence the meaning and the impact of technology should be examined in a broader social context, as 'a technology is always, in a full sense, social' (Williams, 1981: 227). Accordingly, PSB 2.0 is constructed as a policy arrangement based on a set of normative values that derive from a revised definition of PSB that can extend to the online world.

As the literature has shown, there is a certain consensus on the specific defining criteria of PSB (Born and Prosser, 2001; Scannell, 1989) that intended to develop a 'new kind of access to virtually the whole spectrum of public life' (Scannell, 1989: 140). Born and Prosser (2001) identify these elements in principles of citizenship, universality and quality (Born and Prosser, 2001: 671). This certainly constitutes a useful construction, which could offer a valid starting point for the development of PSB 2.0. However, these values behind PSB need to be reinterpreted and adjusted to PSB on the Internet. Therefore, this chapter sets out to explore four normative criteria for PSB 2.0: citizenship, universality, quality and trust.

Citizenship for PSB 2.0: Setting the context

The connection between citizenship and PSB has frequently been emphasized by scholars (e.g. Helm, 2005; Graham, 2005; Raboy, 1996). As Raboy maintains:

> In a broadcasting environment that treats the public as a body of clients or consumers, the role of public broadcasting is to address people as citizens. (Raboy, 1996: 9)

But what do we mean by citizenship? And what is the type of citizenship at the basis of PSB 2.0? Harrison and Woods (2001) offer a traditional definition:

> citizenship is usually a status in relation to a given community determined by law, in that the law will set out the qualifications required for entry to that community and outline the rights and duties of citizens. (Harrison and Woods, 2001: 474)

As it will be discussed in the following section, this definition echoes Roman law with its conception of citizenship as a legal status. However, as it is important to take into account that in a modern democracy:

> There is no necessary minimum content to citizenship, although citizens cannot be granted a lower level of protection than that awarded by fundamental human rights, which are inalienable and awarded to all. (Harrison and Woods, 2001: 474)

There also exist much narrower definitions of citizenship. For authors who advance a consumerist perspective, citizenship equals the sum of individual and consumer choices (Negroponte, 1998). As the argument goes, the increase of consumer choices offered, for example, by the Internet, would be a guarantor of contemporary democracies. However, the consumerist argument reduces democratic choices to market choices, a position that overlooks the need for common experience and common ground (Sustein, 2007). The insistence of providing citizens with broadened consumer choices neglects the fact that citizens 'might want to make choices that diverge from those that they make in their capacities as private consumers' (Sustein, 2007: 127).

Elliot (1982) noted that this restricted notion of citizenship was gaining ground in public policy debates. He claimed that western democratic societies were facing:

> a continuation of the shift away from involving people in society as political citizens of nation states towards involving them as consumption units in a corporate world. (Elliot, 1982: 244)

Elliot's view has been backed by a plethora of political economists who underline how, at many levels of democratic life, we can trace a progressive shift towards the imperatives of the market (Mosco, 1996; McChesney, 2000). An obvious example of this shift is the growing importance of corporate lobbies' power in today's political decision-making

(Freedman, 2008). Dahlgren succinctly summarizes this ongoing transformation of citizenship by declaring that 'democracy is increasingly being reconfigured, in conceptual and rhetorical terms, to make it compatible with a corporate view of societal development' (Dahlgren, 2008: viii). He then concludes with an alarming forecast: 'Democracy will become increasingly reduced to market choice' (ibid.: viii).

Thus, in order to elaborate a notion of citizenship that expresses the philosophy of PSB 2.0, citizenship needs to be assigned a broadened value, rather than being reduced to the instances of liberal individualism (Born and Prosser, 2001).

The 'citizens versus consumers' paradigm

The concept of the citizen has been often conceived in a Manichean opposition to the notion of the consumer. As Lewis clarifies:

> Unlike the citizen, the consumer's means of expression is limited: while citizens can address every aspect of cultural, social and economic life, consumers find expression only in the marketplace. (Lewis, 2003)

In fact, the idea of the citizen entails, on the one hand, a horizontal relationship between citizens, with an emphasis on equality principles, and on the other hand, a vertical dimension, which refers to the relations between citizens and their states (Clarke et al., 2007). This notion of the consumer has its domain only in economic relationships, where consumers are 'engaged in economic transactions in the marketplace, exchanging money for commodified goods and services. The individual is self-directing, capable of choosing how their own well-being may be best served' (Clarke et al., 2007: 2).

This radical opposition between the two notions can be helpful to assess which interests have been prioritized in recent development of media systems around the world. Significantly, consumer-driven and market-failure arguments for regulating the media are prevailing in the progressive deregulation of communications throughout Europe. However, the radical conceptual juxtaposition of the ideas of citizen and consumer are to be understood as a consequence of the sociological attempt to defend citizenship from the 'vagaries of the market'. In fact, according to Turner,

> Sociologists have been concerned to understand how the institutions of citizenship protect individuals and groups from the negative

outcomes and unintended vagaries of the market in capitalist society. (Turner, 1997)

However, this study argues that citizenship should be redefined as not negatively opposed to the notion of consumer. On the contrary, it is important to move towards a positive notion of citizenship to offer a normative framework for PSB 2.0.

Yet, very often in contemporary media policy-making, the notion of citizenship seems to be out of fashion. For example, in its document 'Citizens, communication and convergence' (2008), the independent broadcasting regulator in the UK, Ofcom, points out that 'the need for Ofcom to consider separately the interests of citizens and consumers stems from section 3(1) of the Communications Act 2003. This requires Ofcom to

(a) further the interests of citizens in relation to communications matters;
(b) further the interests of consumers in relevant markets, where appropriate by promoting competition (Ofcom, 2008).

However, Ofcom also acknowledges that:

> It is notable that the section sets out a mechanism for furthering consumers' interests – promoting competition – although it is recognised that this will not always be appropriate. The Act does not specify a particular mechanism for furthering citizens' interests. (Ofcom, 2008: 4)

Moreover, as it appears from the same document, when Ofcom defines the interests of citizens, it does not draw on an holistic understanding of citizenship. Rather, it leans on a 'market gap argument' by indicating that citizenship measures should fill the gap left by the market by adding public interest measures. It again states:

> All these things are relevant to citizens' interests. Competition, investment and innovation can lead to increased economic growth and productivity, which is to the benefit of society as a whole. (Ofcom, 2008: 10)

Hence, if the two concepts – citizens and consumers – have been traditionally opposed as two divergent entities, current policy-making seems to be restricted to satisfying mostly the interest of consumers.

This view is substantiated by public management studies that show how the main focus of contemporary administrative reforms in the US and, significantly, in Europe (New Public Management) is on consumer sovereignty rather than on citizens' sovereignty (Kettle, 2000: 1–2). In fact, according to Aberbach and Christensen (2005), the New Public Management reform calls on:

> public organizations to put customers first, and to orient their services to satisfy consumer preferences and demands [...] The basic idea is that through consumer sovereignty public organizations will produce better outputs (defined as outputs more in line with what citizens want) and that this furthers a fundamental goal of administration in a democracy, which is to serve the public and help it achieve its goals. (Aberbach and Christensen, 2005: 233)

This trend is also highly relevant for media policy, as the latter is not immune from the dominant philosophy of today's decision-making. In the UK context, the inclination to conceive citizens as consumers is manifest. New Labour's policies regarding public services spurred the idea of the 'citizen-consumer', an idea that, on the one hand, puts an emphasis on the importance of choices for citizens, while, on the other hand, contributes to the lessening of the social component of the notion of citizenship (Clarke et al., 2007). This approach certainly echoes Anthony Giddens's argument that: 'Citizenship is not dead, or dying, but found in new places, in life-politics [...] and in consumption' (Scammell, 2000: 351).

The danger of reducing citizens to consumers in media policy

According to Collins and Sujon (2007), the reduction of citizens to consumers is not a risky scenario. More precisely, these scholars argue that the shift in media policy thinking, promoted in the UK by the Peacock Committee's engagement with 'consumer sovereignty', is the only reasonable way to strengthen audiences' power, finally posing questions of media accountability. The endorsement by Collins and Sujon of the 'consumer sovereignty' argument can be read as the last expression of a stream of scholarship, beginning in the 1980s, that stressed the ability of audiences to realize an active media consumption by liberating them from the passive role of viewers (Morley, 1980).

However, there are reasons why the dogma of consumer sovereignty would be detrimental for democracy. If we limit the dynamics of democracy to individual choices and preferences, then we totally lose the collective dimensions of citizenship. The notion of the 'citizen-consumer' automatically curtails any possibility, if not the very idea, of common goods. Was democracy supposed to bring a degree of social integration? Or was it just supposed to protect a sum of individual freedoms? Is society something more than just a balance sheet stating its members' consumer choices?

Cass Sustein (2007) makes another very fruitful argument on the topic of citizenship in contemporary society. He claims that the role of citizens differs greatly from the role of consumers. Indeed, he explains:

> Most citizens have no difficulty in distinguishing between the two roles. Frequently a nation's political choice could not be understood if viewed only as a process of implementing people's desires in their capacity as consumers. (Sustein, 2007: 128)

This can be demonstrated by a simple example. While many people in the UK might like to watch reality shows and sports contests in their capacities as consumers, when asked by Ofcom in its second PSB review (Ofcom, 2009), they showed a strong support for the BBC's PSB remit. Consistently, Sustein's conclusion is that, 'in their role as citizens, people might seek to implement their highest aspirations when they do not do so in private consumption' (Sustein, 2007: 128).

This chapter has tried to show how problematic the current shift towards a society made of consumers instead of citizens really is. If citizenship is seen simply as a collection of individual freedoms – as in the neo-liberal approach – then there is no room for collective rights and solidarity. Consequently, it is necessary to deconstruct the notion of consumer-citizen and to retrieve (and rebuild) an idea of citizenship that is consistent to the public service ethos.

Towards a broader conception of citizenship: Citizenship and its different meanings

This section aims to start developing a more inclusive notion of citizenship that is not defined purely in opposition to the consumer paradigm and is coherent with a PSB ethos that expands into the online world.

Clearly, it is important to notice that citizenship can take very distinct meanings as a result of different theories of democracies. As Dahl acutely observed many years ago, 'there is no single theory of democracy: only theories' (Dahl, 1965: 1). The same reflection could be applied to the concepts of citizenship. Therefore, in order to define a concept of citizenship it is worth revisiting different concepts of democracy and their views on citizenship.

In a famous essay, Pocock (1930) underlined how the Greeks and Imperial Romans provided two opposed classical models that established the term for all subsequent theoretical debates around democracy. As a consequence, among the numerous theories of democracies, most of them have been reconnected to this ideal: the republican and the liberal.

According to the Athenian ideal of the citizen, which is defined in Aristotle's *Politics* (1995) as one who governs and is governed, all citizens are equal in decision-making and obedience to laws. However, Aristotle ties citizenship to the ownership of private property, therefore restricting it to a select group of people: men of known lineage, patriarchs, warriors and landowners. This greater emphasis on political participation has strongly characterized further conceptualization of democratic theories.

On the contrary, the ideal of Roman citizenship developed by Gaius at the time of Imperial Rome ceased to be a political entity and became a legal entity instead. Equality under the law becomes the main element. Therefore, each citizen had freedom to act under the protection of the law, and benefited from a series of rights and immunities.

The political and legal conception of citizenship has rightly been associated with two main streams of political thought: on one side, a republican political thought that sees the political participation element and communality as the crucial factors in a democracy; on the opposite side, a liberal political thought that sees the respect of individual rights as the cornerstone of a democracy.

Different theories of democracy, different theories of citizenship

A brief analysis of how citizenship has been conceived in different ways according to each conception of democracy can be revealing. For classical liberals, the individual is at the centre of political concerns. Moreover, in order to guarantee freedom to each individual, a set of rights is assigned to him or her through laws. There are of course insoluble discrepancies between the thought of liberal thinkers like John Locke and Thomas Hobbes in seventeenth-century England[5] and the views of nineteenth-century thinkers like John Stuart Mill or Alexis de Tocqueville[6] – but this is not the place for engaging in a detailed discussion. However, liberal thinkers all considered citizenship as a set of rights to be defended to secure individual freedom. As a consequence the law becomes a 'necessary evil that should seek to preserve as much of the natural liberty of individuals as compatible with social life' (Bellamy, 2008: 43).

If in classical liberal thinking the dimension of 'communality' and the tension towards the 'common good' is completely absent, the meaning of citizenship is even more diminished by elite theories of democracy. The strong pessimism about the future of liberal democracy that characterized social science thinking in the twentieth century created the basis for the growth of elite theories that see democracy merely as a competition between elites.

For elite theorists like Joseph Schumpeter democracy should be understood as a method for arriving at political decisions by means of competitive struggle for the people's vote' (Schumpeter, 1976: 269), not as an expression of a 'common good' or 'popular will', which, according to him, did not objectively exist.[7]

At the same time, it is evident from this construction that the lack of faith towards the abilities of citizens shrinks the concept far below the one of 'informed citizens' that we find in participatory democracy and below the sum of individual freedom as envisaged by classical liberals.

Citizens here are just requested to 'replace one government by another' (Schumpeter, 1942), while a deep understanding of structural and governmental problems is beyond citizens' capacity.[8] Citizens therefore become 'isolated and vulnerable individuals, in a world where real politics is conducted by competitive elites' (Scammell, 2000: 7).

This conception of citizens could not be further from participatory theories of democracy that are distinguished by Baker (2002) in two very different accounts: the republican, derived from the Greek tradition, and liberal pluralism. The participation element is crucial for normative legitimacy in both of the traditions, but the commitment for common good is missing in the liberal pluralistic account. For liberal pluralists, interest groups are the basis of democracy. Therefore the subject of politics is neither the people nor the individual voter, but the group.[9] Liberal pluralists recognize that each person has his or her own interest and each group its own aim; therefore, conflict becomes inescapable. 'Treating people as equals and as autonomous means that the properly functioning democracy should respond fairly to the different concerns of each' (Baker, 2002: 137). As a consequence, citizens are expected to participate in political decision-making in order to create fair compromises between the groups.

For republicans that derive their thinking from Aristotle, Machiavelli and Rousseau, the need for a vibrant civic life is crucial for democracy: it involves a continuing commitment to the common good and the civic virtue of citizens. They underline that people are not just self-interested, but can be social, communal. Republicans want to make the community the central point of reference for the good polity, not because they undervalue individuals, but because they believe that citizens can have liberty only when the community is united on agreeing about what constitutes liberty and what must be done to defend it. One of the most famous modern accounts of democracy, with strong roots in republican thinking, is the idea of deliberative democracy developed by Jürgen Habermas.

In his view (Habermas, 1974) citizenship means much more than protecting individual freedoms. He says that citizenship should entail a commitment to a common good, while legitimate lawmaking should result from the public deliberation of citizens. For Habermas, the status of citizen should comprise 'a guarantee of an inclusive opinion, and will, and formation in which free and equal citizens reach an understanding on which goals and norms lie in the equal interest of all' (Habermas, 1996: 22).[10]

Towards a definition of citizenship for PSB 2.0: Which theory of democracy?

As discussed in the preceding sections, the concept of citizenship is assigned different meanings according to different concepts of democracy. In moving towards a definition of citizenship that should underpin PSB 2.0, this study draws on a more complex definition of democracy (Fraser, 1992; Baker, 2002) that takes its inspiration from Habermas's account; from the postmodern critique carried on by Mouffe (1999); and from the Gramscian idea of conflictual dimensions (Gramsci, 1996).

Where the first conceptualization of the democratic deliberative theory by Habermas (1974) was focused more on the idea of a 'rational consensus' among citizens to achieve a common good, his more recent discussions on democratic theory seem more open to admit the presence of different groups and interests in society, and that 'compromises make up the bulk of political processes' (Habermas, 2006). However, this account still avoids placing power at the core of the political process. It is Mouffe (1999), with her notion of 'agonistic democracy' (1999),[11] who explains that 'the main question of democratic politics is not how to eliminate power, but how to constitute forms of power that are compatible with democratic values' (Mouffe, 1999: 753). Here the 'conflictual dimension' of Gramsci (1996) becomes relevant, as Mouffe asserts that 'every consensus exists as a temporary result of a provisional hegemony, as a stabilization of power and that always entails some form of exclusion' (Mouffe, 1999: 756).

It can be argued that postmodern societies need to embrace a conception of democracy that keeps alive the tension towards a common good and collective aims. However, it should take into account both the presence of different groups and interests in society, and the relations of power that are constitutive of the social. Consequently we can envisage a new '*enixe* democracy' that assigns to citizens the duty to participate both as individuals and as groups to political life to reach a common aim. At the same time, '*enixe* democracy' requires that citizens never stop renegotiating the common good, given the establishment of different types of hegemonies in democratic societies.

Citizenship for PSB 2.0

After having established the type of democracy that should underpin PSB 2.0, it is crucial to provide a clear definition of citizenship that gives it a social, economic and cultural foundation. The account by T.H. Marshall (1964), first developed in his *Citizenship and Social Class* in 1949, becomes useful. According to Marshall, there were three stages in the historical evolution of citizenship. Firstly (from the seventeenth to the nineteenth century), citizenship was essentially a legal notion, which assigned a series of civil rights, from the freedoms to own property and exchange goods to the liberties of expression and religion. Secondly, from the nineteenth century to the start of the twentieth and after much social struggle, citizenship gained political rights to vote that gradually extended from 'all property owners, then all adult and males, and finally women as well' (Bellamy, 2008: 48). Thirdly, from the beginning to the mid-twentieth century, citizenship extends to social rights, from welfare and security to education, health care and pensions.

Even though this account has been widely criticized[12] for having adopted an evolutionary perspective to the historical development of citizenship (Giddens, 1995), or for being too focused on Britain (Jessop, 1978; Turner, 1990), this arrangement still provides a useful tool for understanding and delineating the notion of citizenship.

The strength of Marshall's account can be seen in its ability to combine the two main approaches to citizenship, the political–republican one and the legal–liberal one. In fact, he conceived the acquisition of rights as an endless renegotiation of legal rights through the exercise of political activity.

Some authors have noted that Marshall's account needs to be enriched today by the cultural dimension of citizenship (Born and Prosser, 2001; Turner, 1990, 1997). By adding the cultural component we could bring issues of identities inside the legal status of citizens and shed light on the obligations of participation in the political community in a multimedia society (Turner, 1990, 1997). However, it can be argued that the civil, political and social rights dimension of citizenship should be enhanced by the communication rights dimension, as recently reformulated by the United Nation's World Summit on the Information Society (WSIS).[13] In fact, the WSIS Geneva Declaration On Principle intends to promote 'a people-centered, inclusive and development-oriented Information Society, where everyone can create, access, utilize and share information and knowledge, enabling individuals, communities and peoples to achieve their full potential'.

The right to freedom of opinion and expression therefore becomes a necessary precondition for communication rights. But communication rights entail also the right to privacy, the right to freedom of thought, the right to education, the right to freedom of movement and to freedom of association, and the right to participation in cultural life. Moreover:

> Without communication rights, freedom of expression can privilege the powerful. With them, it can achieve its full potential. Communication rights have implications for social and collective rights, beyond those of the individual, since they assert the right of cultural and ethnic groups, of language communities and others. Support for diversity is also integral to communication rights, through the high value attached to mutual respect and tolerance. (CRIS Campaign, 2005)

Embracing this new conception of citizenship that comprises not three but four dimensions of rights means embracing the particular conception of democracy that we have described earlier – *enixe* democracy. *Enixe* democracy requires that citizens are given the opportunity to fully participate in politics and therefore are able to renegotiate the common good, given the continuous establishment of different types of hegemonies in democratic societies.

Universality for PSB 2.0

The principle of universality has been advocated since the very beginning of PSB in Europe. However, it is certainly crucial to distinguish between what it meant at the foundation of PSB and what it means today.

In 1924 John Reith, considered the father of the BBC in Britain, was already talking of the responsibility for the BBC to 'carry into the greatest possible number of homes everything that is best in every department of human knowledge, endeavour or achievement' (Reith, 1949: 101).

Again, in the early 1980s, the Broadcasting Review Unit in London drafted the main principles of PSB, later submitted to the Peacock committee (1986),[14] and recognized *universality of availability* and *appeal* as two of the main aims of PSB (Broadcasting Research Unit, 1985).

According to the Unit, universal availability meant that PSB should be available to all members of society and that no one should be excluded because of geographic or socio-economic circumstances. Moreover, universality of appeal meant that PSB should be able to cater for the different interests and tastes of society (Tracey, 1998).

As a survey of European PSB (Betzel, 2008) shows, notwithstanding national differences, PSB in Europe has been committed to principles of universality. This propensity is also shown by the relevance assigned to the universality principle by the policy documents coming from the European Union and from the Council of Europe. In fact, the Resolution of the Council (1999) states: 'Broad public access, without discrimination and on the basis of equal opportunities, to various channels and services is a necessary precondition for fulfilling the special obligation of public service broadcasting' (Council of Europe, 1999, Art. 4). Moreover, it clarifies: 'public service broadcasting must be able to continue to provide a wide range of programming in accordance with its remit [...] It is legitimate for public service broadcasting to seek to reach wide audiences.'

An even more detailed declaration of principles is offered by the 2007 Recommendation of the Council of Europe, describing PSB as 'a reference point for all members of the public, with universal access offered' (Council of Europe, 2007). It also clarifies that:

> The principle of universality, which is fundamental to public service media, should be addressed having regard to technical, social and content aspects. Member states should, in particular, ensure that public service media can be present on significant platforms and have the necessary resources for this purpose. (Council of Europe, 2007)

In contemporary discussions around the principle of universality, it has become common to distinguish between 'universality of content' and 'universality of access' (Jacubowicz, 2008; EBU, 2002; Collins, 2007) instead of using concepts of appeal and availability.

The EBU report *Media with a purpose* (2002) provides a clear definition of universality of content as:

- universality of basic supply on generalist channels (including mass-appeal entertainment programming), which will be central to what public service broadcasters offer to the public;
- universality across the full portfolio of services, some of them specialized or tailored for specific audiences (Ebu, 2002).

It should be noted that within the context of PSB 2.0, it is more appropriate to talk of 'universality of content and services', given that besides offering a diversity of content – with attention to all types of minority interests, including high culture and educational programmes – the offer should comprise a wider range of services. It should include online services catered on a diversity of tastes and groups, but also interactive forums, social networking sites and search engine tools that we certainly cannot refer to just in terms of 'content'.

Even more relevant for the idea of PSB 2.0 is the understanding of 'universality of access'. Jacubowicz (2008) clarifies that it

> can no longer be understood as a couple of terrestrial channels available to the entire population, but as presence on all relevant media and platforms with significant penetration, but also the ability to deliver a 'personalized public service' in the 'pull', online and on demand environment. (Jacubowicz, 2008: 13)

However, achieving universality of access for PSB 2.0 entails a more far-reaching discussion that needs to draw a line between two different concerns regarding access. On the one hand, there are issues of access to the technology and more specifically the networks; on the other hand, there is access to content that brings about discussions on copyright, which must carry rules and issues of *retrievability*.

Figure 4.1 shows the components of universality of access: access to networks, content, retrievability and media literacy.

To begin with, universality of access for PSB 2.0 means that access to the networks is guaranteed. This refers to the condition of being connected to a broadband network, a mobile network or a phone network. Here, the first problem manifests itself, because certain areas might not be connected (digital divides). Moreover, citizens are already required to pay for

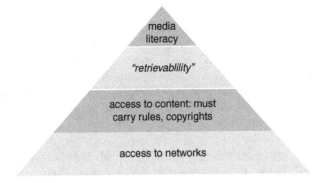

Figure 4.1 Components of universality

being connected (through IP providers), even though they receive content from PSB online just by paying the licence fee. This is certainly a situation that was not envisaged at the time when public broadcasting was born, and universality of access meant that the broadcasting signal had to be available regardless of geographical and social location. This changed situation carries the concern that, unless PSBs own a broadcasting network, in order to achieve universality of access to networks, they will always have to rely on private providers. Furthermore, this situation is complicated by the prospects, already advocated by network providers, of requiring content providers to pay a premium for heavy usage of bandwidth.

As for the second point (access to content), it is clear that having just access to the network is not sufficient if the content itself is restricted online. But the principle of universality enshrined in PSB 2.0 requires that content is available universally on the Net.

This consideration brings into the discussion two much-discussed issues: 'must-carry' rules and copyrights issues.

As for the first problem, public service content should be available on all significant delivery platforms, as 'must carry' content. This view is backed by the Recommendation (1999) on Measures to Promote Media Pluralism of the Council of Europe Committee of Ministers. According to this, must-carry rules could be envisaged, where necessary, for other distribution means and delivery platforms over cable systems. Furthermore, all distribution networks should carry public service television and data channels, on a reasonable, non-discriminatory basis (Council of Europe, 1999).

Regarding the second problem (the diffusion of digital right management),[15] it seems to already be the preferred practice of PSBs offering online content. This is confirmed by the decision of offering video content on the i Player for seven days in the UK (BBC Trust, 2007b). In Germany, programmes and video content will be available on the Net for just seven days, while major sporting events will be available for only 24 hours (Schulz, 2008).

However, this solution should not be considered as the only option available. For example, the idea of licensing PSBs' content under a creative commons licence could certainly constitute another alternative for achieving universality.

Finally, universality for PSB 2.0 also has to consider issues of *retrievability*. In an age of information abundance, PSBs should be visible and easy to find online. If PSB content online is produced conforming to PSB ethos, but is not easy accessible, then universality is mined. Above all, to achieve universality of access, it is fundamental that citizens have the ability to use new technologies. Media literacy therefore becomes a crucial variable for attaining universality.

Quality for PSB 2.0

The problem of quality has caused debates since broadcasters began transmitting. From Europe to the US, notions of quality in the media have taken centrestage in political debates about the future of the media (Blumler et al., 1986). Quality has been the constant promise of governments around the world when heralding their new policies for the media.

Murroni and Irvine (1997) explain that in Britain, 'since the Thatcher revolution, quality assurances have been presented as a solution to the problems of poor service provision' (Murroni and Irvine, 1997: 1). From that time, the term has been employed in several White Papers on television reform, including the *1988 White Paper on Broadcasting* (Mulgan, 1990) and the *2006 White Paper on the Future of the BBC* (DCMS, 2006a). Consistently with this tradition, Ofcom has, among its most important statutory duties, the responsibility of 'ensuring a wide range of TV and radio services of high quality' (Communication Act, 2003, Art. 3).

However, very often in policy debates as well as in literature, a definition of quality is taken for granted. This reflects the difficulty of giving a unique definition. Quality is not a static concept; rather it changes accordingly to certain social and ethical values and different visions of society (Murroni and Irvine, 1997; Mulgan, 1990). Mepham (1990) powerfully declares that:

> Quality, whether we are talking about the quality of TV programming, of books, of football matches or of people, can only ever be

given meaning with the purposes that give these things a place in people's lives, the values which they serve. (Mepham, 1990: 56)

Hence, the determination of the notion of quality clearly depends on the function and the role that we intend to ascribe to PSB 2.0, being directly dependent on the idea of citizenship, universality and trust. In moving towards a normative definition of quality for PSB 2.0, it can be useful to recall the main efforts to define the notion when referring to television. Murroni and Irvine (1997) identify five meanings resulting from five different views:

1. The consumer view, according to which 'quality can be defined by consumption';
2. The producer view, which sees quality deriving from innovative production 'achieved through a set of ethical values, favouring integrity, progress and artistic merit';
3. The manager view, which considers quality as a 'good return on investment';
4. The curator view, which 'defends prestige productions and indigenous language programming';
5. The regulator view, which 'seems close to producer choice: praise goes to the channel who appears to interpret viewers' demand in the most innovative, artistic and effective way'. (Murroni and Irvine, 1997: 2–3)

Mulgan (1990) lays out similar, sometimes clashing types of television quality. However, he claims that these categories should be balanced because

any desirable broadcasting system will support a range of different, and often contradictory qualities: it should, for example, sustain a balance between the producers' freedom of expression and the viewers' freedom to choose, and between the needs of diversity and those of social solidarity. (Mulgan 1990: 7–8)

Mulgan then draws up a list of seven types of quality, namely, quality in terms of production values; quality as viewers' preference and market demand; quality as intrinsic aesthetic of the medium; quality as the driver of communal values and experience; quality as a means to guarantee wide spread access and individual participation; quality as truth-telling and fairness; and finally quality as diversity (ibid.). A variety of other quality categories emerged from a large-scale study supported by the Japan Broadcasting Corporation (NHK) in 1990.

The research involved a quality assessment of television in three different continents (USA, Europe and Asia, i.e. Japan) and resulted in the publication of *Quality Assessment of Television* by Sakae Ishikawa (1996). Here, several authors (including Albers, 1996; Leggatt, 1996; Rosengren et al., 1996) systematically described the criteria on which television professionals based their production of quality programmes.

Rosengren et al. (1996) offered four dimensions of quality, each tapping a different relationship of the communication chain: *descriptive quality* stresses the relationship between message and 'reality' as the basis for setting quality standards; *receiver use quality* focuses on message effects, uses and gratifications criteria as the basis for quality assessments (message receiver relationship); *sender use quality* is defined in terms of societal functions fulfilled by television and mass media in general (message-sender relationship); finally, *professional quality* looks at quality from the point of view of professionals.

A powerful recommendation is derived from the NHK project: this is to prefer quality assessments of professionals over those of audiences. For example, Ishikawa (1996) views quality assessments of professionals as a more valid instrument than those of the viewers. Similarly, Rosengren et al. (1996) regard 'professional quality' as the most central, and possibly ultimate, yardstick by which all their other types can be assessed.

The validity of this argument is certainly enhanced by the recent finding of a survey conducted by Costera Meijer (2005). Her 2000–2001 study for the board of governors of the Dutch Public Broadcasting system entailed interviews with TV programme-makers and managers. In her analysis, she discovered that 'TV professionals' were relying on five different 'logics' or 'vocabularies' to express quality (Costera Meijer, 2005: 38). These vocabularies referred to what she called the marketing logic; the artist logic; the artisan vocabulary; the teacher vocabulary; and the moderator vocabulary.[16] These findings seem to give more evidence to the supposed superiority of the producers' view over others, given the richness of the different dimensions that producers are able to take into account when evaluating quality.

The same standpoint is backed by Born and Prosser (2001). They strongly argue in favour of giving primary normative attention to what the producer judges as quality, since 'production is ontologically prior to consumption' (Born and Prosser, 2001: 679). For them, 'producer intentionality in combination with the conditions bearing on production together determine the character of the output' (ibid.: 679).

Before ruling out the possibility of defining quality from the viewers' perspective, it is useful to clarify what the viewers' view means. For some authors the audience perspective translates into a categorical free market perspective (Peacock, 1986; Jacka, 2003). According to this vision, quality equates to popularity and audience size indicates people's satisfaction and preferences. The best newspaper would be the one with the largest sales, the best TV channel the one with the largest number of viewers. However, this biased vision, far from being of any scientific value, is certainly spurred by the logic of business and profit that is abundant in today's media ecology (Belsey and Chadwick, 1995). Disguised as an ideal of consumer sovereignty, the association of ratings with quality is exploited by neo-liberal economists to justify low-budget productions and other cost-saving tactics, under the banner of 'giving the public what they want'.

However, there are more accurate accounts of the viewers' view. Comparisons of audience figures with audience appreciation data have consistently indicated that, while not independent, audience preferences and viewership are distinct measures (Leggatt, 1996). As Mulgan (1990) logically explains: 'When asked, people consistently felt the need to criticize the quality of the programme they enjoyed' (Mulgan, 1990: 7). This view is certainly also supported by numerous audience studies that revealed the complexity of audience behaviour, such as the research conducted by David Morley in *Family Television* (Morley, 1986).

Likewise, in a more recent survey conducted in Israel by Shamir (2007), the audience demonstrated the ability to employ 'production value considerations in assessing television programs' and 'perceive them as distinct from their gratification and involvement with the program' (Shamir, 2007: 16). By showing the complexity of the audience's assessment of quality, these findings shed new light on their usefulness compared to the views of the producers.

Drawing on Rosengren et al. (1996), it can be argued that quality for PSB 2.0 is to be conceived as a relation between a programme or online service and a set of values. It is therefore a criterion that needs to be normatively defined according to certain values, but it also needs constant renegotiation. If PSB 2.0 builds upon the ideals of *enixe* democracy,[17] where citizenship is enhanced by the communication rights dimension, then a peculiar notion of quality is needed – a quality that, far from being reduced to high ratings, aims to combine a set of values coming from the producers with the needs of the viewers.

Undoubtedly, there is a strong relation between quality and trust, especially with reference to the Internet. Quality as a principle therefore entails a culture of avoiding deception, the same culture that is needed to build trust (O'Neill, 2002). Impartiality, accuracy, balance, fairness, objectivity, rigour, self-awareness, transparency and truth (BBC Trust, 2007a) are all essential components of trust, but also of quality.

Moreover, quality points to originality, innovation and experimentation among new services and programmes of PSB 2.0 and across the full online offering. The pressure of delivering constant news and programmes, fostered by the increased competition in the media market, has already damaged the quality of output, according to Born and Prosser (2001). Davies (2008) says the situation is worsened by 'rapacious capitalist practices favored by more efficient digital production', which increase the cost-cutting in journalistic resources that reduces quality. As a consequence, quality for PSB 2.0 can work as a tool of resistance against the progressive commercialization of the Internet and become an instrument to strengthen the role of citizens, rather than consumers.

Trust for PSB 2.0

Trust has not so far been considered as one of the normative elements of PSB. However, it can be argued that it is necessary to assign greater relevance to trust in a normative discussion of PSB 2.0. Even though information is abundant today, there are many spaces of disinformation and misinformation. For this reason, issues of trust are critical.

It is maybe worth here recalling the argument of Michael Shudson (2003) that 'information does not necessary bring participation' and that we cannot simply consider the Internet as a democratic tool because of the amount of information it delivers.

But there are also optimists who believe that information abundance is just a blessing, and that the Internet has brought much more 'good journalism' (Beckett, 2008). According to his view:

> The Internet means that the journalists have lost their effective monopoly over news production. The means of production have changed and so too has the power relationship. (Beckett, 2008)

However, as Habermas (2006) highlighted:

> The price we pay for the growth in egalitarianism offered by the Internet is the decentralized access to unedited stories. In this

medium, contributions by intellectuals lose their power to create a focus. (Habermas, 2006)

As a consequence, there is even more of a need today to be guided through the mass of information available online. Thus, trust assumes a greater relevance.

Discussions on trust regarding the BBC in Britain have begun to resonate more and more often as recent scandals, from fake phone-in competitions to the 'Queengate' documentary row, have sparked debates over how trustworthy the BBC is and about how it can increase this trust and restore public faith. This trend is also apparent in the policy work conducted by Ofcom, who, in their second review of public service broadcasting, conducted several surveys on the trustworthiness of channels in the UK (Ofcom, 2008).

As then Director-General of the BBC Mark Thompson highlighted in a discussion on trustworthiness, the media must also be blamed for generating distrust in politics and in public institutions in general (Thompson, 2008). This matter was been at the centre of an infamous speech by then Prime Minister Tony Blair, in which he referred to the media as 'the Feral Beasts'.

This has been the subject of the theories developed by Robert D. Putman in *Bowling Alone* (1995, 2000), where he blames US media for having eroded social capital in the US. Moreover, in John Lloyd's study in *What the Media are Doing to our Politics* (2004), the press and broadcasters are held accountable for damaging the political system in the UK. However, for the scope of this analysis, it is useful to draw a clear line between the supposed effect that media could exert on trust towards institutions and trust towards the media. This latter form of trust becomes one of the most important normative principles for PSB 2.0. In order to increase trust, PSB 2.0 should encourage a public culture in which 'publishing misinformation and disinformation [...] is limited and penalized' (O'Neill, 2002).

As the philosopher Onora O'Neill explained in her famous Reith Lecture series in 2002, trust is not destroyed if we avoid deception in communication. This belief certainly echoes principles of autonomy derived by Kant's philosophy, according to which 'autonomy is a matter of acting on principles that can be principles for all of us' (O'Neill, 2002). As a consequence, issues of impartiality, transparency and accountability become fundamental for notions of trust.

The governing body of the BBC, the BBC Trust, seems to be aware of the importance of impartiality in building trust (BBC Trust, 2007a), and spent time and resources on establishing the twelve guiding principles for impartiality that every programme and content-maker at the BBC should follow:

> Impartiality involves a mixture of accuracy, balance, context, distance, evenhandedness, fairness, objectivity, open-mindedness, rigour, self-awareness, transparency and truth. But it is also about breadth of view and completeness. (BBC, 2008)

But as explained earlier, since trust is a process that needs to be negotiated, citizens should be given reliable ways of detecting impartiality. This is the field where accountability plays a relevant role.

Undoubtedly, the guidelines used by the BBC in the UK are a valuable instrument to hold the PSB accountable. But, as Lady O'Neill warns, if accountability is pushed too much further, with too many perfect administrative controls and too many sophisticated complaints systems, it could 'build a culture of suspicion, low morale and may ultimately lead to professional cynicism, and then we would have grounds for public mistrust' (O'Neill, 2002). Therefore it is crucial to attain the right balance in establishing systems of accountability. Thus PSB 2.0 needs, on the one hand, to encourage internal standards and a culture of avoiding deception, while, on the other hand, giving the citizens an opportunity to check on PSB's online activities and assess them.

Thus, the more interactive nature of the Internet should be seen as an enormous advantage to encourage checks and assessments. In fact, we could argue that the ability to share information easily on the Internet is helping to build trust, just as the dialogue between the citizens and the PSBs is. Also new practices of integrating user-generated content with PSBs' production, as many European PSBs are doing, should be encouraged to enhance a stronger bond between the public and PSBs.

Conclusion

This chapter has aimed to establish a normative framework for PSB online that has been named PSB 2.0. It identified four normative criteria inherent in a revised definition of PSB that can be applied to the online world: citizenship, universality, quality and trust. More specifically, the chapter elaborated on a concept of citizenship that draws on a composite definition of democracy that combines complex theories of democracy (Fraser, 1992; Baker, 2002; Mouffe, 1999; Gramsci, 1996) into the idea of *enixe* democracy. It then developed citizenship as a multi-dimensional notion that, far from being reduced to market choices, embraces four dimensions of rights (civil, political, social and communication rights).

The definition of universality has been also amply discussed by focusing on its four components, which are all relevant in the online world: issues of access to networks and content, retrievability and media literacy. Furthermore, issues of quality as related to the Internet world have been framed as a relation between a programme/online service and a set of values. These values originate from ideas of impartiality, accuracy, balance, fairness, objectivity, rigour, transparency, truth, originality and innovation. Finally, the chapter has pointed at the paramount importance of a 'culture of avoiding deception' online (O'Neill, 2002) as a crucial component both of quality and trust. Indeed, trust becomes another critical normative criterion for PSB 2.0, conceived as a way to build a dialogue between the citizens and PSBs, but also a tool of resistance to online misinformation and information abundance.

5
Comparing Histories of PSB in Denmark, France, UK, Spain and Italy

Comparative data about the media and technology context of France, Spain, Italy, UK and Denmark

Before setting out to discuss and analyse the commonalities and differences of public service broadcasting histories in the European countries considered, it is necessary to describe historical developments in broadcasting and technology in all the countries as well as their Internet and technological take-up.

In 2008 France reached 25.28 million TV households in total, and the share of all-day viewing by channel is certainly revealing about the weight of France Télévisions in the television market (Table 5.1). The most successful and established TV channel is still TF1, which was privatized in 1987.

Spain reached 17.5 million TV households in total in 2008, and the share of all-day viewing by channel showed the position of TVE, squeezed between strong commercial competitors like Telecinco and Antena 3 (Table 5.2).[1]

In 2008 Italy had a total of 24 million TV households and clearly showed (and still shows today) a highly concentrated TV market with the enduring duopoly of RAI, the public media holding, and Mediaset, which controls Canale 5, Italia 1 and Rete 4 (Table 5.3).

Table 5.1 France: Share of all-day viewing by channel

	TF1	France2	France3	M6	France5	Canal*	Arte	Others
2008	27.2	17.5	13.3	11	3.3	3.3	1.8	22.6

Source: CSA and Mediametrie.

Table 5.2 Spain: Share of all-day viewing by channel

	Telecinco	TVE1	Antena3	Cuatro	LaSexta	La2	FORTA	Others
Jan-Oct 2008	18.4	16.7	16	8.8	5.3			
Dec 2008						4.7	14.1	16

Source: Sofres.

Table 5.3 Italy: Share of all-day viewing by channel

	Rai Uno	Rai Due	Rai Tre	Canale 5	Italia 1	Rete 4	La 7
2008	21.8	10.6	9.1	20.3	10.8	8.3	3.1

Source: Auditel.

Table 5.4 Denmark: Share of all-day viewing by channel

	TV2	DR1	TV3	Kanal4	Others
2008	31	29	5	5	30

Source: Nordicom, 2009.

Table 5.5 UK: Share of all-day viewing by channel

	TV2	DR1	TV3	Kanal4	Others
2008	31	29	5	5	30

Source: OFCOM.

Meanwhile Denmark counted in 2008 just 2.5 million households. The data indicates the straightforward competition for viewing between DR – totally funded by licence fee – and TV2, the second advertised-based public channel[2] that the Danish government has been willing to privatize since 2000 (Table 5.4).[3]

The United Kingdom had 25.5 million TV households in total in 2008, in a market where the BBC has traditionally enjoyed a wide audience (Table 5.5).

Having showed the position in the market of each PSB TV channels before the digital take-up, it is useful to juxtapose these data to the level of public funding each PSB receives, as this clearly affects the PSBs' policies and practices online.

The next table (Table 5.6) highlights the evident discrepancies in levels of public funding between the countries considered. The first prominent difference is the high reliance on advertising of France Télévisions, RTVE and RAI compared to the BBC and DR.[4] Moreover, Table 5.7 relates the total funding of each PSB to the number of households and reveals the wide imbalance between DR and the BBC on the one hand and the southern PSBs on the other, with a stronger public investment in the UK and Danish case.

Table 5.7 provides a clear-cut picture of resources available to each PSB per household in 2010. Even though the spreadsheet considers also the advertisement funding available to France Télévisions and TVE, the disparity between resources is striking: 194.76 euros per household in Denmark and 226.65 euros in UK against 130 euros in Italy, 113.63 euros in France and 75.21 euros in Spain.

Table 5.8 is another interesting table, which shows the overall audience of PSB in all European countries; again important differences are pointed up between Italy, France, Spain on the one hand and UK and Denmark on the other.[5]

Finally, data about the Internet and technological take-up of each country are also crucial for an assessment of policies of PSB online. As

Table 5.6   Types of funding (€) of the five PSBs

Country /PSB		Grant	Licence fee	Advertising	Sponsorship	Other	Total income
UK	BBC	442,3	4565,5	0	0	975,2	5983,1
DK	DR	5	445,9	0	0	34,1	485,2
FR	FRANCE TV	0	1879,5	738,5	84,5	225,2	2927,7
IT	RAI	0	1588	1039	97	242	2966
ES	RTVE	436,9	0	679,3	0	50,7	1166,8

Source: DR, NRK, BBC and annual financial reports (2010).

Table 5.7   Costs of PSBs in the five countries by HH

Country	PSB	Funding (€)	HH cost by total funding
UK	BBC	5983,1	226,65
DK	DR	485,2	194,76
FR	FRANCE TV	2927,7	113,63
IT	RAI	2966	130,54
ES	RTVE	1166,8	75,21

Source: DR, NRK, BBC and other financial reports (2010).

Table 5.8 Europe: Public Service television daily audience market shares
1999–2007

Country	1999	2001	2003	2005	2007
Austria	59	56	52	49	44
Belgium (CFR)	22	23	20	18	21
Belgium (VLG)	31	34	38	36	40
Bulgaria	70	32	25	19	15
Croatia			71	54	49
Cyprus	21	19	17	21	19
Czech Republic	32	29	30	30	32
Denmark	67	66	69	69	66
Estonia	18	17	17	17	16
Finland	43	43	44	44	44
France	42	42	41	39	37
Germany	43	43	44	44	48
Great Britain	50	48	46	51	50
Greece	10	10	14	15	16
Hungary	17	15	19	18	17
Iceland	43	41	43	44	49
Ireland	50	43	41	41	40
Italy	48	47	45	43	42
Latvia	18	18	18	17	15
Lithuania	10	9	12	14	14
Norway	39	41	44	44	42
Poland	51	48	53	52	47
Portugal	33	26	29	29	29
Romania	39	36	35	24	17
Russia	48	44	44	48	39
Slovakia	18	20	22	25	23
Slovenia	32	34	35	34	32
Spain	49	50	49	43	37
Sweden	47	42	41	39	35
Switzerland (Al.)	35	34	36	35	35

Sources: EAO, 2008 and Nordicom, 2009.

shown in Table 5.9, the level of Internet access is very different across
the countries, with Denmark already ranking in top position in 2002.
Internet access in Denmark rose from 56% in 2002 to 86% in 2010,
followed by the UK (50–80% in 2010), while in Spain it increased from
28% to 59% in 2010, in France from 23% to 74% and in Italy from 34%
to 59%. However, the broadband penetration rate shows a different picture (Table 5.10). While Denmark is still in top spot with a stable 80%,
broadband connection in Spain jumped from 29% in 2006 to 57% in
2010, while in France it reached 67% in 2010, from 30% in 2016. While

Table 5.9 Internet access in EU27 per country 2002–2010 (share of households, percent)

	2002	2003	2004	2005	2006	2007	2008	2009	2010
European Union (27 countries)			41	48	49	54	60	65	70
European Union (25 countries)			43	48	51	56	62	67	
European Union (15 countries)	39	43	46	53	54	59	64	68	
Austria	33	37	45	47	52	60	69	70	73
Belgium				50	54	60	64	67	73
Bulgaria			10		17	19	25	30	33
Cyprus	24	29	53	32	37	39	43	53	54
Czech Republic		15	19	19	29	35	46	54	61
Denmark	56	64	69	75	79	78	82	83	86
Estonia			31	39	46	53	58	63	68
Finland	44	47	51	54	65	69	72	78	81
France	23	31	34		41	49	62	63	74
Germany	46	54	60	62	67	71	75	79	82
Greece	12	16	17	22	23	25	31	38	46
Hungary			14	22	32	38	48	55	60
Ireland		36	40	47	50	57	63	67	72
Italy	34	32	34	39	40	43	47	53	59
Latvia	3		15	31	42	51	53	58	60
Lithuania	4	6	12	16	35	44	51	60	61
Luxembourg	40	45	59	65	70	75	80	87	90
Malta				41	53	54	59	64	70
Netherlands	58	61	65	78	80	83	86	90	91
Poland	11	14	26	30	36	41	48	59	63
Portugal	15	22	26	31	35	40	46	48	54
Romania			6		14	22	30	38	42
Slovakia			23	23	27	46	58	62	67
Slovenia			47	48	54	58	59	64	68
Spain		28	34	36	39	45	51	54	59
Sweden			:	73	77	79	84	86	88
United Kingdom	50	55	56	60	63	67	71	77	80

Source: Eurostat, 2010.

the gap between Northern European countries and Southern Europe is still wide, both France and Spain have been conspicuously investing in broadband infrastructure, much more than other Southern European countries such as Italy, for example.[6]

These data concerning the technology take-up as well as the previous data discussed regarding each media market and PSB funding become

59

Table 5.10 Broadband access in EU27 and per country 2002–2010 (share of households, per cent)

Household internet connection type: Broadband

geo\time	2003	2004	2005	2006	2007	2008	2009	2010
European Union (27 countries)	:	15	23	30	42	49	56	61
Euro area (EA11-2000, EA12-2006, EA13-2007, EA15-2008, EA16-2010, EA17)	:	:	23	31	42	50	56	63
Belgium	:	:	41	48	56	60	63	70
Bulgaria	:	4	:	10	15	21	26	26
Czech Republic	1	4	5	17	28	36	49	54
Denmark	25	36	51	63	70	74	76	80
Germany (including former GDR from 1991)	9	18	23	34	50	55	65	75
Estonia	:	20	30	37	48	54	62	64
Ireland	1	3	7	13	31	43	54	58
Greece	1	0	1	4	7	22	33	41
Spain	:	15	21	29	39	45	51	57
France	:	:	:	30	43	57	57	67
Italy	:	:	13	16	25	31	39	49
Cyprus	:	2	4	12	20	33	47	51
Latvia	:	5	14	23	32	40	50	53
Lithuania	2	4	12	19	34	43	50	54
Luxembourg	7	16	33	44	58	61	71	70
Hungary	:	6	11	22	33	42	51	52
Malta	:	:	23	41	44	55	63	69
Netherlands	20	31	54	66	74	74	77	:
Austria	10	16	23	33	46	54	58	64
Poland	:	8	16	22	30	38	51	57
Portugal	8	12	20	24	30	39	46	50
Romania	:	:	:	5	8	13	24	23
Slovenia	:	10	19	34	44	50	56	62
Slovakia	:	4	7	11	27	35	42	49
Finland	12	21	36	53	63	66	74	76
Sweden	:	:	40	51	67	71	79	83
United Kingdom	11	16	32	44	57	62	69	:
Iceland	:	45	63	72	76	83	87	88
Norway	23	30	41	57	67	73	78	83

Source: Eurostat, 2010.

relevant when studying PSBs' national and institutional online policies. In fact, they highlight important imbalances that need to be taken into consideration when investigating the institutional and structural factors that impact on these polices. The next sections focus on the historical developments in broadcasting in all five countries. Without at least some cursory knowledge of political, social and cultural developments in these countries, the context in which current practices and policies are executed may not be understood. The different interpretations of Public Service Broadcasting in the three countries can be traced back to power relations between governing authorities *vis-à-vis* society/the public/their citizens

DR and its political, cultural and historical legacy

The history and development of public service broadcasting in Denmark cannot be approached without understanding the political, cultural and social *terroir* in which it flourished. It is therefore necessary to highlight briefly the main characteristics of Danish democracy and then to move on to explain the role of Danish Radio (DR) in this context.

The Danish political model has been placed by political scientists within the so-called Nordic Political Model, an idea that originated in the 1930s (Hilson, 2008) and referred to Sweden, Norway, Denmark, Finland and Iceland. Certainly, the ideal of Scandinavian countries as 'specific egalitarian social democratic community of destiny was contrasted against the capitalist and Catholic European continent' (Hilson, 2008). In general, the Nordic countries' political culture has been dominated by the will and ability to find peaceful solutions to political and social conflicts. (Christiansen et al., 2005) It is characterized by the struggle towards a wide consensus between political forces and the aim of including civil society, industry and the State in making decisions about their society (Jespersen, 2004; Svendsen, 2009).

Moreover, one of the defining features of Nordic states has been the development of a specific welfare state system, clearly one of the most far-reaching and ambitious in Western Europe. As part of the Nordic model, the Danish welfare state meant much more than a mere system of social security based on financial transfers from state authorities to citizens. As Jens Otto Krag, the architect of the Danish welfare state, has claimed, it constituted 'a project to hold Danish society together' (Jespersen, 2004: 30). Welfare benefits, provided mostly by the public sector, were comprehensive and universal. Universal in this context means that 'social programs, old age pensions, health care, child-care, education, child allowances and health insurance are not targeted for the poor, but instead cover the entire population with no consideration given to their ability to pay' (Hilson, 2008: 90).

Jespersen points out that the Danish welfare state 'permeates the whole of society in all its aspects, from the system of taxation to the way in which the citizens conduct themselves. It would not be an exaggeration to talk of a whole philosophy of life' (Jespersen, 2004: 77). Through a development of a large public sector, the aim was to provide the system with comprehensive educational, social and cultural services and 'to transform economic affluence into social welfare beyond purely material progress' (Sørdergaard, 1996).

To use the category developed by Gosta Esping-Andersen in his highly influential book *The Three Worlds of Welfare Capitalism* (1990), the Danish welfare state constituted a 'social democratic system of welfare' whose main aim was to 'de-commodify' citizens. Esping-Andersen (1990) referred to de-commodification as 'the degree to which people can make their living standards independent of pure market forces' (Esping-Andersen, 1990: 3). Therefore, de-commodification means that 'citizens can freely, and without potential loss of job, income or general welfare, opt out of work' (ibid.: 23).

Moreover, it is worth noticing that the way the welfare state developed in the 1960s to transform the mainly agricultural economy of Denmark into an industrial economy already showed the characteristic of Danish political culture that was so crucial for the foundation of DR, the Danish broadcasting corporation. The way in which the reforms of the 1960s were carried out indicated the importance of achieving a wide consensus within Danish society:

> The emergency legislation in the 1930s and the implementation of the welfare state which started to take shape around 1960 were also conducted through a tightly knit co-operation between politicians, the state and business and labour market organizations. Together they took responsibility for the comprehensive regulations and limitations of the economic freedoms of the citizens necessary to ensure that everything continued to function. This amalgamation of government power and the interest of business and other organizations or, to put it another way, the merging of the state and civil society, has continued to be a characteristic of what has subsequently been called the 'Danish model'. (Jespersen, 2004: 160)

Since the principles of universalism, equality and democracy can be found at the core of this drive to reform Danish society, it is understandable why cultural policies received so much importance as a part of this project of democratization.

It is important to be aware of the high value assigned to educational and cultural policies to achieve the project of a more egalitarian Danish society and to abolish social distinctions. Certainly, these ideas were uppermost in the mind of the Danish government during the years in which DR was established. Thus, Tufte and Tufte rightly assert that the founding of PSB in Denmark is an extension of social democratic ideals and the 'wish from the political intellectual elite to promote education for all, to spread information and to democratize culture' (Tufte and Tufte, 1996).

It can be argued that even though it was not explicitly stated at its inception, DR, the Danish broadcasting corporation, was clearly part of this particular welfare state model. Certainly, it was part of its philosophy. Naturally this approach has had its consequences on the high level of political control DR was subjected to, especially if compared with today's DR, transformed after the reforms that took place in the 1980s (Svendsen, 2009; Nissen, 2009).

However, Tufte and Tufte (1996) are certainly right when they relate the roots of DR's ethos to philosophical ideas that developed much earlier than the welfare state, and they date this back to the beginning to the legacy of the Enlightenment and Reformation:

> Television as public broadcasting represents a continuation and development of a strong Danish tradition of popular enlightenment dating back to the early 19th Century and strongly linked to the social movement and philosophical ideals of that time. These movements and ideas strongly influenced the writing of the first Danish constitution (1848) and were fundamental for the founding of the Danish democracy. (Tufte and Tufte, 1996: 46)

In the present author's opinion one philosopher who certainly had a bearing on the important ideals at the basis of Danish democracy, of which DR has later become one of its most crucial instruments, is N.F.S Grundtvig. This philosopher probably affected the ideas of how Danish citizenship and democracy is conceived more than any other European political movement.[7]

Grundtvig lived between 1783 and 1872 in Denmark. He is well known for his work as a theologian, which brought him to formulate his groundbreaking thinking on the relationship between church and state and its call for a more secular society. However, his ideas about democracy and the role of education are those that have influenced Danish society most obviously and which can be considered the seeds of modern welfare state Denmark. Jespersen comments:

> His fundamental idea in the area of education was to establish a 'school for life' where the living word could stimulate and enlighten people. [...] this idea was the first seed of the 'folk high school' movement in Denmark, which in a few decades became the biggest popular educational project of the century, aimed especially at rural youth, who had always been deprived in educational terms. (Jespersen, 2004: 106)

Moreover, Grundtvig was the first thinker to introduce the word *folkelig* (popular) into the discourse about democracy and the State: every institution, law and regulation needed to be 'popular' in order to be respected.[8] For the first time the concept of *folke-lighed*, 'the equality of people', started resonating in the minds of Danish citizens.

Grundtvig was interested in the question of how to enlighten people (certainly, an idea inherited from the Enlightenment) and transform them into responsible citizens in Denmark's new democracy. Jespersen continues:

> Grundtvig thought that this democratic project could be carried out just 'by reaching out the groups previously marginalized or considered incapable of managing their affairs there they actually here, taking them seriously and striving to draw them into a national community trough broadly targeted education and enlightenment. (Jespersen, 2004: 108)

What is fascinating about Grundtvig's concept of democracy and the State is that he strenuously believed that belonging to a State should be a matter of choice. One could choose to join or to remain outside, but choosing to join the State meant accepting certain obligations, such as equal treatment for citizens. There was a 'spiritual obligation to the whole concept' (Jespersen, 2004: 109). Interestingly, Grundtvig's ideas have been embraced across the political spectrum in Denmark, not just by the Social Democrats. These ideas might explain why Danish democracy tends to be based on a wide consensus that leads minorities to struggle for an agreement. Grundtvig's ideas were also influential because they permeated the articles of Denmark's constitution. He was a member of the national constitutional assembly between 1848 and 1849.

Grundtvig's legacy might also help explain the concept of universal solidarity towards fellow citizens, which is solidly imprinted in Danish society. It should be noted that the right-wing Venstre party, which currently rules Denmark, has not dared to dismantle the cornerstones of the Danish welfare state.

A brief history of DR

DR ('Statsradiofonien', renamed Danmarks Radio in 1959) was established in 1925 as a public service institution and had a monopoly over radio and television broadcasting until 1981 (Petersen, Prehn and Svendsen, 1992). Until that point, the DR consortium consisted of one television channel (DR), three national and nine regional radio channels. Christian Nissen, Director General of DR from 1994 to 2004, elucidates that:

> the mission of DR can be explained by referring to two different schools of ideas. First, the Social Democratic Party that established DR did so on the conviction that in order to create a social democratic culture besides welfare policies, cultural policies were needed. And second, the *Folkehøjskole* (folk high school) movement that stressed the importance of giving the citizens the tool to participate in democratic life and the ideals of enlightening people through education played another important factor. (Nissen, 2009)

As a consequence, the broadcasting vision under which DR was born and developed emanates from a wider consensus that stretched over the entire spectrum of political parties' visions. Certainly, there was and still is today a broad social democratic consensus that television has to support the basic principle of socializing and enabling all Danes to become well-informed, democratic citizens who are empowered to actively participate in the political sphere.

Given this political/ideological context, it is logical that the mass media must be public and all forms of commercialization of the electronic media, including the use of advertising, should be avoided (Tufte and Tufte, 1996). As Sørdergaard (1996) clarifies:

> the social democratic dominance has further meant that radio and television have primarily been considered as matters of cultural politics, while their economic and industrial aspects, [...] has only had a limited influence. (Sørdergaard, 1996: 13)

The choice of having a public monopoly – a choice that mirrors many other European countries – can also be attributed to the Denmark's small size. Denmark's size has twofold consequences: firstly, a small area of culture and language requires a stronger protection to maintain its identity, so a public monopoly can be assigned the role of protector of culture; secondly, a small country equals a small market, which is less attractive to commercial organizations than bigger markets. As Lund and Berg (2009) observe, 'in small media markets with limited linguistic reach, an all commercial media system would result in market failure' (Lund and Berg, 2009: 32).

As a means of 'enlightenment' in the tradition of Grundtvig, DR aimed to give all Danes the same access to culture and thereby unify the nation. According to Sørdergaard (1996): 'DR represented a middle-strata culture', with

> [the] norms and values of the new middle strata of civil servants emerging from the developing welfare state, again deeply rooted in the social and cultural reform ideals of the modernizing Danish welfare state. (Sørdergaard, 1996: 13)

The Radio Law of 1926 defined radio as a public service and placed it under the scrutiny of the Radio Council, a cross-party body reflecting the balance of power in parliament. When television was launched in 1954 it was subject to the same program me policy requirements. More precisely, TV 'should not merely [be] entertainment but was charged with broadcasting programmes of a diverse, cultural and informative nature' (Sørdergaard, 1996: 14).

As already stressed, since its inception broadcasting was one of the most important tools for the Social Democrat government to deliverits cultural political strategy of abolishing social distinctions to create a unified culture. If, formally, the Radio Law gave DR independence from the State and the market, the Radio Council put DR under the indirect control of parliament. Humphreys argues that the Danish broadcasting council 'became known as the country's "mini-parliament" and its politically appointed members were referred to as "radio politicians"' (Humphreys, 1996: 156). Svendsen agrees with Humphreys when recalling that:

> In those days, at the time of monopoly there was also a bit of a tendency towards 'clientelism', but later on DR ideally developed more as a professional organization. No question that at the time, The

Radio Council certainly regarded DR as part of the political system. (Svendsen, 2009)

However, it is also true that the government never exerted control in the history of DR. Rather, DR was managed to reflect the party balance in parliament and was run on the basis of a high standard of 'professionalism'. This twofold characteristic defines the so-called Nordic-corporatist model developed by Hallin and Mancini (2004) in *Comparing Media Systems*:

> Democratic corporatism is characterized simultaneously by the presence of a wide range of parties and organized groups with distinct interest and ideologies rooted in historic divisions of society and by widely shared agreement on the rules of the game by which these groups share power, resolve their differences and come to collective decisions about the common good. The media are characterized historically by a similar duality. (Hallin and Mancini, 2004: 143)

Surely the monopoly position of DR helped in delivering these important sets of cultural policies as part of the welfare state. As Sørdergaard (1996) explains:

> the programming policy of DR could not be unequivocally rooted in the social elite's cultural norms, as was the case for most other areas of cultural politics, but rather came to be based in a common denominator of elite culture and popular culture without coinciding with either. In reality DR represented a middle-strata culture [...] accorded with the norms and values of the new, middle strata of civil servants emerging form the developing welfare state. (Sørdergaard, 1996: 17)

During what Bondebjerg (1996) has called the 'classic public service period' of Danish broadcasting (1964–1980), DR developed into 'one of the most central cultural and journalist media institutions with a very broad and diversified range of programmes' (Bondebjerg, 1996: 41).

Nevertheless, DR's monopoly came to an end in the early 1980s. This was partly because of viewers' increased dissatisfaction with DR's output, partly because of the desire of DR employees to offer more independent news and better satisfy their viewers, and partly out of growing competition from foreign television, in particular Swedish and German programmes. At the beginning of the 1980s, a Media Commission was established to reform media policy and introduce a second national television channel. TV2 was a compromise between two political factions: the Social Democratic Party, which viewed funding TV through advertisements with suspicion, and the right-wing party that gained the political majority in 1982. TV2 was allowed to carry advertisements, but was subjected to similar obligations of output as DR and gained a third of its income from the licence fee. With the breaking of the monopoly, the old Radio Council was also abolished, while in 1988 DR was restructured. It was given a new independent, professional board, albeit appointed by politicians. For almost two decades, it has had a new service contract that established new obligations and objectives (Svendsen, 2009). With the introduction of TV2 and more local and international competition, DR was forced to deliver broadcasting that met public demands.[9] By the 1990s, TV2, which was focused on entertainment and popular genre programmes, became the most watched television channel in Denmark.

Currently, there are four main players in the Danish television market: TV2, MTG/Viasat, Scandinavian Broadcasting Service (SBS) and Danish Broadcasting Corporation (DR).

France Télévisions and its political, cultural and historical legacy

Public broadcasting in France has been the ground of animated political conflicts throughout its history. This is clearly a consequence of the highly political role assigned to television in the Gaullist vision of French society that persisted in the minds of French politicians for decades and which involved close political supervision and interference (Kuhn, 1995). One could also argue that the concept of television as an arm of the government is still very much alive in contemporary France.

President Pompidou's pronouncement of 1970 that ORTF – the body managing French broadcasting – was the 'voice of France' and should therefore reflect the government's views is consistent with this vision (Sergeant, 1999; Vedel, 2005). It comes as no surprise that all governments in France have tried to use television to gain public approval and pursue their agenda. In fact, this has been reflected in the numerous series of changes to the broadcasting regulatory framework. As Levy (1999) highlights, 'between 1972 and 1998 [...] there were seven major changes in French broadcasting law (1972, 1974, 1982, 1986, 1989, 1992 and 1994)' (Levy, 1999: 170).

As in all other European countries, public service television was started in France as a State monopoly. Under the Vichy regime, a government ordinance of March 1945 assigned the monopoly of broadcasting system to the State. This legal framework was kept by the post-war government of General de Gaulle. Under the firm supervision of the Minister of Information, and then of Culture, broadcasting was run by a public broadcasting body – firstly, the *Office de Radio diffusion- Télévision de France* (RTF) and later *Radiodiffusion Télévision Française* (ORTF) (Kuhn, 1983, 1995; Sergeant, 1999; Humphreys, 1996). Indeed, the 'legal principle of the state monopoly had in practice quickly become equated with the political control of broadcasting by the government of the day' (Kuhn, 1983: 67).

Humphreys (1996) observes that this administrative and centralized 'etatiste' tradition was a typical feature of French history. For this reason,

> whoever won the presidency disposed of extensive powers of patronage [...] Even cohabitation (the state of affairs when the president lost his parliamentary support base to the opposition) merely transferred uncommonly strong executive powers in most policy fields – including broadcasting – to the prime minister and his cabinet. (Humphreys, 1996: 146)

Kuhn (1983) shares the same view that 'the history of French broadcasting since the second world war has been characterized by a degree of governmental control unequalled in other Western liberal democracies' (Kuhn, 1983).

During the entire period of state monopoly the political grip on television went hand in hand with its highly normative value of being the main governmental tool to promote culture and education. The important feature of French television as a governmental tool to deliver cultural policies has always been its strong focus on protecting national and culture and language, and to reflect this specificity in its programmes (Sergeant, 2009). The State was in control of RTF's budget and the President directly nominated RTF's Director General. Even in 1964, when RTF was transformed into ORTF, the governmental influence was maintained. This meant that very little autonomy was given to the newly introduced management board (Kuhn, 1995; Humphreys, 1996).

Many authors agree that, particularly during the reign of De Gaulle (1959–1969), public television in France was simply a weapon of State propaganda (Humphreys, 1996; Kuhn, 1983; Vedel, 2005). Despite an early attempt to change the structure of ORTF, things did not change much under the presidency of Pompidou. As stated previously, for Pompidou, ORTF was still the voice of France and had to act like a loyal ılly to the presidency. Some authors (Vedel, 2005; Humphreys, 1996) ʒee the advent of Valéry Giscard d'Estaing's presidency between 1974 to 1981 as an important twist in French television history, with his deciʒion to break ORTF up into seven public companies:

- three television companies – TF1, Antenne 2 and FR3;
- one radio company – Radio-France;
- Télédiffusion de France – a company in charge of managing the technical process of broadcasting;
- Société Française de Production – a production company in charge of providing high-cost programmes to broadcasters;
- Institut National de l'Audiovisuel (INA) – entrusted with maintaining the public broadcasters' archives of programmes, professional training of public broadcasters' employees and research in the field of new broadcasting technologies.

Under this new arrangement, the public television channels were financed by a mixture of licence revenue and income from commercial advertising. Although in the original Common Programme of 1972 the Socialists and Communists had previously guaranteed to abolish advertising in the State broadcasting services, this policy had not actually been carried out.

This reform aimed to bring greater variety and quality of programming, as well as more political independence. Political influence on French public TV became less invasive under Giscard d'Estaing's presidency (Humphreys, 1996). Kuhn, however, states that Giscard d'Estaing proved himself 'no more willing or able than his predecessors to set the broadcasters free' (Kuhn, 1983: 69). Partisan political coverage was the rule, in order to favour the president, his policies and supporters. As Beaud, Flichy and Sauvage (1984:17) explain, 'L'information etait traité de façon à reintroduire le faits dans l'ordre des verites officielles' ('The information was treated as a way to present the facts under the order imposed by the official truth').

When the socialists came into power under the leadership of Mitterand in 1981 (until 1986), many observers believed that the restructuring of the broadcasting system would become one of the most likely new reforms. Yet instead of reviving the values of public service, especially in the light of traditional socialist opposition to private ownership in broadcasting, the socialist government began liberalizing the French airwaves (Vedel, 2005).

The Broadcasting Law of 1982[10] aimed to free state broadcasting from political control and establish the Haute Autorité de l'Audiovisuel – the

High Authority for Broadcasting – also responsible for nominating the directors of public television channels. Competition to public television arrived in 1984, in the form of a terrestrial pay TV channel, Canal+. In 1986, shortly before the general elections, two more private free-to-air television channels were granted licences by the government, La Cinq and TV6 (later M6).

It should be noted that the 1982 reform did not change the legal nature of French television, but rather it retained its status as a public service. Consequently, the public channels were required to fulfil obligations laid down in a *Cahier des Charges* (charter). These stated, for example, that news coverage had to be carried out according to principles of 'honesty, independence and pluralism': The channels also had obligations to spread and protect French culture, to guarantee access to different groups of French society and to increase the knowledge of citizens.

As previously mentioned, the reform aimed to diminish the historic grip of government on TV by introducing the High Authority for Audiovisual Communication (*Haute autorité de l'audiovisuel*). The authority was given powers to control broadcasting in order to guarantee independence from the State (its most crucial power was to nominate the Director General of governors of the board). It was also charged with checking the compliance of the broadcasters with the public objectives set out in the *Cahier des charges*. However, as Kuhn (1995) observes:

> it proved very difficult for the Socialists to make a clean break with the tradition of political interference, since their support in principle for the application of public service ideals to political output clashed in practice with their desire to have their policies presented in a favourable light. (Kuhn, 1995: 177)

The victory of a right-wing government led by Jacques Chirac in March 1986 saw the further liberalization of French broadcasting with the Law on Freedom of Communication in 1986.[11] This set up a new legal framework for a dual broadcasting system. Many of the public service obligations established by the 1986 law are imposed on both private and state-funded broadcasters. The public channels have detailed programming obligations listed in the *Cahier des charges*, particularly in relation to their educational, cultural and social missions. Private broadcasters have to comply with regulations approved in consultation with the *Conseil d'Etat* (the highest administrative court) for issues related to advertising, broadcasting of programmes of French and European origin during peak hours and contributing to the development of audiovisual programme production.

The new law also established a new regulatory agency, the National Commission for Communication and Freedoms (*Commission nationale de la communication et des libertés*, CNCL). However, with the privatization of TF1, the main public channel, by Chirac's government in 1987 a radical alteration in the television market took place in France. After 1987 private channels led by TF1 gained the largest audience ratings, while the two remaining public channels, Antenne 2 and FR3, lagged behind.

Under the new socialist government that came to power in 1989, the existing regulatory authority was replaced by the Higher Council for Broadcasting (*Conseil supérieur de l'audiovisuel*, CSA) with much broader competences.[12] The previous CNCL had never enjoyed a high degree of professional credibility and independence from the government, but kept perpetuating the historical pattern of governmental influence described earlier.[13]

Yet, the CSA's lack of political independence is still often highlighted (Dagnaud, 2000; Dagnaud, 2009; Sergeant, 2009; Vedel, 2005). Because the CSA commissioners are appointed by political authorities, or have previously been associated with the television industry, they are suspected of lacking neutrality. This criticism has usually arisen when the CSA appoints heads of public television stations. At the same time, it should be emphasized that, prior to the start of the Sarkozy presidency, the Council has survived switches in government between left and right over an eighteen-year period and its existence has constrained the freedom of the President and government to interfere directly in the management of public television.

The 1986 reform is also extremely important for having explicitly defined the obligations assigned to PSBs. The Law on Freedom of Communication 1986(Freedom of Communication Law, 1986) states:

> The public broadcasters must serve the public interest and are in charge of fulfilling public service missions. They must provide the public, taken in all its components [diversity], with a set of programmes and services characterised by diversity and pluralism, quality and innovation, respect for people's rights and democratic principles as defined by the constitution. They must supply a wide range and diversity of programmes, covering the areas of news, culture, knowledge, entertainment and sports. They must contribute to the democratic debate within French society as well as to the social inclusion of citizens. They must ensure the promotion of the French language and reflect

the diversity of cultural heritage in its regional and local dimensions. They must contribute to the development and diffusion of ideas and arts. They *must* also spread civic, economic, social and scientific knowledge and contribute to media literacy. They have to ensure that the deaf and people who are hard of hearing can access their programmes. Public broadcasters must provide honest, independent and pluralist news and contribute to the pluralist expression of social and political forces on an equal basis and according to the recommendations issued by the CSA. Finally, public broadcasters must take part in French external audiovisual policies and contribute to the diffusion of French language and culture abroad. They must develop new technologies and services in order to continuously enrich their programmes. (Freedom of Communication Law, 1986, Art. 43-11)

The number of public television channels on terrestrial networks expanded in the 1990s, while its commercial rivals actually decreased. After the failure of La Cinq in 1992, the fifth terrestrial network was assigned to be shared between ARTE – the Franco-German cultural channel – and the educational channel La Cinquième (later renamed France 5); both are now part of France Télévisions. France Télévisions was established by the Law on Freedom of Communication of 2000 as a holding company. It runs three national television channels – France 2, France 3 and France 5 – and one digital channel, France 4. Radio France Outre Mer (RFO) is also part of France Télévisions, and operates public television and radio channels in French territories outside metropolitan France, and several thematic channels transmitted via cable and satellite.

Created in 1964 under the name Antenne 2, France 2 offers news and general programming, including feature films, sports, current affairs, entertainment and talk-shows. It is the main competitor of TF1, the most successful broadcasting channel in terms of audience share (31%). France 3, founded in 1969, has a clear obligation to deliver regional and local news. It broadcasts bulletins produced by 13 regional directorates and 37 local bureaus. France 5 – established in December 1994 under the name La Cinquième – is an educational channel devoted to educational and cultural programmes and documentaries. Today, France 5 and ARTE benefit from separate digital terrestrial networks but they used to share the same frequency. More recently, France Télévisions has taken advantage of the launch of digital terrestrial television to expand its programming. It launched France 4, aimed at 25–49-year-olds, with a strong output of cinema, concerts and theatre festivals.

The BBC and its Charter renewal

The BBC is constitutionally established by a Royal Charter that last ten years, and this is complemented by an Agreement between the BBC and the Secretary of State for Culture, Media &Sport. The apparent conflict between liberal market theory as the dominant political ideology in UK communication policy and the public interest argument in support of Public Service Broadcasting is certainly apparent in the debate for the latest renewal of the BBC Royal Charter, which was granted to the BBC on 19 September 2006 and took effect from 1 January 2007. Thus, while the structure and function of the BBC has been guaranteed for the next ten years, the new reform also introduced a set of checks on the BBC that in some scholars' view could 'lock the BBC into a much more precisely defined set of responsibilities and outputs' (Barnett, 2006: 20), which could be seen as 'a means of reassuring competitors that the BBC will, indeed, be "tamed" [...] in its ability to operate freely within the market-place' (Barnett, 2006: 18).

The complex system of controls to prevent the BBC from unfairly competing with commercial operators has been widely transformed by the most recent reform. The first and most important aspect of this change has been the introduction of a BBC Trust.

The BBC Trust: Guarantor of BBC independence

The BBC Board of Governors has been abolished and replaced by the BBC Trust, which, according to the Department for Culture, Media & Sport, is responsible for 'setting the overall strategic direction of the BBC, including its priorities, and exercising a general oversight of the work of the Executive Board' (DCMS, 2006a: 7) In this way the two bodies become completely independent from each other, given the BBC Trust's duty of holding the Executive Board to account in the public interest.

According to the government's White Paper (DCMS, 2006a),[14] the BBC Trust has to carry out its control on BBC through a 'triple lock system' (DCMS, 2006a: 3). 'Firstly, every service will be run according to a new, detailed service licence' (ibid.: 3).[15] Secondly, all the content will have to comply with 'new criteria of quality, originality, innovation, challenge and engagement' (ibid.: 3). Thirdly, 'any significantly changed or new BBC service will have to undergo detailed scrutiny via a Public Value Test to determine how it will serve the public interest, and to weight that against any impact on the market' (ibid.: 3).

The first two requirements throw out one of the main points of the argument that the BBC can indeed unfairly compete with commercial operators. Indeed, Cave et al. (2004), in their study *Regulating the BBC*, claimed that 'the absence of a satisfactory definition of PSB is a clear impediment to the development of a fully justified view of the appropriate arena for use of the licence fee' (Cave et al., 2004: 261). However, the new provisions offer exactly the specificity that is required. More precisely, 'the service licence is the most important means by which the Trust will hold the Executive to account for delivery of individual services. It also provides the link between the BBC's public purpose and its services' (DCMS, 2006: 29), while the new 'six public purposes' (ibid.: 6) of the BBC give a detailed definition of PSB.[16] Moreover, the second 'lock' requires that every type of content fulfils the new public service criteria mentioned above. Thus, in summary,

> every BBC programme or item of online content is required to demonstrate at least one of these public service characteristics. For the first time, then, every single element of BBC output – not just channels and stations, but individual programmes – will be vulnerable to challenge by commercial rivals as well as members of the public for not meeting one of those criteria. (Barnett, 2006: 20)

Approval process for new services: The Public Value Test

The third form of check established by the reform concerns the approval process for new BBC services. Whereas before the new Charter, consent was given by the Secretary of State following approval by the Board of Governors (Cave et al., 2004: 262), today proposals for significant change to existing services or for new services are subject to a Public Value Test. As will be explained in Chapter 7, the test consists of a public value assessment carried out by the BBC Trust of the consumer-citizen benefits of the proposals and a market impact assessment carried out by Ofcom. Moreover, the White Paper explains,

> we are also committed to sustaining a vibrant, dynamic commercial sector. This means balancing the flexibility we will give to the BBC with strong measures to give the wider industry greater clarity and certainty about the BBC's activities. (DCMS, 2006a: 28)

These new arrangements contrast with the previous greater flexibility recognized to BBC with the former Charter, when the Secretary of State consents to a new service were typically very broad, raising criticism about the risk of the BBC intruding into the market sphere without any formal consultation process (Cave et al., 2004: 262).

Furthermore, 'for the first time in BBC history, there is an explicit injunction to take into account not only the public interest, but the commercial interest as well'(Barnett, 2006: 20). Therefore, not only will this third lock prevent the BBC from intruding into the commercial space, but some commentators fear that, in balancing public and commercial interests, 'the BBC Trust is likely to face enormous lobbying pressure from the commercial sector to be as restrictive as possible' (Barnett, 2006: 21).

Yet, as will be discussed further in Chapter 7, in conducting the first Public Value Test in April 2007, the BBC Trust showed itself capable of fair judgement. On this occasion the BBC Trust gave final approval to BBC on-demand proposals for the online seven-day catch-up TV service through the BBC i Player. As the Trust makes clear in the conclusion paper of the Public Value Test,

> 'in assessing the BBC Executive's proposal, we were guided by the public interest in two senses. The first of these was to be satisfied that the new on-demand propositions would be genuinely valuable to the public. The second was to take care that, in providing new offerings, the BBC would not limit choice elsewhere. In brief, we have not altered our view that each of the proposals is likely to deliver significant public value, enough to justify the likely market impact'. (BBC Trust, 2007b: f2)

TVE: Its political, cultural and historical legacy

Television Espanola (TVE) was created under the dictatorship of General Franco. It had a peculiar funding system based largely on advertisement in condition of public monopoly as well as public resources (Bustamante, 1989; Escobar, 1992). This distinguishing twofold feature of Television Espanola, which on the one hand was subject to strict political control, while on the other was largely commercially oriented, has influenced its role and activities right up until the time it was reformed and into the present day.

The centralization of radio and television broadcasts, along with a strict control of telecommunications, characterized the dictatorship of Francisco Franco (1939–1975). Televisión Española started broadcasting in 1956, while a second state-controlled-television channel was launched in 1965. Both channels were at all times regulated by the state; a situation that lasted almost thirty years. The interim *Transición* government established after Franco's death exposed the need to regulate radio and television services. Nevertheless, the liberalization of radio was only fully accomplished in 1977, when the government of Adolfo Suárez granted 300 licences to broadcast in Frequency Modulation (FM). However, by 1976 the SER network had already transmitted the famous *Hora 25* for the first time, evading the State's monopoly on radio broadcasting. Two large communication groups also took advantage of this confusing situation: Antena-3 Radio and Radio 80. These movements rejuvenated radio, with SER, COPE, Radio Rato and Cadena 13 becoming leading stations. However, it should be noted that local unauthorized stations flourished under the shield of illegality.

Meanwhile, TVE also started undergoing a radical reorganization. The TVE board of directors was created in 1976, and aimed to advise, orientate and determine all the programmes emitted by the station. A year later, TVE was transformed and configured as an independent and commercial organization. However, it was hard to cancel thirty years of political and state control in less than a year.

During Franco's dictatorship 'Radio and television were media for non-polemical entertainment, and for information which was controlled, slanted or restricted with the Spanish population in mind' (Escobar, 1992: 242). After Franco's death in 1975, despite the changes in audiovisual legislation, TVE has been distinguished by a strong political influence as well as a strong commercial orientation (Bustamante, 2008). As Bustamante highlights as regards TVE:

> The two prime functions of television are political persuasion and the acceleration of the economic process. [...] Both elements are crucial to understand the development of Spanish television during the years of dictatorship. [...] But this model, shaped during two decades (1956–76) and stamped in the collective memory of society, is not foreign to the concepts and decisions taken in the period of democratic transition and to the tardy democratization of television. (Bustamante, 1989: 69)

The most significant example of this long-lasting pattern can be found in the wording of the first law concerning television: Act 4/1980, of 10 January 1980, the Statute of Radio and Television. This law states that the Director General of RTVE has to be nominated by the Government, while the Administrative Board has to be chosen by each house of Parliament.[17] At the same time, this law maintained the commercial model based mainly on advertisements.

The relative novelty of the Spanish regulations in comparison with those of other European countries is clearly the result of the undemocratic nature of the State's previous political regime. The Statute of 12 January 1980 reaffirmed radio and television as State-run services, exclusively owned by the State according to Art. 1.2. The law that provided the first legal basis of this television monopoly was not passed until 1980 with the approval of Act 4/1980. For the first time in Spanish history, the law provided a definition of television services, and settled some basic principles of the television regulatory system that are still valid today.

Art. 1 of the 1980 Law defines television broadcasting as an 'essential public service legally entitled to the State' and, as a consequence, affords the State the power of assigning broadcasting rights as well as administrative 'concessions' for the management of television services, as the unique method to start developing private broadcasting activities.[18] It goes without saying that in the years following the establishment of Spanish democracy up until Act 10/1988, when private broadcasters were legally recognized, TVE enjoyed a monopoly position as the only receiver of TV advertising, with the exception of the autonomous television channels.[19]

However, Act 10/1988 radically changed the Spanish television market and the position of TVE within it. The State monopoly was broken and three analogic commercial national broadcasters were granted administrative concessions: ANTENA 3, TELE 5 and CANAL PLUS. Furthermore, in the mid-1980s, local cable and analogue terrestrial television stations were launched but were considered 'illegal' because of the inexistence of regulatory provisions on the issue. The laws that recognized their legal status came with the approval of Act 41/1995 (22/12/1995), on local television, and Act 42/1995 (22/12/1995), on cable telecommunications.

The evolution of the legal framework explains why, when the competition of commercial broadcasters arose in Spain, financial and institutional crisis at TVE, which had for many years become a self-funded institution through advertisement, was inescapable.[20] As Bustamante observes (1989):

> we can see that in eleven years (1976–87), income from advertising has risen by 1265 percent while the state subsidy in the same period increased by 14 percent. [...] In 1976 state subsidy represented 15 percent, with an increase of 27 percent in 1980, but by 1986 state subsidies were reduced to 1.8 percent and in 1987, the income from advertising constituted more than 94 percent of the total income. (Bustamante, 1989: 72)

Clearly, the total subordination of PSB in Spain to the advertising industry and the absence of a cultural policy for public television – with the only exception being the limits on importing foreign material – has given rise to the extreme commercialization of TVE, so that it has never really distinguished itself from its commercial competitors. Since the 1980s, the Spanish socialist party has also backed a neo-liberal ideology, which has always accused PSB of being just a replica of commercial broadcasters and a burden on taxpayers.

In effect, since the start of the new democratic era for Spain, TVE has never been legitimized as public service television. It was never really independent from Government control and was oriented to populist entertainment. Besides, the strong competition for advertising that has arisen since the end of the 1980shas also triggered a radical financial crisis that has increased its uncertainty in terms of mission, strategy and market positioning. This is also reflected also in the incredible loss of audience share: from 1990 to 2006 TVE1's share has decreased from 52% to 18.2% (Figure 5.1).

The historical context helps explain the importance of the reform of RTVE undertaken by the Zapatero Government in 2005, in particular by the

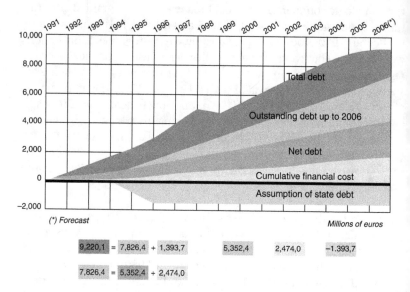

Figure 5.1 The growth of debts accumulated by RTVE 1991–2006 (Informe Anual RTVE, 2005)

17/2006 Act regulating State radio and television (Spanish TV Law, 2006) As will be further explained in Chapters 7 and 9, this law is the result of a report on the situation of RTVE produced by a government-appointed committee, the so-called *'Informe de los Sabios'*,[21] which proposed a radical change of its organization, funding and structure.[22] More precisely, the *Informe* recommended establishing a more independent management of RTVE, a transparent system of accounting, fixed limits for advertisement and increased state funding for RTVE.[23]

RAI and its tradition

Public Service Broadcasting in Italy is provided by RAI, under a 20-year Licence Convention between the State and RAI, which specifies the conditions of utilization of the licence and a Service Contract – *contratto di servizio* – that clarifies the objectives and the remit of the PSB.

At a time where the European debate on the evolution of PSB became intense (1997–2007), RAI has undergone different reforms concerning its accountability and independence, its supervision, its remit and objectives.

However, the expected reform to secure total independence of Italian PSB from the government was never really passed, nor was the path suggested by the RAI Act of 1975 and subsequent Constitutional Court decisions taken.

The policy framework of RAI is set out by the Broadcasting Law, the Licence Convention and the Service Contract between the Secretary of State for Communications and RAI, which indicates all remits and obligations of the providers of PSB.

The so-called 'Gasparri Law' (from the name of the Minister who sponsored it) (Gasparri Law, 2004) and the subsequent Act of 2005 (Consolidated Broadcasting Law, 2005), which sets out the Italian broadcasting framework, details the main duties of PSB, including:

- Broadcasting an adequate number of radio and television programmes devoted to education, information, training, promotion of culture, and theatrical, cinematographic, television and musical works, including works in the original language, that are recognized as being of great artistic value or highly innovative.
- Allotting broadcasting time, in accordance with the legislation, to: all parties and groups represented in Parliament [...]
- Broadcasting children's programmes at appropriate hours.

- Preserving, and providing public access to, historical radio and television archives.
- Reserving a quota of no less than 15 per cent of the overall annual revenue forthe production of European works, including those made by independent producers.
- Creating interactive digital services of public utility. (Gasparri Law, 2004, Art. 17).

RAI's funding is based on a mixed system of licence fee and advertisements. While the public funding that RAI receives is – as seen in Table 5.7 – much higher than other Southern European counterparts, the high level of tax evasion accounts for the necessity of RAI to produce commercial programmes to attract higher ratings. The commercialization of RAI's output has also been enhanced by the sole competition of the other commercial competitor – Mediaset – given the lack of pluralism of the Italian television market (Figure 5.2).

The ongoing duopoly of the public service broadcaster RAI and former Prime Minister Silvio Berlusconi's Mediaset group is visibly at odds with the principle of media pluralism explicitly enshrined in Art. 11(2) of the Charter of Fundamental Rights of the European Union and acknowledged by the jurisprudence of the European Court of Human Rights (ECHR) based on Arts 10 of the European Convention on Human

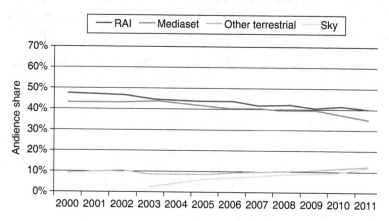

Figure 5.2 Audience of RAI and Mediaset channels 2000–2011
Source: AGCOM Report 2012 (in Italian).

Rights. In particular, in a recent case regarding Italy, the European Court of Human Rights observed that

> in such a sensitive sector as the audiovisual media ... the State has a positive obligation to put in place an appropriate legislative and administrative framework to guarantee effective pluralism. [...] This is especially desirable when, as in the present case, the national audiovisual system is characterised by a duopoly. (European Court of Human Rights, 2012)

The following chapter analyses the extent to which these historical, political and cultural legacies have influenced the online expansion policies of the five European PSBs studied. Has the distinctive ethos of each PSB institution continued to characterize its Internet expansion? Or is a convergence of political and institutional policies on PSB observable?

6
The Impact of Historical, Political and Cultural Legacies on PSB Online in Europe

This chapter aims to analyze the national and institutional policies on PSB online in the countries selected. It highlights how the historical, political and cultural factors that characterize the ethos of each PSB framework have dictated the development of PSB online in each case considered.

National and institutional policies on RTVE online

As described in Chapter 6, when the competition of commercial broadcasters was introduced in Spain by Act 10/1988, TVE began to suffer a crisis of resources. Year by year, the level of accumulated debt became more and more serious. From 1991 to 2006, the debt of Radio televisión Española (RTVE) – the public broadcasting corporation that since 1973 incorporated the public radio (RNE) and Television (TVE) – grew to 9 million euros (RTVE, 2005). For the historical and institutional reasons highlighted – namely, the lack of dedicated resources and the deep structural crisis of TVE – investments in online ventures were feeble until the new reform brought in by Act 17/2006 (Spanish TV Law (2006). The reform had an important bearing on the development of the Internet activities of RTVE because it readjusted its organization, funding and structure and drove the growth of RTVE online.[1] As Bustamante, a member of the 'council of wise men' that drafted the reform – the *Informe*–explains (2008):

> With the reform we had to face two issues combined. On one hand the transformation of TVE into a more democratic PSB. On the other hand we had to face the new digital and online scenario. (Bustamante, 2008: 2)

The turning point in the history of the Internet activities of RTVE dates back to the Zapatero reform of 2005–2006. Although RTVE.es started its activities in 1996, before the reform, the online activities were initially very minimal. As demonstrated in an EBU–BBC survey in 2006, RTVE was positioned last in the European ranking of EBU member websites (EBU and BBC, 2007). According to the survey, 4.9% of the active online audience visited TVE's site in the month of June 2007 (EBU and BBC, 2007). During the same period of 2007, the reach of DR online was 36.8% and of the BBC websites was 59.6%, whereas RAI's online sites attained 11% and France Télévisions 16.7 % (EBU and BBC, 2007).

The reasons for this delay in the development of RTVE online and its consequent low ranking among European countries was the grave financial crisis faced by RTVE in the 1990s, the mishandling of the budget, the inefficiency of the organization and the continuous turn-over of managers according to the different political affiliations in power. From its launch in 1996, the RTVE portal was characterized by a lack of resources, to the extent that the online content was updated just once a week. As Carmen Caffarel, General Manager of RTVE under the first Zapatero government, declared at the time of the first relaunch of the portal in 2004: 'The portal of RTVE was attended just by three people in the morning and the content was sometimes not updated in weeks' (Diarios, 2004: 22).

From Parliamentary discussions of 2004 we can appreciate for the first time what type of online offer was envisaged. An MP from the Socialist Group, Rosa Lucia Polonio Contreras, declared:

> The Internet portal of RTVE should be not just a complement to pub-lic service, but should be itself conceived as a public service, being one of the activities of RTVE as a public entity. Therefore our group consider that RTVE can neither remain being unconnected to the new media scenario, neither can start integrating in the information society with so many disadvantages in comparison to the private competitors. (Diarios, 2004: 22; author's translation)

This quote is relevant in showing once again the double character of PSB philosophy in Spain that persisted in the online world: on the one hand, the need to deliver classic PSB output, and on the other, a strong commercial requirement to be competitive in the market in order to collect advertising revenue.

As mentioned earlier, even though the online activities of RTVE were launched in 1996, it was only in 2004 under the direction of Carmen

Caffarel that the organization of RTVE's online services started to progress. New streaming content produced by TVE and by the National Radio (RNE) enriched the platform, and the number of professionals working for the portal reached 12. In June 2005, the number of pages viewed per month was 1.1 million, and in December of the same year, that figure reached 13.4 million (Figure 6.1).

However, it was the reform of 2005–2006 that brought a radical innovation to the Internet department of RTVE. The draft of the reform – the '*informe*' – that paved the way to the new law on RTVE recognized the absolute need for RTVE of creating a

> portal with its own identity and resources and with the autonomy to develop its potential. The portal would serve as a technological platform that could modernize and better the new structure of RTVE, in order to [...] become the best point of reference for the development of the Group. (Informe, 2005: 126, author's translation)

In order to appreciate the contrasting ideas behind the vision of RTVE online within the institution, it is worthwhile to juxtapose the wording of the draft of the reform – the *informe* – with the Annual Report of RTVE of the same year. According to the draft of the reform:

> The Internet of RTVE should offer radio, TV, and multimedia services that are adequate for a two-way communication. That means that it should be strongly participative and democratic for the citizens, according to a vision of public service. (Informe, 2005: 127)

This quote certainly illustrates the aspiration – for the 'council of wise men' that was asked to reform the public television of Spain – to achieve

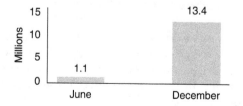

Figure 6.1   Page views per month, RTVE.es 2005
Source: RTVE Informe Anual 2005.

an authentic public service in the online sphere. In contrast, the wording of the Annual Report of RTVE 2005 states that:

> The presence of RTVE online becomes crucial both from the point of view of the public service and the business. (RTVE, 2005)

Once again, the debate around PSB online in Spain mirrors the debate about public service television. Even if there is, in the spirit of the reform, the urge to secure the aims of a PSB institution, this idea always clashes with the strong commercial orientation that has traditionally characterized TVE with its prerequisite of obtaining resources through advertising. According to Art. 5 of Act 17 of 2006, the objectives of the public service have to be defined by a 'Mandato Marco',[2] endorsed by the Parliament every nine years. The first Mandato Marco signed at the end of 2007, in line with the Informe, gives new relevance to the Internet activities of RTVE:

> It is part of the public service of RTVE to produce, develop and transmit through different platforms–radio, TV, interactive media and internet – quality, equal and diverse content for every type of public and genre [...] in order to satisfy the needs of information, culture, education and entertainment of the Spanish Society and to reflect its identity and cultural and linguistic diversity, and in order to promote pluralism and participation. (Mandato Marco, 2007)

Hence, the 'agreement on the foundation of RTVE as a corporation',[3] establishes a new separate division for the Multimedia and Interactive Services of RTVE (Acuerdo RTVE, 2006).

Practices of RTVE online

The Multimedia division launched in 2008 employed 70 professionals, a big change to the previous organization where just 12 people were employed. A new portal – RTVE.es – was launched on 20 May 2008 under the supervision of the first director of New Interactive Media of RTVE, Rosalia Lloret. For the first time in RTVE history, the accounting transparency required by Act 17 of 2006 allowed the new division to have a separate budget for a period of three years as a result of the Contrato Programa.[4]

Notwithstanding the great delay of RTVE's online presence, as appreciated by the new President of RTVE, Luis Fernandez,[5] the new portal RTVE.es has increased unique users from an average of fewer than

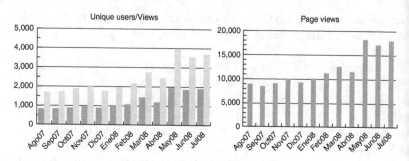

Figure 6.2   Page views and unique users, RTVE.es 2008
Source: OJD Interactiva, July 2008.

1 million a month in 2007 to an average of almost 2 million in 2008 and up to 7 million in 2010 (ODJ Interactiva, 2008, 2010) (see Figure 6.2).

Since its transformation in 2008, an ambitious plan to upload both radio and broadcasting content produced by TVE and RNE (Radio Nacional de España) was undertaken, with a goal for the online archive of making available more than one million hours of programmes. Furthermore, the news offer was enhanced by news services produced by a separate online news division. As Rosalia Lloret (2008) explains:

> We have a very similar platform to the BBC i Player, Television a la carta. In fact, you can watch everything that is broadcast on TVE for 7 days after the transmission. (Lloret, 2008)

She also explains the promise to deliver more news:

> We have 1000 people working for the news at TVE and we already collect the news produced by TVE but also by Radio National. The result is a very multimedia website, where we offer video and audio, but also texts. (Lloret, 2008)

Notwithstanding the reform and the accomplishments of the new division, a strong entertainment and commercial vocation was apparent in the new portal. This trait was explained by the prominent reliance of RTVE on advertisements (accounting for approximately 65% of its total funding) up until the 'counter reform' of 2009.[6] Hence, in 2008 Lloret confirmed that:

> We believe that the portal should also spur the online advertisement market that in Spain is still stagnant at 7%. (Lloret, 2008)

However, the abolition of advertisements might have a high impact not only the budget of RTVE.es, but also on its content. The strong commercial orientation that has so far characterized RTVE on the web could diminish and more space could be given to news, public affairs and educational content. Although this outcome could be guaranteed just by solid public investment, the current finances of RTVE seem to have been returned to the realm of uncertainty, as in the pre-reform years. If the resources are put in doubt, the recent progress of RTVE.es could be jeopardized. In fact, in April 2010 RTVE reached 7 million unique users per month and surpassed the success of its commercial competitors online by 1 million unique users (ODJ Interactiva, 2010). According to ODJ Interactiva, in April 2010 the number of unique users of Antena 3 and Telecinco were both about 6 million. This result also confirms that RTVE.es on the web is more a competitor of the commercial broadcasters than of online news providers. Thus, RTVE is still placed in the category of 'entertainment media' by OJD Interactiva, being separated from the websites of newspapers such as *El Mundo* or *El Periodico* that are listed as providers of news. *El Mundo* online enjoyed its supremacy as an online news provider at least until April 2010, when it had 25 million unique users and 377 million page views (OJD Interactiva, 2010).

In a nutshell, RTVE's online expansion has been constrained by a radical institutional and structural crisis that afflicted Spanish PSB between 1991 and 2006. The inadequate resources invested by RTVE delayed the development of its online output until the radical change brought by Act 17/2006. Since then, the Multimedia division launched in 2008 with its 70 professionals has implemented a clear strategy of expansion. Still, a strong entertainment and commercial vocation characterizes RTVE's online content.

Public and institutional policies of DR online: First came the practices and then the policies

In the words of the former 10-year CEO of Denmark Radio (DR), Christian Nissen, DR's online activities started in 1994 as an 'underground experiment' (Nissen, 2009). In fact, it was the inventiveness and curiosity of some Internet-savvy employees working in radio and TV that brought to launch the first web pages for DR's programmes.

During those years, DR was undergoing a massive reorganization, given that the objective was to turn DR into a more competitive institution and certainly more dedicated to its audience (Nissen, 2009). The challenge of this fundamental reform for DR was contained in an important policy document issued by DR, *Danmarks Radio 1995–2005*, which contained strategies for programmes, TV channels and radio. It also showed a deeper reflection on the core values of DR.[7] However, the plan approved on 8 November 1994 enclosed in a book of more than 100 pages never mentioned the word *Internet* (Nissen, 2009).[8]

Certainly the Board of Directors knew about the onset of the online world, but did not consider the Internet as a new possibility of expansion for DR. Thus, the change came very soon and it was unexpected (Nissen, 2009).[9]

In fact, in the following six months, some programme unit teams were beginning, without any formal assignment from the Board of Directors, to run their own web pages. As Nissen recalled:

> What they were starting doing online was interesting, but not under the control of the Board of Directors. That was quite disturbing...for this reason I decided to look into that and to establish a program team to explore the new possibility offered by the online world. (Nissen, 2009)

After a couple of months, at the beginning of 1995, the leader of the project presented its vision for DR online at a board meeting. The presentation was not convincing, because it lacked a monitor to display the plans for web pages, activities and new territories. Nissen (2009) explained:

> Then, after a month, the project leader came back to the Board meeting with a computer, showing how the webpages of DR might look like. That was the beginning of Dr.dk. (Nissen, 2009)

As shown by this brief account, DR online started really as an experiment. In fact, it launched on 5 January 1996, as a six-month trial and it was not subject to a legal framework (Søndergaard, 2009).[10]

The budget allocated to DR was not independent from radio and TV at the beginning. Radio and TV employees who wanted to take part in the new online initiatives were doing so during their normal working hours. In fact, for the first two years, they had very few people – four or five – working exclusively for DR.dk platform (Brügger, 2009).

National policies and the legal framework of DR.dk

As in several other countries of Europe (Svendsen, 2002) the Danish Broadcasting Act sets out some of the most important principles for

DR: it establishes its nature as a public service institution, its broad obligations, independence and organization. Chapter 2 Art. 10 of the Broadcasting Act of 2007 clearly states:

> The overall public service activities shall, via television, radio and the Internet or similar, provide the Danish population with a wide selection of programmes and services comprising news coverage, general information, education, art and entertainment. Quality, versatility and diversity must be aimed at in the range of programmes provided. In the planning of programmes' freedom of information and of expression shall be a primary concern. Objectivity and impartiality must be sought in the information coverage. Programming shall ensure that the general public has access to important information on society and debate. Furthermore, particular emphasis shall be placed on Danish language and culture. Programming shall cover all genres in the production of art and culture and provide programmes that reflect the diversity of cultural interests in Danish society.[11]

In addition to the Broadcasting Act, the policy framework for DR is specified by a 'Media Political Agreement' negotiated every four years by parties in Parliament. This agreement integrates and implements the Danish Broadcasting Act and is flexible enough to allow for amendment during the four years of its remit. It specifies the licence fee for the period and also clarifies general objectives for DR. Accordingly to the 2006–2010 Media Agreement[12] DR provides public service content

> In the form of text, sound and images that meet cultural, social and democratic needs of the Danish society – in all relevant technological platforms. DR will have to be able to produce public service that is specifically developed for these platforms. (Danish Media Agreement, 2006)

However, the Media Agreement can set also more specific duties for DR, for example:

> DR must establish a digital combined children/history channel. This channel is part of DR's total public service provision and funded exclusively by license fees. (Danish Media Agreement, 2006)

Moreover, the Media Agreement can settle other media policies issues not necessarily referred to DR, such as the development of digital take-up or decisions concerning TV channels other than DR. Also, it often reflects on the other important piece of policy that shape DR's activities, the service contract. In fact, the service contract between DR and the Danish Minister for Culture lays out the objectives and aims of DR for the period that coincides with the Media Agreement.

> The purpose of the contract is to specify the tasks DR is expected to perform and to identify the scope within which the public service activities can be carried out. (Public Service Contract, 2007)

National policies on DR online

As discussed in Chapter 5, the strong tradition of popular enlightenment in Denmark has determined the main characteristic of Danish PSB. Accordingly to this ethos, DR should constitute an instrument of education for all the Danish people, should enhance the protection of the Danish heritage and pursue social inclusion. As soon as it was clear that the Internet had a remarkable potential for inclusiveness of the Danish public, Internet activities started being conceived as the third arm of DR. As Søndegaard (2009) explains:

> the online idea of PSB rests very strong within the idea of reaching a lot of the population, because sometimes it's not easy in Denmark to reach certain parts of the population, therefore it's a way to reach the public. (Søndergaard, 2009)

The Broadcasting Act of December 2000 added (§10) the Internet as one of the platforms that DR should develop. For the first time, the Act was contemplating the idea that 'public service shall be provided via television, radio and internet or the like'.[13]

It is clear from the wording of the general policies developed then by the Danish government that the ethos characterizing DR the broadcaster should be informing DR's online activities. In fact, Broadcasting Act 2002, for example, clarifies that the same aims of DR should be achieved throughout all the platforms at its disposal. The Internet therefore was seen as another important tool to reach the widest possible Danish public, including the part of the population that was more difficult to access through broadcasting alone:

> The overall public service activities shall provide, via television, radio and Internet or similar, the Danish population with a wide selection

of programmes and services comprising news coverage, general information, education, art and entertainment. The programming shall ensure that the general public has access to important information on society and debate. Furthermore, particular emphasis shall be placed on Danish language and culture. The programming shall cover all genres in the production of art and culture and provide programmes which reflect the diversity of cultural interests in Danish society. (Broadcasting Act, 2000)

As Nissen (2009) recalls:

According to the service contract, DR has to be for the many and the few. In fact, as a PSB, we should broadcast for the whole nation, therefore we should also reach minorities (cultural, age-range). That is a difficult task for a broadcaster, and in fact, at DR we tended to put minorities' programs later at night. But the internet gives you a great opportunity to cater for minorities. (Nissen, 2009)

The importance of reaching the wider Danish public is reaffirmed by the service contract between DR and the Minister of Culture (Public Service Contract, 2007), which clarifies the tasks that DR is expected to perform through 'television, radio, Internet or similar' and identifies the scope within which the public service activities can be carried out. More precisely, the main purposes of DR, according to the service contract, are to:

- Strengthen citizens' capacity efficiency in a democratic society;
- Reflect Denmark and the Danes;
- Stimulate creativity and culture;
- Promote knowledge and understanding.[14]

What emerges from these policies is that the principles that constitute the ethos of DR should inform all the platforms of the Danish broadcaster. Certainly, the same ethos has to characterize the online offer. So, for example, 'News' has always constituted a priority for DR the broadcaster, but the same pattern is replicated by the offer of DR online. Moreover Art. 2 of the Public Service Contract (2007) states that 'DR shall launch a news channel on the Internet during the contract term'. Moreover, it is clear from the policy documents (in particular from the public service contract) that DR online has also received a specific additional mandate to strengthen DR's connection with younger audiences and to enhance the educational offer of DR. Indeed, the Public Service Contract (2007) clarifies in Art. 2 that 'DR must pay particular attention to the use of all technological platforms, including the Internet, for educational programmes and services'.

Practices of DR online

DR's web platform is one the most advanced and most successful in terms of unique users among European PSBs, in a country that continues to stand top intechnological development globally.[15] As shown in Table 6.1, in March 2009 DR.dk led the ranking of online websites and also the online news website for unique users in Denmark.

Among DR's online activities, a prominent space is given to the delivery of news online, as one of the main statutory objectives of DR. Moreover, both DR channels are streamed online, as well as all the radio channels. Besides the TV/radio platform, a new web channel, Update, has been launched with the aim of giving the public the choice to get constant updates about programmes by clicking on very small clips of 5–7 minutes. The success of Update on the web has led DR to the decision to launch its digital version on the digital TV platform (Westman Hertz, 2009; Busck Porsbo, 2009). Additionally, DR Online has had since the very beginning of its activities the ambition to enhance the connection of DR with a younger audience. As a consequence, DR has built a successful youth community online, called Skum,[16] where children can share news, tastes, readings and discussion forums. Additionally, there

Table 6.1   Ranking of online websites, Denmark, 2009

No	Release	Users	Visit	Pageviews
1	dr.dk	1,946,586	18,297,854	106,205,678
2	krak.dk	1,771,745	8,335,098	39,427,294
3	tv2.dk	1,591,634	20,116,935	150,653,671
4	msn.dk	1,487,273	35,266,040	101,482,303
5	ekstrabladet.dk	1,421,650	25,919,328	102,636,413
6	dba.dk	1,249,757	8,219,605	117,278,140
7	eniro.dk	1,239,958	13,115,657	50,814,986
8	degulesider.dk	1,230,271	5,149,408	21,476,774
9	dmi.dk	936,724	9,801,731	35,705,203
10	bt.dk	931,497	12,717,046	60,939,234
11	rejseplanen.dk	829,255	2,574,816	11,926,666

Source: FDIM (2009) Foreningen af Danske Interaktive Medier, Ranking of top Danish Internet sites, March 2009.

s another important community, for a younger audience, known as T,[17] where different programmes for children are available.

> With Skum we have been the pioneer in the creation of the first youth community online. It started as the biggest youth community online in Denmark, but now there is a lot more of competition. For us the aim is always to make of Skum an alternative space to commercial online places for entertainment. We have succeeded in stimulating kids in building their space online. (Westman-Hertz, 2009)

The interactive character of the web has also given DR the idea of launching an online space where children can play and learn, called Oline,[18] which addresses a younger audience from three to seven years old. The Danish public has given Oline a positive reception (Westman-Hertz, 2009).

Besides these initiatives, the educational aims of DR online have been achieved through other strategies. A platform called Skole[19] (meaning school) has been developed to offer public schools, through the payment of a small fee, a variety of educational content ranging from history to science. And one of the most important achievements of DR online has been the creation of an impressive online archive, called Bonanza,[20] which is available to the public. The project of digitalization of the archive (the Cultural Heritage Project) started in 2007 with 75 million Danish Kroner (more than £9 million). Bonanza was launched in early 2008 and showcased an offer of up to 2,000 TV programmes:

> Our focus is first as a big 'wish list' where people let us know their wishes...100,000 people voted for that...so we started with the favourite top 5, then the top 10 and so on...TV, radio...in 2009 it would be more personal. We'll go more in details with each year... and everything in Bonanza is available forever. (Busck Porsbo, 2009)

Moreover, the Bonanza project was informed by a lucid participatory strategy, as the policy document that explains the aim of the new Archive clarifies:

> Bonanza was developed as a web concept involving the public in the digitalizing and prioritizing of their archived cultural heritage. The site contained snippets of archived material in ten categories each containing 100 programmes. For 12 weeks the public voted to decide, which favourite show should be made available on-demand

first. Each week a new category had one show voted to the top and it was immediately digitalized and made available online forever for everyone to watch. The voting generated substantial traffic and Bonanza was an instant hit. (Bonanza, 2008)

The Cultural Heritage Project is actually more ambitious then Bonanza itself. Its digitalization will end not before 2013 and involves the most important cultural organizations in Denmark, including state museums, national libraries and DR to create an even wider cultural archive online for the Danish people.

At the moment, DR has created an independent editorial area behind Bonanza, and new digital TV channels have emerged from the initiative: DR K (DR Culture and History channel), which broadcasts a daily Bonanza-branded two-hour slot from 6pm to 8pm, and DR Ramasjang (DR children's channel), which will broadcast archived children's programmes.

Evidently, this important achievement would have not been possible without an enabling copyright framework. In fact, since the start of the project, DR was committed to find a broad clearing agreement with the group of copyright holders with interests in the archives. Following the common Danish practice of extended collective agreements, on 1 January 2008, an agreement was reached between DR and all the copyright holders represented by the copyright manager Copy-Dan. The arrangement covers the rights inthe materials that constitute the archive, with 26 different organizations of copyright holders represented in the archives of DR (Busck Porsbo, 2009).

Finally, DR online has strongly invested in health information websites. The health website has aroused a controversy among DR's commercial competitors, because it involves different health institutions.

In summary, the strong public broadcasting ethos of DR characterized by an extensive offer of PSB outputs like news, public affairs, educational and cultural programmes is reproduced in its online offer. Since its launch DR online has been conceived independently from the broadcasting offer and has invested in the huge potential of the Internet to enhance the inclusiveness of the Danish public.

France Télévisions online: The regulatory framework

As showed in Chapter 5, the policies of PSB in France have been characterized by three main features: first, the frequent changes of legal framework that mirrored changes in political majorities in government; second, the firm interest of various governments not to lose their grip on PSB's output – especially news; and third, the *'exception culturelle'* that boosted the protection of French culture, language and the nation.

Brun-Buisson (2001) highlights the differences between *service public* in French and *public service* in Anglo-Saxon usage. According to him, when public service is concerned, there is a clear attitude in France to confuse *intérêt public* with *intérêt général*. The latter does not necessarily equate to the public interest, but it is rather something that the State defines through its public enterprises. More precisely, for Brun-Buisson:

> public service broadcasting in France is manifestly guaranteed through public enterprises, owned by the State and exploited by the State. (Brun-Buisson, 2001:21)

This *'etatiste'* pattern that characterizes public service broadcasting in France determines another distinctive trait of the policies that inform France Télévisions: that the most important policies regarding PSB in France come from the State rather than from France Télévisions.

The foremost document that frames the duties of France Télévisions is the Law of 1986 on the 'freedom of communication' (Communication Act, 1986).[21] This has been modified several times by Parliament and was radically changed by the reform of 2009 (Communication Act (2009). The law sets the most important principles that France Télévisions, as the provider of PSB, should follow:

1. Pluralism and diversity of output
2. Cultural enrichment
3. Objective information
4. Integration, solidarity and respect of civil rights
5. Protection of culture and language
6. Provision for education
7. Bring French culture to the world.

The second tier of legal provisions is represented by the *sde mission et charges* that is adopted by a Decree by the Government where the objectives of PSBs are listed. Until 2009, there were different *ssdes charges* for each channel, but the reform of 2009 introduced just one *cahier des charges* for France Télévisions. Every year each channel had to complete a review to state in which ways the missions and duty have been satisfied, while the CSA[22] controls the application of the *cahier des charges*.

The third tier is represented by the *contrat d'objectifs et de moyens*,,which constitutes a contract between the government and each channel to achieve the objectives requested by the law and by the decree, and which indicates the resources and the budget given to achieve those aims (Scirpo, 2009). In fact, it can be argued that one of the ways in which the State has exerted its control over France Télévisions has been the budget of French PSB. Historically, the budget has always been imposed by the government. At the beginning, it was imposed annually by the so-called 'budget law,' the *loi de finance*, a mechanism that made it difficult for PSB to plan a strategy for its future, especially in times of crisis for advertisement income.

However, a big change was achieved by the promulgation of the first *Contrat d'objectifs et de moyens 2001–2005 entre France Télévisions et l'Etat* (COM, 2001–2005), an agreement between the State and France Télévision, whichwas introduced by the audiovisual reform of August 2000 and allows for a better long-term planning for France Télévisions.

Policies on France Télévisions online

The new opportunity for France Télévisions of developing online activities is mentioned for the first time in the COM of 2001–2005. Interestingly, the new chances offered by the web are indicated by the document as an instrument to achieve the specific expectations of universality, diversity and pluralism of offer (COM, 2001):

> The websites and the interactivity have to fulfil two important aims: the universality of the public – that means they should address all the people without excluding and discriminating (COM, 2001–2005: 5–6)

More specifically, the 'universality of the public' relates 'not to an audience that is profitable', but to an audience that is 'socially legitimate' (COM, 2001–2005: 6–7) without discrimination. As requested in the COM 2001–2005, France Télévisions had to connect with the public not just through broadcasting but through the whole range of new platforms and interactive services. In fact, the COM 2001–2005 repeatedly mentions digital terrestrial television as one of the most important areas of development, where major public funding has been invested, thus neglecting the online offering.

In 2001, the development of new interactive services of France Télévisions and therefore the online activates were assigned to a newly created division called France Télévisions Interactive (FTVI), which, accordingly to COM 2001–2005, had to:

> Increase the offer of interactive content and services on different platforms (on the internet specifically through the creation of regional portals, interactive television). (COM, 2001–2005:3)

From its launch in 2001, FTVI had to face many problems generated by the lack of coordination in the new France Télévisions: each channel had its own strategy, with no central cooperation and no central plan. When it was launched – and before the new reform of 2009–FTVI was in charge of the design and development of the web activities of France 2 and France 3, while France 5 has always had a separate department. As David Botbol, Head of Online News of France Télévisions, recalls:

> France Télévisions started in 2000 with the online [project], at the time each channel was trying to do something, but for lack of expertise and strategy there was no great impulse to use the online to the fullest. It was difficult in fact for TV channels to use the web. France Télévisions at the time was already a group under the coordination of Marc Tessier and he decided to create an online department to put together all the resources scattered in the group and he hired more people to bring in more expertise. (Botbol, 2009)

Laurent Souloumiac, the new director of FTV, showed commitment to enhance the presence of France Télévisions on the web. At the time of this appointment he explained that:

> The objective is to increase the presence, the importance and the profit of France Télévisions on the web. One of the aims in fact is to increase the users of our internet pages and the entire management of France Télévisions agrees that these new developments are part of the overall strategy of the group. [...]FTVI is indeed an entity that is complementary to the broadcast offer on matters of interactivity. (Souloumiac, 2002)

However, the online activities have never really been conceived as a new 'arm' for the French PSB to achieve its aims, but rather as an activity that could complement and enrich the broadcasting offer. This attitude has partly to do with the resistance shown by the professionals within France Télévisions towards the expansion into the new medium. As Botbol (2009) explains when referring to the online news:

> Many people in the channels felt that online news was not important. Journalists working on the web were considered of a lower league. The main difficulty is represented by the lack of this kind of culture, so changing this culture is the real challenge.

Yet, the defensive strategy towards the web has more to do with the lack of political will and interest inonline activities. The objective of preserving the status quo has probably been stronger than the need to envisage a solid strategy change in France Télévisions.

The *Cahier des charges* of France 2 and France 3, adopted in 2002, for example, stressed once again the role of the Internet as a tool to 'enrich and complement' the broadcasting offer. The Internet is never conceived as a separate entity from broadcasting:

> France 2 should develop, according to its mission, new programmes and services on the different platforms for audiovisual communication in order to extend, complete and enrich its offer of programmes. (*Cahier des charges*, 2002: 10)

The Communication Law of 1986, as modified by Law 719 of 2000, also stresses the importance of using new technologies to 'develop new services that can enrich or complete the existent broadcasting offer'. (Freedom of Communication Law, 1986, Art. 3).

Furthermore, even the most recent COM for 2005–2010 fails to mention the Internet as a separate tool to deliver the PSB ethos. In fact, the section dedicated to new technology explicitly refers to digital terrestrial platforms, on demand or mobile, but not to the online world. One would think that the reform of French public television of 2009 would have prompted a change in this approach towards online activities. However, despite the efforts of creating a more centralized strategy for France Télévisions, the policy-makers involved in the process of reform did not consider it necessary to invest more in online activities. Rather, once again the defensive attitude and the tendency of preserving the status quo seemed to prevail.[23]

The report of the Copé Commission that constituted the basis for the reform[24] barely mentioned the opportunities offered by the Internet. More surprisingly and very revealing of the lack of interest of politicians and policy-makers for the Internet, advertising has not been banned from the web pages of France Télévisions. This constitutes a clear sign of the lack of concern regarding Internet expansion.[25] Finally, the *Cahier des charges* of France Télévisions approved on 23 June 2009 (*Cahier descharges*, 2009) once again assigned to the Internet the role of contributing to the enrichment of the broadcasting offer and failed to recognize its potential as another autonomous tool for France Télévisions to deliver its remit.

Practices of France Télévisions online

The online offer of France Télévisions is not yet centrally organized. Instead, each channel has developed a service that replicates the main offer on television with no efforts to produce something specific for the web (France Télévisions, 2008). Yet, the two portals of the main PSB channels, France 2 and France 3, have improved their reach since their launch. For example, before the first reorganization of France Télévisions, the average number of viewed pages for the two most important websites of France 2 and France 3 were 1.9 million per month in 2002. However, from 2002 to 2008, the average of unique users of the websites was 5.8 million (+ 37% against 2007), with 253 million page views (+79 % against 2007). Still, it ranks just 26th on the top Internet websites for August 2009 (Mediametrie, 2009).

In 2009 there was a first attempt to join forces as a single institution to produce coherent activity online: the launch of a news portal called *France Télévisions Info*, which unifies and retransmits the video news produced by france2.fr, france3.fr and rfo.fr. Yet, overall the development of the practices of France Télévisions online from 2000 to 2008 showed an increased presence of videos on the platforms (France Télévisions, 2008). This tendency stresses even more the lack of autonomy of the online offer from the broadcasting offer of each channel. For example, the *Rapport Annuel* 2008 (France Télévisions, 2008) stresses that the new offer has reached 2,500 hours of video retransmissions for major elections and sport events, such as the Roland Garros French Open tennis tournament, Le Tour de France and Olympic Games (France Télévisions, 2008:141).

Given the specific mission and history of each channel,[26] their online offer essentially replicates online the philosophy of each broadcaster. For example, France 2, the generalist and information channel, brings online its information videos, news bulletin (JT) and reportage, with the most important new bulletin, 'JT de 20 heure', attracting 8 million visits each evening (France Télévisions, 2008:57). Then, France 3, with a clear mission for local news, has a web portal that mirrors the mission of providing for local information, but also culture. In 2008, a new catch-up service dedicated to culture called *Culturebox* was launched on France 3.fr, as well as a *Toowam Web TV* for the youth. Also, France 4, the channel dedicated to the young, and specifically to the age range between 15 and 34 (France Télévisions, 2008) France4. fr, offers the same youth video and programmes, with websites like Pliés en 4 and Rachid au Texas that are nothing more than website replicas of the TV programmes.

On the other hand, the website of France 5, which has always been developed independently from the other channels and came very late to be part of France Télévisions, has developed a more independent platform, clearly more autonomous from the activities of its television channel. France 5 constitutes the exception to the general hostile attitude towards the web of France Télévisions, but precisely because of its different tradition and mission as being more education-oriented.

The educational material available on France 5.fr web platform that targets teachers and school children is certainly one of the most important achievements of France Télévisions. In February 2008, France 5.fr launched a new service called 'Le Wiki des documentaries', a sort of Web 2.0 similar to Wikipedia but dedicated to documentaries. In addition it launched curiosphere.tv, a Web TV that provides educational and cultural videos free of charge. France 5 has also launched a number of educational initiatives financed by the Ministry of Education, such as www.lesite.tv, which offers educational material for disabled people, with 600 minutes of video and a service for schoolchildren on payment of a small fee by each school.

To sum up, the national framework of France Télévisions online assigned to the Internet the role of a complementary tool of the broadcasting offer. The new reform of 2009 (Communication Act, 2009) failed to recognize its potential as another relevant instrument to achieve the remit of France Télévisions. As a result, the online offering of France Télévisions is not yet centrally organized, but every channel has a different offer according to its specific obligations. Among the channels of France Télévisions the most innovative and successful online offering is that of France 5, vocationally focused on educational programmes.

The next section complements this chapter's analysis with a discussion of the Italian policy framework of its PSB online, RAI.

RAI online: Constrained by political negligence

RAI (Radio Televisione Italiana) is the provider of Public Service Broadcasting in Italy under a 20-year licence convention with the State.

The broadcaster started its transmissions in 1954 and maintained its monopoly until the early 1980s, when private competitors entered first the local markets and later the national one. During the years of the monopoly, RAI played an important role in the cultural development of the country (Hibberd, 2001:234). It also contributed to the unification of the fragmented Italian public (Monteleone, 2001) through the deployment of successful educational policies. However, in line with the Hallin and Mancini model (2004), the broadcaster never freed itself from control by political elites. In fact, RAI has for many years been subject to 'lottizzazione' – the distribution of posts and power according to political affiliation (Hallin and Mancini, 2004; Mazzoleni and Vigevani, 2005) – and subsequent reforms adopted to re-establish RAI's accountability, independence and supervision have never succeeded.

However, with the arrival of competition – and more precisely the commercial television empire of Silvio Berlusconi in the 1980s – RAI has unmistakably broken with its tradition by competing with new commercial rivals for its audience. As Hibberd (2001) puts it, 'no other European public service broadcaster [...] was forced to break so clearly with its old programming formats' (Hibberd, 2001:237). Hence, RAI's regulatory framework, mixed funding structure and strict links to political majorities are all fundamental elements of the online expansion of RAI.

Similarly to France – as can be plainly inferred from the policies developed by the Italian government and RAI itself concerning its online offering – the Internet was never considered a crucial part of the public service remit of RAI.

The first policy documents to affirm the importance of RAI exploring new media opportunities were the service contracts[27] signed under the centre-left coalition for the period 1997–1999[28] and 2000–2002. However, the Contract of 2003, signed by the centre-right majority, shifted the main priority to digital television take-up.[29] The same is true for the Gasparri Law (Law 112 of 2004), strongly advocated by Prime Minister Berlusconi to secure his unconstitutional dominance of the television market in Italy (Constitutional Court, 1988, 1994).

It was only when the new service contract of 2007 was signed by the centre-left majority that the new media expansion of RAI became relevant again. Art. 6 of the Service Contract for the period 2007–2009 declares that:

1. RAI will define a clear strategy to add value to its own productions and its audiovisual rights on every multimedia platform, from the digital terrestrial and satellite offer to IPTV, mobile and Internet;

2. RAI will enhance and update the service offered on its portal www. rai.it in order to enlarge the actual production with new content for the Internet;

3. RAI will make available, within the limits of copyright law, every type of content produced by RAI to every internet user [...]. Moreover, RAI will allocate increasing resources to the acquisition of the copyrights of the programmes [...]. (RAI, 2007b)

Nevertheless, it is interesting to note that the final draft of the Service Contract 2007 had a more progressive spirit than the official version of the contract. This was perhaps a sign of the resistance encountered inside RAI to implementing the new strategy. In fact, the final draft of the Service Contract of 2007 stated that:

RAI will make available on the portal www.rai.it every type of content produced by RAI to every internet user.

RAI will negotiate the acquisition of copyrights of programs and it will allocate 7% of all its resources to the production or the acquisition of content broadcast by the TV channels [...] and it will offer to the users the opportunity to download every type of content under Creative Commons License. (RAI, 2007a, Art. 6(3))

As is clear from the text, the two versions showed wide discrepancies. In fact, the official contract took a more restrained approach that failed to secure a clear budget for the online offering, and abandoned the idea of providing free online content under a Creative Commons License.[30]

If the policies developed by the left coalition and the right coalition seemed extremely dissimilar, the lack of a continuous strategy owing to scarce resources and a constant turnover of managers demonstrated the insufficient commitment of both the political majorities in power for a strong PSB online. Moreover, the former CEO of RAI NET indicated that one reason for the slow development of an online strategy was the 'lack of competence of the leadership of RAI in the field of new media and new technology' (Contri, 2009).

Between 1997 and 1999, in one of several reforms of the Italian PSB of that decade, RAI was reorganized into five segments, each with a specific remit: RAI NET, responsible for web activities; RAI SAT, for satellite channels (and the subsequent agreement with Sky); RAI WAY, for transmissions services; RAI TRADE, for the commercialization of RAI production; and RAI CLICK, a joint venture between RAI and Fastweb.

Thus, we can trace the beginning of the online expansion of RAI to 1999, with the creation of RAI NET aimed at 'enhancing the brand of RAI on the web' and the launch of the first, official portal, www.rai.it (Contri, 2009). If at that time it was clear that the main Internet activities of RAI had to be directed by RAI NET, in 2005 the picture was further complicated by the creation of RAI New Media, a new directorate with the aim of coordinating the five divisions. However, RAI New Media has never performed its harmonizing functions, rather focusing on the DTT (digital terrestrial TV) transition (Contri, 2009).

Interestingly, RAI NET provided the infrastructure for the websites of RAI and other multi-platform services. However, two important divisions of RAI – RAI Educational[31] and RAI International[32] – were completely independent from RAI NET and could 'decide by themselves their own online strategy' (Zela, 2009). Besides, many programmes and channels are today still running their websites independently (Rai News24 and Trebisonda, to name only two).

This complex organization of web activities explains in part the lack of a clear and centralized strategy forRAI online. Additionally, the resource allocation for RAI's Internet activities seems contradictory. Every year since 1999 when 20 million euros were invested to establish RAI NET, RAI NET has been assigned 0.2% of the whole budget of RAI, or 6 million euros. Also, the staff employed at RAI NET is very limited, with just '6 journalists and 30 technicians that have to take care of all websites' (Contri, 2009).

The former CEO of RAI NET surprisingly kept his position from January 2003 to March 2008, despite changes in government, and under his guidance a huge growth in page views and unique users was achieved. Data from Audiweb–Nielsen Online (2008) shows an increased interest in www.rai.tv, especially after the launch of the new portal rai. tv with an average of 2.8 million unique users every month in 2007, against an average of one million in 2003. However, despite the growth, the Internet offering of RAI is still mainly entertainment-oriented with a surprising lack of investment in news and public affairs. The news offering, in the form of text, blogs of newsrooms and interactive forums, is in its infancy on RAI's portal. Up until 2008, the service offered by RAI Net was not continuous across the week and was suspended during the weekend. Until recently no updates to the news and no upload of programmes were made from Friday evening to Monday morning. In 2008 the two most important providers of online news were still enjoying an unchallenged dominance of the online news market with seven million unique users for La Repubblica (Nielsen NetRatings, 2008) and six million for Il Corriere della sera (ibid.).

Thus, RAI's portal seems the perfect replica of its TV offering, with most of the TV channels' content available online, but with no initiatives catering for the web. Consequently, the offering online mirrors the entertainment-oriented inclination of RAI's broadcasting output. With 'scarce resources available to RAI NET', explained Contri (2009), it is necessary to collect advertisement fees on the web; therefore the entertainment offering 'seems the only option' (Contri, 2009).

Yet an overview of the online presence of RAI would be incomplete without an analysis of the well-developed web activities of RAI Educational (RAI Edu). This division of RAI, dedicated to educational programmes that promote history, culture and science, has launched material on the web since 1997. So far,

> RAI Educational web manages 30 websites of educational programmes. The amount of money dedicated to RAI Educational as a whole totals 0.3% of RAI's overall budget, while on average, 20% of the budget of nine million Euros goes to the web activities. (Zela, 2009)

Some of the programmes offered on the web by RAI Edu in 2008 were the online editions of successful TV programmes, such as the *Divertinglese* and *Divertipc*, devoted to the learning of English as a second language and ICT alphabetization, or *La Storia Siamo Noi* ('We are history'), devoted to history. Others, like Medita, were specifically created for the Net. Medita.rai.it, a multimedia project launched under an agreement with the Minister of Education, consisted of a digital multimedia library dedicated to schools, and is 'currently the most important online encyclopedia in Italy' (see www.medita.rai.it) and one of the biggest in Europe. In 2008 it comprised 2,500 audio visuals, hundreds of multimedia learning objects and 1,100 hours of videos. The material has been designed to act as a complementary didactic activity.

To sum up, the relentless change of government and of its politically controlled management at RAI has thwarted the expansion of RAI on the web. Even though RAI started developing its online output in 1999, the investments were minimal because the Internet has never been considered a priority. The growth registered by RAI's portal in 2007 – with an increase from one million unique users per month in 2003 to 2.8 million per month in 2007 – was more due to the obstinate work of the isolated management of RAI NET than to a central strategy drawn by the Executive Board. RAI's presence on the web has from the start showed a strong commercial orientation, with mostly fictional and reality shows on offer, as a consequence of its high reliance on advertisement revenue and scarcity of funding. Yet, the achievement of the educational department, with its strong focus on the online offer, constitutes the exception to the dominant paradigm.

Conclusion

This chapter has investigated the institutional and public policies on PSB online in European states. The findings show that the policy framework of PSB online in the cases considered is principally framed within each national milieu. Owing to different national political, cultural and historical legacies, Public Service Broadcasting online continues to express nationwide peculiarities. More precisely, the online expansion of the PSBs considered seems to follow a path-dependent model. Once each PSB adopted a distinct 'path' and therefore a typical broadcasting ethos, it did not reverse course in its Internet activities.

There is a clear correspondence between each PSB's online and offline ethos ingrained in each country's specific cultural context. Thus the strong tradition of a public broadcasting ethos of the DR characterized by an extensive offer of PSB outputs like news, public affairs, educational and cultural programmes is reproduced in DR's online offer. Following the same pattern, RTVE's and RAI's platforms on the web are characterized by a strong entertainment and commercial orientation. News or public affairs sections are not adequately developed, and therefore citizens in Italy and Spain opt to obtain their news online from the main online newspapers rather than from their PSBs. Additionally, in the case of France and Italy, the lack of resources and political support has led to insufficient investment in the Internet offer, with the result of creating an online replica of the two broadcasters' offer. The dissimilarities of the policy frameworks of the PSBs online confirm the usefulness of the Hallin–Mancini model (2004) because the dissimilarities between the different clusters are still evident.

DR recognized the potential of the web back in 1996 and was encouraged to develop it, while the online policies of TVE, RAI and France Télévisions were virtually nonexistent at that time. As a result of the crisis in Spain's PSB, no resources were invested in new services or long-term strategies until the 2005 reforms. In France and Italy investments in the web by France Télévisions and RAI have been minimal, with priority going to digital terrestrial TV implementation rather than online. Since the official launch of DR online, it was at once clear that 'DR online' constituted 'the third arm of the DR' rather than just being a complementary service to broadcasting. The same conclusion cannot be drawn for

France Télévisions or RAI, where there is still no clear-cut and centralized strategy and where most of the services constitute a mere replica of the broadcasting offer. RTVE, notwithstanding its delay in the online world, thanks to renewed political support has been able to make a much more sophisticated online offer.

Interestingly, the Southern European cases investigated show substantial differences in their Internet expansion, although they all belong to the same Mediterranean model characterized. Because of their intense politicization, the three PSBs have developed diverse responses to the Internet world. Hence, thanks to the recent political backing RTVE has been able to build up an online offering that has outshined RAI's and France Télévisions'. Yet, as Chapter 8 will elaborate, despite RTVE online moving beyond its historical legacy since 2007 as a weak PSB, the counter-reform of Zapatero of 2009–2010 (Law 8/2009) that abolished advertisments on RTVE.es could bring the clock back to 2004. With no resources invested and no possibility of RTVE.es collecting online advertisement revenues, the quality of the online offering of RTVE might stagnate. The creation of more strictly interpreted public service content will ultimately depend on the political willingness of the government to sustain a stronger RTVE.

The following chapter examines the influence of the European Union framework on PSB online by focusing on the recent policy-making of the European Commission. It also discusses the case of BBC online and its impact on the European framework.

7
European Union Influence on PSB Online

The European regulatory framework on Public Service Broadcasting was sketched out in Chapter 2 above. The present chapter aims to explore the European Commission's policies on the online activity of PSBs – and to assess the impact of those policies at the national level. In particular, it will summarize relevant decisions on State Aid and examine the adopted Communication on State Aid to Public Service Broadcasters, issued on 2 July 2009. This document, hereafter referred to as Communication 2009, departs from its 2001 forebear, which encouraged online and new media initiatives by PSBs, by imposing strict controls on their expansion. Finally, the analysis turns to the national and institutional policies of BBC online, whose parent organization remains one of the most influential PSBs in Europe. The influence of the BBC's policy framework on Brussels' policy-making is assessed and the possibility of a policy transfer between the UK and Brussels that might lead to 'bottom-up' Europeanization is explored (Harcourt 2002).

Foundations of the European framework

As described in Chapter 2, European institutions since 1997 have repeatedly affirmed that PSBs must pursue effective online media provision if they are to fulfil their remit in the digital age.[1] Moreover, the EU regards online media as an essential tool for social cohesion that can still function in the knowledge-based economies of the future. As noted, the regulatory framework for PSBs in Europe is based on competition policy, and specifically the State Aid rules set out in Articles 106 and 107 of the Treaty on the Functioning of the European Community. The European Commission and the European Court of Justice thus play a crucial role in developing regulatory frameworks for Public Service Broadcasting.

In order to understand this role, we must examine the Commission's case practice regarding State Aid, and assess the principles it has followed in applying these articles to PSBs. Recent Commission decisions reveal a shift in its approach to PSB online; in fact, Brussels seems increasingly reluctant to encourage their new media ventures, and has arguably extended its scrutiny beyond manifest errors.

Early decisions of the European Commission

Commentators have been divided in their appraisals of recent European decisions regarding the traditional PSB offer. Prosser (2005), for example, believes that the Commission has usually allowed Member States wide discretion in defining the scope of their public service remit. Likewise, Humphreys (2007) claims: 'In its decision making so far, the Commission has plainly been generally supportive of public service broadcasting' (Humphreys, 2007: 109). But other authors such as Scharpf (1999), Harcourt (2005), Michalis (2007) and Katsirea (2008) are not so optimistic, and have identified in the decisions of the European Commission an ongoing trend of 'marketization'.

Both arguments have their merits, and both have been true at different periods in the history of the EU. The European Commission was initially open towards attempts by PSBs to expand their broadcasting offer (Humphreys, 2007). But, since 2002, as complaints by commercial competitors increased, we can detect a clear shift in the Commission's attitude towards new media and specifically towards expansion online.

Indeed, until 2003, the Commission took a technology-neutral stance when deciding State Aid for PSBs, and allowed Member States wide discretion to define their remit. For example, in its decision regarding the BBC's new 24-hour news channel it stated: 'the public service nature of a service cannot be judged on the basis of the distribution platform' (European Commission, 1999: Para. 57). It added that, once a government has defined a certain service as a 'public service' (as defined in Art. 106 (2)), 'such service remains a public service regardless of the delivery platform' (ibid.). This reasoning demonstrates a relaxed attitude towards the expansion of PSB into new media, and upholds the right of Member States, under the Amsterdam Protocol, to define the remit of their PSBs.

The Commission's declaration of 22 May 20002 follow the same line. Ruling on the funding of nine new digital channels for the BBC, it cited the 1999 Resolution of the Council,[2] stating:

> Public service broadcasters can develop and diversify their activities in the digital age, as long as they are addressing the same democratic

social and cultural needs of the society. (European Commission, 2002: Para. 27)

Cold feet: The Commission's shifting approach to PSB online

While the pre-2002 Commission was encouraging the expansion of PSB online, its decision regarding the BBC Digital Curriculum (European Commission, 2003) signalled a paradigmatic shift in the Commission's PSB policy (Widermann, 2004; Michalis, 2007; Katsirea 2008).

The decision concerned public funding for a new e-learning service by the BBC, provided free to schools and students. The Commission considered whether the new initiative could be considered an 'ancillary service' alongside the BBC's current provision, but took the view that its educational remit was limited to traditional broadcasting and did not cover the new initiative.[3] Acting for the first time beyond the limits of manifest error, the Commission defined three new criteria that would guide future EC policies on PSB online and severely restrict the freedom of Member States to define the online remit of their PSBs.

The three principles developed by the European Commission's reasoning are certainly consistent with market-failure and non-technology-neutral logic. First, a new PSB online offering must be 'closely associated' with the 'core offer' of television and radio services.[4] Secondly, the online offer must be 'distinctive from and complementary to services provided by the commercial sector' (European Commission, 2003: Para. 41). Thirdly, it must be clearly delineated in advance so that commercial competitors can plan their responses accordingly (Ridinger, 2009).[5] These criteria conflict with some of the Commission's earlier decisions,[6] and impose clear limits on Member States seeking to determine their PSBs' remit.

The Commission maintained this direction when it ruled regarding the Dutch PSB, NOB.[7] As Widermann (2004) has pointed out, the Commission's formal opening of procedure:

> ...reversed the burden of proof. It said that a Member State can only be said not to have committed a manifest error in including online services in the public service remit under Article 86(2) if the Member State can prove that: there is a need for these services and that they are of a special character i.e. they are not also offered by commercial providers. (Widermann, 2004: 9)

In fact, in its initiating letter on 3 February 2004 (European Commission, 2004), the Commission abandoned its previous technological neutrality.

In Para. 84, it once again draws a line between PSBs' broadcasting and new media activities:

> The Commission points out that the case-law of the Commission differentiates greatly between broadcasting services and information society services. The range/scope of the broadcasting communication is defined by the broadcasting service and includes in principle no services of the information society. Although the Broadcasting Communication does not exclude all internet activities from the public broadcaster of their application/use, this does not mean that all new media services delivered by public service fall within the application/use as broadcast communication. Similar to the illustrated BBC Digital Curriculum, similar services can only be judged on the basis of broadcast communication if they stay closely related to broadcasting services (European Commission, 2004: Para. 84, my translation)

The Commission criticized NOB's provision of SMS and I-mode as vague and likely to create uncertainties for competitors. Furthermore, it considered the provision of these services to be outside the PSB remit (Donders and Pauwels, 2008). Once again, then, the Commission demonstrated a move away from technological neutrality to a more pro-market position. The ruling led to new media laws, which anticipated the requirement of Communication 2009 (European Commission, 2010) by subjecting all proposed new PSB services – including paid ones – to 'prior evaluation'.[8]

We can see further evidence of this shifting attitude in the case of the Danish broadcaster TV2 (European Commission, 2004a). As Mortensen (2006) details, the prospective sale and privatization of TV2 was blocked by Commission decisions and by lawsuits over its State Aid. Mortensen notes the Commission's elaboration of its public service criteria, as expressed in its decision of 19 May 2004 (European Commission, 2004a):

> The Commission acknowledges that TV2's internet pages that are limited to informing the user about its public service television programmes fall within its public service broadcasting task. There is therefore no manifest error in treating the operation of these pages as covered by the public service task. In contrast, TV2's commercial internet service should be regarded as a purely commercial activity, as it offers interactive products on individual demand like games or chat rooms, which do no differ from similar commercial products. Since such services do not address the democratic, social and cultural

needs of society they cannot constitute services of general economic interest under Article 86(2) of the EC Treaty. Indeed, the Danish authorities considered these activities to fall outside the scope of TV 2's public service'. (European Commission, 2004: Para. 91–92)[9]

Thus the Commission reaffirmed the terms of BBC curriculum case, confirming its new, more restrictive attitude. It took the same position in its rulings on the German licence fee system (European Commission, 2007) and the Flemish and the Irish PSBs (European Commission, 2008a and 2008b). The former case involved an investigation into the German PSBs, ZDF and ADF, leading to an agreement between the Commission and the German government on their future funding regime (European Commission, 2007). In the process, the Commission made several important observations regarding the scope for PSB activity in the new media.

First, it expressed concerns about the absence in the German framework of:

[a] sufficiently clear definition and adequate entrustment of the public service remit (in particular as regards new media activities and additional digital channels), excluding activities which would be regarded as 'manifest errors' (in particular as regards the inclusion of commercial activities as well as mobile services), (European Commission, 2007: Para. 75)

Moreover, it lacked:

a general authorization of public service broadcasters to offer such loosely defined new media services and the resulting lack of predictability for third parties bears the risk that other market operators are discouraged to develop and offer such new media services. (European Commission, 2007: 230)

These complaints draw a clear line between the Commission's approach to old and new media. The Commission also places the burden on PSBs to clearly indicate in advance the specific character and scope of their new media offering.

Furthermore, the Commission outlined a requirement that online services should differ from those the market already offers in terms of 'specific features' (Para. 232). They should also display 'added value' (Para. 362), given that their 'specific contribution to the democratic, social and cultural needs is not always evident' (Para. 231). Thus, once again, the Commisson yields to a strong market failure paradigm. While in one section it claims to follow the principles of technological neutrality,[10] in practice it commands much stricter controls on PSBs' online activities than in any other medium.

The same approach is manifest in the EC's decisions regarding the Flemish PSB provider VTR[11] (European Commission, 2008a) and the Irish PSBs RTÉ and TG4 (European Commission, 2008b). The Commission ordered VTR to conduct *ex ante* reviews of all new online services in a way consistent with Communication 2009, which was still under discussion at the time (European Commission, 2008a). The same type of controls were demanded in its decision on Irish PSB (European Commission, 2008b).[12] Again, the Commission required the introduction of a public value test and a market impact assessment for any significant new activities (European Commission, 2008b).

This overview shows how far the Commission has moved beyond 'a check for manifest error' (European Commission, 2001), gradually subjecting PSB online and new media activities to ever stricter controls. These measures seem calibrated to meet the goals of commercial operators who demand that PSB activity be contained – especially on the Internet.

Negotiating a new standard

In July 2009 a new Communication on State Aid to PSB succeeded the existing (2001) regime. As Neelie Kroes, the European Commissioner for Competition Policy, put it, the Communication of 2009 was needed to 'consolidate our existing case practice' (European Commission, 2008c: 2) and take 'full account of the new media environment' (ibid.). By Kroes' own admission, the document was a response to the concerns of commercial operators:

> Certain initiatives by public broadcasters have led their commercial competitors to complain in increasing numbers to the Commission. And in recent years these complaints have spread beyond the broadcasting sector. For instance, newspaper publishers and other private content providers fear that State Aid may be used excessively to fund on-line activities of public service broadcasters. (European Commission, 2008c: 2)

These complaints were principally drawn from a consultation process involving public and private stakeholders that began in 2008. The first consultation was held between 10 January and 10 March that year, and asked stakeholders whether they felt a new Communication was needed. A total of 121 replies from commercial and public stakeholders reached Brussels[13] and, despite the opposition of Member States and PSBs, the Commission decided to go ahead with the updating process. Consultation on a first draft ran from 5 November 2008 to 15 January 2009 involved a meeting of experts from the Member States (in December 2008), and 90 stakeholder submissions;[14] the second draft consultation ran from 7 April to 8 May 2009 and elicited 70 replies.[15] The final, updated Broadcasting Communication was published on 2 July that year and came into effect on 27 October. Broadcasting Communication was adopted and took effect on 27 October. The new document codified all the changes seen in case law since 2002, abandoning technological neutrality and setting a demanding 'added value' test for new media ventures by PSBs. In fact, according to Art. 48: 'a manifest error could occur where State Aid is used to finance activities which do not bring added value in terms of serving the social, democratic and cultural needs of society'.

Therefore, when venturing online, PSBs must define their online remit according to market failure. Not only is it incumbent upon them to demonstrate 'added value', but they must do so *ex ante*, prior to the launch of any and each new service. Art. 88 makes this clear:

> In order to ensure that the public funding of significant new audio-visual services does not distort trade and competition to an extent contrary to the common interest, Member States shall assess, based on the outcome of the open consultation, the overall impact of a new service on the market by comparing the situation in the presence and in the absence of the planned new service. In assessing the impact on the market, relevant aspects include, for example, the existence of similar or substitutable offers, editorial competition, market structure, market position of the public service broadcaster, level of competition and potential impact on private initiatives. (European Commission, 2009)[16]

Evidently, both private sector broadcasters and publishers have heavily lobbied the EC to keep public funds – and PSB – out of potentially profit-making new media projects. On the opposite side, Member States and public broadcasters have battled to keep their autonomy in defining the remit of PSB. They have called for the principle of subsidiarity as defined by the Amsterdam Protocol of 1997.[17]

Communication 2009 represents a compromise between these interests – but not a victory for PSBs. Indeed, its first draft placed even stricter limits on Member States seeking to define a new media remit, and incorporated *ex ante* requirements, which, if retained in full, would have restricted the ability of Member States to decide for themselves the most appropriate mechanisms of assessment.[18] Nevertheless, the test outlined in the final Communication remains a major change for European PSBs. Obligating prior assessment of public service remits for all Member States arguably goes far beyond mere controls for manifest error.

Private competitors, meanwhile, have been unsurprisingly enthusiastic about Communication 2009. Angela Mills Wade, the director of the European Publishers Council (EPC), has said:

> For the private media companies the introduction of ex-ante scrutiny for new ventures which can play havoc with our online and mobile services and the need for an independent control body are the most important milestones. (EMB, 2009)

Moreover, the Director General of the Association of Commercial Television Europe (ACT), Ross Biggam, has congratulated the Commission 'for having come up with a balanced and workable text' (EMB, 2009).

The *ex-ante* test

Notwithstanding its presence in Communication 2009, the *ex-ante* test had been an explicit requirement at least since the EC's decision on Dutch PSB (European Commission, 2006). Its application, in turn, follows a logic established in 2002: PSB online is legitimate only if it shows 'distinctiveness' from the market, 'added public value' compared to commercial offers, and 'predictability' for commercial competitors. The test is a key vector by which the expansion of PSB online is treated differently from – and more strictly than – its broadcasting activities. Evidently, the reasons for this policy shift have to be found in the willingness to placate the continuous complaints of the commercial competitors, especially publishers of online press that were heavily lobbying the Commission. In the words of the competition officials:

> This test at the national level (i.e. by a national body rather than the Commission) addresses the legitimate concern of commercial media, including the print media, that public broadcasters might use public money to offer new online services which are not remotely similar to a TV or radio broadcast, which do not add any clear value for society

and which considerably distort competition. In several Member States, the debate focused on the question whether broadcasters could start using public service compensation to finance a kind of 'electronic online press'. (Repa, Tosics, and Dias, 2009: 8)

Interestingly, the test has been conceived in the hope of limiting future complaints of commercial outlets. However, it does not in itself forbid the Commission from opening an investigation if it finds that a test was unfair or ineffective.

The first application of Communication 2009 came on 28 October that year, with the case of ORF, the Austrian PSB (European Commission, 2009). The Commission's main remarks concerned the unclear definition of the public service remit with particular reference to ORF's online activities. Notably, according to previous ORF conditions, only 'online services and teletext which are connected with broadcast programmes as part of the service provision remit and serve to fulfil the programme remit'[19] were to be regarded as part of the PSB's offer (European Commission, 2009a: Para. 29). Despite this limitation, the Commission considered 'the remit for online services and for special interest channels was too unspecific' (European Commission, 2009a: Para. 83).

According to the decision:

It was necessary for the public service obligations to be defined more specifically with regard to online services taking into account the existing offer on the market. It should be clear which of the population's needs are supposed to be covered by the broadcasting institutions with their online services and the extent to which these online services, described in greater detail, serve the democratic, social and cultural needs of society. (European Commission, 2009a: Para. 83)

Ultimately, the Austrian government agreed to withdraw a number of its online offers (ibid.: Para. 93) and to establish a new media authority that would regulate the remit of PSBs online and test the 'added value' of new services against their market impact. The Commission's decision on the Dutch PSB followed a similar pattern (European Commission, 2010), closing with the adoption of an *ex-ante* test according to the principles now enshrined in Communication 2009:

The Dutch authorities will ensure that the prior evaluation process will take place in a transparent way. As part of this prior evaluation process interested parties will be consulted and the market effects of new audiovisual services will be assessed and balanced against the benefits of the new service for Dutch society. (European Commission, 2010)

Communication 2009: A critical appraisal

The recent policy-making of the European Commission regarding PSB's new media activities shows a stronger market-failure and non-technology-neutral approach. This outcome can certainly be explained by the increasing influence of private broadcasters and publishers on EU policy-making. Proof of this trajectory is the number of complaints that have been filed by the publishing industry against PSB, which call for the downsizing of PSB activities online. Regrettably, the European Commission has been progressively more inclined to satisfy commercials operators' demands, rather than considering the public interest.

This recent more restrictive attitude of the European Commission towards PSB online seems to conflict with the increasing recognition and constitutionalization of the principles of public services in the Lisbon Treaty that was ratified on 1 December 2009. For the first time, all new EU laws will have to be checked for compliance with the Charter of Fundamental Rights, which explicitly recognizes and protects access to services of general economic interest (public services).[20] Likewise, the treaty introduces a new legal basis for services of general interest (SGI) and also a series of principles contained in a protocol that assign a fundamental role to SGI in the European Community. The SGI Protocol, in particular Art. 1, once again recognizes:

> The essential role and the wide discretion of national, regional and local authorities in providing, commissioning and organizing services of general economic interest as closely as possible to the needs of the users. (Protocol on Service of general Interest, 2009)

This renewed recognition of public services (services of general interest in the words of the treaty) is clearly in contradiction with an assessment of the Commission that is increasingly based on market criteria and that results in a restriction of the remit of PSB online. Moreover, it could be claimed that a stricter control is incompatible with both the Amsterdam Protocol on PSB and the Protocol of SGI of the Lisbon Treaty that assigns the widest discretion to Member States to define the scope of PSB.

Surely, as Humphreys (2009) demonstrates, the German and the UK cases show that the increased pro-market inclination of their national policy frameworks has led to stronger controls on PSB online even independently from the EU's influence (Brevini, 2010a and Brevini 2010b). However, the role played by the Commission in fostering a pro-market approach is hard to deny. As explained, the Commission has encouraged the adoption by national authorities of a stricter policy framework for online PSB in states such as Denmark that had previously presented an enabling framework towards PSB online.[21] Importantly, this new European framework is impacting on all other European states that had so far resisted the pressure of commercial operators.

Additionally, as this chapter has examined, the adoption of Communication 2009 is just the last stage in a process of change of the European policy on PSB online that has been developing since 2002. However, it could be argued that a Communication is not an appropriate legal act for imposing such new requirements that do not already exist under EC law. In particular, Articles 107 and 106(2) EC do not expressly require any *ex ante* assessment of new services, and the Commission could not query the compatibility of the aid with competition policy just because no *ex ante* assessment has been carried out by the Member States. It could also be argued that the European Commission lacks the competence in deciding on general criteria determining the remit of PSB, and therefore is in breach of the principles of subsidiarity that are once again reiterated by the Lisbon Treaty.

Furthermore, Communication 2009 seems to conflict with the decision taken by the Court of First Instance (now the General Court) in October 2008 regarding Danish broadcaster TV2. This explained that:

- The mission of Public Broadcaster can be broad and should be defined in relation to the needs of society and not in relation to the market.
- Member States can draw up a broad definition of public broadcasting delivered through 'television, radio, internet and the like'.
- There is no need to take account of the activities of the commercial operators for the purpose of defining PSB's remit. (Court of First Instance. 2008)

European influence or BBC policy transfer? The importance of the BBC online framework

The recent European Commission policy-making on PSB online that led to Communication 2009 would be incomplete without an analysis of the BBC policy framework given the considerable influence exerted by the BBC model on all other European models of PSB. For this reason, it seems useful to conclude the chapter with an analysis of the BBC online case. In fact, as the chapter unfolds, the UK case shows a domestic policy framework that has become more hostile towards BBC online activities. The following sections examine these developments.

Histories of bbc.co.uk

The BBC's activities in the online sphere dates back to the mid-1990s, when the Director General John Birt first talked of the possibility of building the third great arm of the BCC, an online public service. The evolution of the policies related to the online activities of the BBC have to be put in the context of the reform of the Corporation, spurred certainly by the European influence dictated by State Aid decisions regarding PSBs (Craufurd Smith, 2001; Levy, 1999) and by the compulsory review of the Royal Charter that takes places every 10 years, discussed in Chapter 5.[22]

Since the beginning, the BBC seemed to recognize that the Internet could enable new opportunities to connect with citizens. However, as in the 1990s the Internet was a relatively unknown medium, the activities of the BBC online were limited to text based on its core programmes and services, like BBC Radio 1, CBBC, the Planets, News and Sports. It was later in 1997 that the new project BBC online was launched. The approval of the Secretary of State[23] arrived in 1998 after a one-year pilot and a public consultation.

As we gather from the letter sent by the BBC to the Secretary of State seeking consent for its public service online,[24] the objectives of BBC Online, established by the original approval were clear:

I. Act as an essential resource offering wide ranging, unique content
II. Use the internet to forge a new relationship with licence fee payers and strengthen accountability
III. Provide a home for licence fee payers on the internet and act as a trusted guide to the new media environment.
(Letter from the BBC to the Secretary of State, 9 October 1998, cited in Graf, 2004)

As the Graf Report (2004) on BBC online observes,

the BBC's 'third arm' of public service broadcasting, BBC Online shares BBC television and radio's wider public purpose which is, broadly, to 'enrich people's lives with great programmes and services that inform, educate and entertain'. (Graf, 2004: 17)

After becoming a permanent service, BBC Online kept growing, thanks to its vast investments and its capacity of bringing the public online. After becoming a permanent service, expenditure on BBC Online increased massively from £23 million in 1998, to £40.7 million in 2000 and £57 million in 2001 (£51.9 million for the Home Service and £5.1 million for the World Service respectively). Page views almost doubled in one year from 176.7 million in 2000 to 322.3 million in 2001, while the total number of BBC Online users grew from 3.8 to 4.9 million in March 2001 (BBC, 2000: 80) (see Figure 7.1).

As we can infer from Figure 7.1, the total number of BBC Online users grew from 3.8 million in March 2000 to 4.9 million in March 2001.

As shown in Figure 7.2, the News division online was already the most successful of BBC online services, with a peak of high of 120.6 million paged views in March 2001, followed by the Sport division, launched in 1999, and by the Education division. Given the government's approval and wide-ranging opportunity to expand its service, the BBC consolidated its position in the online world. In 2002 the new search engine tool was launched with total costs of £414,268 (BBC, 2002). In addition, the first radio player was launched offering the opportunity to listen live to all the radio programmes offered.

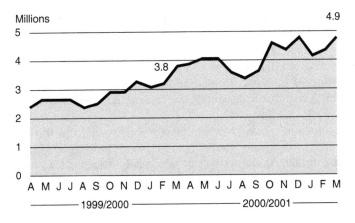

Figure 7.1 BBC online reach of UK internet users 1999–2001
Source: BBC Annual Report and Accounts 2000–2001.

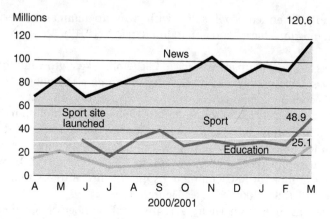

Figure 7.2   BBC online page impressions for News, Sport and Education 2001
Source: BBC Annual Report and Accounts 2000–2001.

Commercial pressure on BBC Online

Political support for BBC Online initiatives started fading under the pressure of commercial operators in the United Kingdom. Many claimed that BBC Online was expanding too much and that its activities comprised the production of services that had not been foreseen at the time of its launch and approval. In particular, the British Internet Alliance became very active in lobbying the government to reduce the large-scale expansion online of the BBC.

Hence the government announced in 2004 the first independent review of BBC Online, to be conducted by Philip Graf. The Graf Report,[25] concluded that the BBC delivered high-quality service in an effective way and that there was a wide support and public affection for BBC Online. At the same time, some sites were 'hard to justify in terms of the BBC's remit or wider public purposes' (Graf, 2004:10):

> Sites – such as fantasy football, certain games sites, and the 'What's On' listings sites – do not seem to me, to be sufficiently distinctive from commercial alternatives or adequately associated with public service purposes, to be justified by the remit. (ibid.: 10)

Moreover, the Report concluded that there were 'indications' that BBC Online 'may have an adverse impact on competition' (Graf, 2004: 58). As a consequence, the BBC decided to close five websites (Smith, 2006).

This was the beginning of the new phase for the BBC Online, in what can be called the 'public value test era'.[26] It is a period in which, consistently with the reform and the introduction of a triple-lock system (DCMS White Paper; Barnett, 2006), every new service of the BBC is closely investigated and must undergo a public-value and a market impact assessment. Moreover, every new service is subjected to a service licence issued by the BBC Trust.

Here, the similarities with Brussels argumentations are striking. As underlined by Barnett (2006), the pressure brought to bear by commercial competitors on policy-makers to downsize BBC activities was difficult to deny. Therefore, the service licence for BBC Online requires that the BBC delivers one or more of the BBC's public purposes indicated by the Royal Charter,[27] and its content should contain at least one of the 'public service characteristics', namely, high quality, challenging, original, innovative and engaging programming (Agreement, 2007: 7).

In May 2008, the BBC Trust completed the first service review of bbc. co.uk, finding that bbc.co.uk was highly valued by the public and was considered to meets the aims of the licence. However, it pointed out that more management control was needed to make a better use of resources (£116 million spent on BBC Online in 2006–2007 and £182 million in 2007–2008).[28] Moreover, once again, the need for 'distinctiveness' (Review: 13) from the services offered by commercial competitor is strongly demanded. It is also stressed that public values need to be balanced with the market potential negative impact for the market (Review: 14) .Therefore, 'for the first time in BBC history, there is an explicit injunction to take into account not only the public interest, but the commercial interest as well' (Barnett, 2006: 20).

Hence, the first decision to reduce the scope of BBC Online arrived in 2007: the BBC Trust closure of BBC Jam[29] by the BBC Trust. As Scott (2007) observes,

> the Trust's problem was that it hadn't conducted an assessment of the public value to be gleaned from market intervention of this type, and therefore couldn't simply explain to the EC Commission that the public service requirement in the Article 86(2) EC 'get out of jail card' was satisfied. Facing the risk that the BBC's activities may be found subsequently to have involved reliance on unlawful state aid, the Trust adopted a safety-first approach. (Scott, 2007: 1)[30]

Not much later, the Trust decided to refuse permission to expand BBC local video news online.[31] Yet, in conducting the first Public Value Test

(PVT) in April 2007, the BBC Trust showed itself to be capable of fair judgement. In fact, the BBC Trust gave final approval for an online seven-day catch-up TV service, the BBC i Player. As the Trust makes clear in the conclusion paper of the PVT, 'we have not altered our view that each of the proposals is likely to deliver significant public value, enough to justify the likely market impact' (BBC Trust, 2007a, 2007b: 2).

Launched over Christmas 2007, with an overall spend of £3.9 million, by March 2008 the i Player had reached 4.7 million requests for content per week. Meanwhile, the appeal of bbc.co.uk continued to grow, reaching an average of 3.6 billion page views and 16 million unique users per month in 2008 (BBC Trust, 2008), being the third most-visited UK website after Google and MSN (Nielsen Net Ratings, 2008).

The current restrictive attitude towards BBC Online has been reaffirmed by the Digital Britain White Paper (Digital Britain, 2009) adopted on 16 June 2009, which contained the Labour Government's policy strategy for communications and digital content. The White Paper claimed that 'given the current nature of the market, new BBC activity has a higher risk than in the past of chilling or foreclosing market developments' (Digital Britain, 2009: 140). Regrettably, the recent proposals drawn up by BBC executives within the BBC Strategy Review indicate the firm decision to reduce the budget of BBC Online by 25% by 2013 (BBC Strategy Review, 2010: 9).

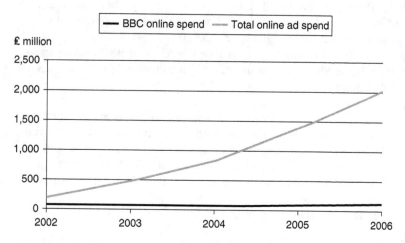

Figure 7.3   Relative increase of BBC's online spend and total advertising spend 2002–2006

A last comment should be made on the evidence for whether BBC Online crowds out commercial competitors. Ofcom, the UK communications regulator, has found that from 2002 to 2006, the 'BBC's online spend increased by over 50 percent in five years, while online advertising spend in the UK rose by over 1600 percent in the same period' (Ofcom, 2008: 79) (see Figure 7.3). The increase in the total online advertising market has been 'faster than in countries in which there is no comparable public subsidy' (Ofcom, 2008: 79). This suggests that the BBC may not have limited the growth of the market – contrary to the concerns of its critics. Surprisingly, these findings were given very little attention in the recent policy discussions about BBC online.

Conclusion: A progressive Europeanization?

This chapter started with an examination of the decisions on State Aid by the European Commission that led to the adoption of Communication 2009. It argued that whereas until 2002 the Commission was supportive of new media initiatives by PSBs, the more recent reasoning – substantiated in Communication 2009 – reveals an increasingly restrictive approach towards PSB online. The document has been highly advocated by commercial rivals of PSB who filed their complaints in Brussels, and it requires stricter controls on PSBs' expansion by imposing an *ex ante* test on new services. Finally, the chapter offers an in-depth investigation of the national and institutional policies of the BBC, which is an historical reference point for all European PSBs. The evaluation of the BBC case shows that from a strong political support of BBC online activities in the 1990s, the UK policy framework has become more hostile towards the BBC's online offer, under growing pressure from commercial operators. Since 1997, thanks to a solid political backing and the vast amount of resources invested, BBC Online became one of the most successful online platforms for information, education, entertainment and participation online. However, the scrutiny over BBC new media activities has progressively intensified, and the introduction of the Public Value Test (PVT), with its market-impact assessment component, has prevented new initiatives from being introduced. Interestingly, the process that led to stronger controls on BBC Online was not triggered directly by Communication 2009, but rather, it had already started during the renewal procedure for the Royal Charter in 2006.It was then that political backing for BBC Online started weakening under the pressure of intense domestic lobbying by commercial rivals.

Hence, it could be argued that Communication 2009 is in the end a 'BBC policy document' and that a mechanism like the PVT introduced within the BBC framework constitutes an example of policy transfer (Dolowitz and Marsh, 2000) between the UK and Brussels. Indeed, the idea of an *ex-ante* assessment with a market evaluation component was first introduced in the UK and then adopted as a new tool by Communication 2009. This could also framed as an example of Europeanization by a 'bottom-up' mechanism (Harcourt, 2002: 737), which occurs when a policy idea from a European Member State is then transferred to the European level. Indeed, there is evidence of continuous contacts between the BBC and Brussels regarding the introduction of the PVT in the UK framework (interview with Matteo Maggiore, January 2009). Furthermore, as Collins (2007) confirms:

> Many European Public Service Broadcasters have, directly or through the European Broadcasting Union (EBU) obtained detailed briefings from the BBC about its approach to public value and the public value test in particular (communication from David Levy, 28.6.2006). (Collins, 2007: 65)

Despite acknowledging the BBC's position as one of the most influential and functional model of PSB in Europe, it is difficult to argue that a 'BBC policy' adopted on a European scale through Communication 2009 could be beneficial to all PSBs in Europe.

Albeit some authors (Thompson, 2006) claim that PVT is an effective instrument for the dimension and reach of the BBC,[32] there are reasons to be sceptical about the adoption of PVT on a European scale. The test could have the detrimental effect of curtailing the possibilities for other PSBs in Europe to achieve their remits online. For example, an *ex ante* test could be a too big hurdle for the PSBs of smaller European States, like Denmark, that need continuous public funding to operate. In fact, small Member States' PSBs operate under difficult conditions of small internal markets, a shortage of resources (sales income, licence fees and public funds), while their dependency and vulnerability to media globalization and concentration is certainly higher than the BBC's. As Chapter 8 will amply discuss, Denmark is one of the first country that has seen its policy framework becoming more restrictive towards PSB online after Communication 2009. The test recently introduced could prove to be too costly for DR and could constitute a new barrier for innovation in the online offering.

Likewise, the frameworks of some States in Southern Europe could be detrimentally impacted by the *ex-ante* test. As Chapter 7 has explained, PSBs in the South of Europe are still characterized by a far less successful and established online offering when compared with Northern European PSB. The new costly bureaucracy of the *ex-ante* test could deter Southern European PSB from experimenting with new online activities, and rather confine their online policies away from the ideals of PSB 2.0. At the time of writing, France and Italy have not introduced an *ex-ante* test in their respective frameworks, although Spain adopted it in the reform of March 2010 (Spanish TV Act, 2010), so an assessment of its impact is premature. Art. 41(3) explains that the new *ex ante* control entails a public consultation and the evaluation of the overall impact of each new service on the market, to be conducted by the Consejo Estatal de Medios Audiovisuales (Spanish TV Act, 2010).[33]

The next chapter scrutinizes the ways in which pressure from the commercial world has dictated the policies of PSB online in European Member States. It also discusses how the mobilization of PSBs' commercial rivals is extremely active both at national and at European level.

8
Commercial Pressure from Rival Competitors: The Impact on PSB Online

Introduction

This chapter examines the impact of the pressure of the commercial world on the policies of PSB online in European Member States. In particular, it aims to find out what are the most important entities contesting the expansion of PSB online; to what extent these entities have succeeded in moulding PSB online policies; and whether we can detect a process of 'marketization' of these policies.

RTVE and its commercial rivals

In Spain, with the introduction of competition in 1988, TVE started losing its prominence in the national audiovisual market. Its lack of funding, coherent planning and a long-term strategy led TVE to an inescapable crisis (López-Escobar, 1992; Bustamante, 1989). The pressure from the commercial front was not limited to the battle for advertising and audience: in fact, TVE was the subject of several complaints filed at the European Commission (EC) by its commercial counterparts. The first of these complaints – and indeed the first complaints in the history of the EC – were filed by Gestevision Telecinco against the Spanish autonomous regional television companies in 1988 and later in 1993 against TVE (Court of First Instance, 1998). At the time, the complaints were mainly related to the funding of TVE and claimed that the double financing system of RTVE was allegedly contrary to European competition law. In France similar complaints were raised by TF1 against France Télévisions. Interestingly, the Commission delayed its decision on these cases while the new protocol on PSB was being approved. In 1997 the Amsterdam Treaty clearly defined that every Member State could freely decide on the means of financing their PSBs (Protocol on PSB, 1997). It was with its 2001 Communication (EC, 2001), however, that the double funding system of PBS found a new legitimacy.[1]

Once the dispute over mixed funding for PSBs was settled at the European level, successive Spanish governments promised to reform PSB and bring it in line with the EC's policy-making and the requirements of Communication 2001. Yet, they all failed to achieve a solid reform of TVE and satisfy the calls from the Commission. In 2005 it was the turn of Spanish Prime Minister Zapatero, who prompted a reorganization of TVE. Not only was TVE in need of a serious reform[2] that could secure clear funding measures and waive the huge debts of the broadcasters, it also needed to comply with Brussels' requirements for transparency and to be redefined in order to avoid further commercial complaints.

If the first Zapatero reform of 2005[3] showed a firm commitment to enhancing the values of RTVE and sustaining a more solid public service output, the policy developed by the same government after 2006 showed a definitive shift. So paradigmatic is the policy shift that it seems to be the result of policy-making by two ideologically different governments. Arguably, the most recent policies regarding PSB in Spain have been strongly influenced by the desire to please and reinforce the commercial sector in times of economic crisis. Also, these policies seem to have been dictated by the desire to secure support in upcoming Spanish elections.

Commercial complaints and their impact on RTVE reform

Zapatero's new reform (Spanish TV Law, 2010) has revolutionized the funding system of RTVE by abolishing advertisements – the main financial resource of TVE since its birth; it has relaxed media and cross-media ownership rules; and has introduced new benefits for sport-rights acquisitions for commercial broadcasters. These are all measures that have the explicit objective of sustaining commercial audiovisual operators. As it can be inferred from the documents, press releases and speeches produced so far by commercial broadcasting associations, the new reform of 2010–2011 has met their expectations (Spanish TV Law, 2009; Spanish TV Law, 2010). On 8 May 2009 (Mundoplus.tv, 2009), Jorge del Corral, the secretary of Uteca (Unión de Televisiones Comerciales Asociadas and Antenas 3), declared his satisfaction with the new measures that the government and parliament, were going to pursue:

> The abolition of advertisement in public television is a landmark decision. We are confident that, given the huge economic efforts

that we – as commercial television and other industrial operators – are undertaking to co-finance TVE will contribute to turning it into a non commercial institution, and turning TVE into a real public television station with public service programmes. (Mundoplus.tv, 2009; my translation)

In contrast, this law has been found deeply unsatisfactory by non-commercial entities such as the Association of Communication Users (Asociación de Usuarios de la Comunicación; AUC) and the Community Media Network (Red de Medios Comunitarios; ReMC). AUC has expressed its disagreement with stopping advertisements on RTVE on at least two different occasions. Firstly, AUC complained about the lack of funding produced by the reform:

> In this time of economic crisis, eliminating advertisements from public television will highly compromise the necessary funding for RTVE to fulfil its remit as a public service. (AUC, 2009a)

Secondly, the same association expressed its reservations about the possibility that in the future private commercial television would contribute to financially sustaining RTVE:

> Our Association believes that the private television stations, after benefiting greatly from the advertising that will no longer run on RTVE, will stop contributing to public television in future years. They will follow the same pattern we have seen in film production funding: instead of contributing they are resisting doing so. (AUC, 2009b)

Furthermore, according to the Community Media Network ReMC, the commercial networks closely influenced the outcome of the new law:

> The vice-prime minister was constantly in touch with Uteca regarding the new audiovisual reform. However, in public documents, the same Uteca is not quoted as an association that has been consulted during the policy making process. Nevertheless, we are sure that the association has been heavily involved since the very beginning of the political process, while all other associations like ours have been excluded by the process. (ReMC, 2009)

The fact that Uteca heavily lobbied the government to draft a favourable law is confirmed by a statement of the president of the association that was given in the aftermath of the reform (Uteca, 2009).[4] Once again, this speech demonstrates how the association was extremely satisfied with the reorganization of RTVE and the prohibition of advertisements as well as by the new law concerning media ownership regulation, Act 7/2009 (Spanish Telecommunication Law 2009). Importantly, the Act reduces media ownership controls and cross-ownership rules.[5] Also, several laws passed following the urgent procedure of the law decree (Real Decreto) were favourable to the communication industry. Overall, the decree contains measures that were highly advocated by the market. They are, more precisely, deregulation measures that allow for a greater consolidation and the lessening of advertising rules and measures that limit the amount of sport-rights and overseas films to be broadcasted by RTVE.[6]

The benefits of the law on the commercial networks are already clear: by May 2010, Telecinco announced an unprecedented, 101% increase in profits (Montalvo, 2010; Prisa 2010), beating even the very optimistic forecasts of market analysts who had predicted 'only' a 68% increase. By Telecinco's own admission, this was due to the elimination of advertisements from RTVE (Telecinco, 2010). Likewise, the revenues of Antena 3 boomed once the reform was passed. According to the data provided by the Comisión Nacional del Mercado de Valores, the Antena 3 Group earned 15.9 million euros in the first quarter of 2010, doubling the profit achieved in the same period of the previous year (CNMV, 2010).

The fragile new funding scheme of RTVE

If the Act of 2006 reaffirmed a mixed funding system – based on State funding for one-third of the budget and advertisement for two-thirds – the new law bans advertising and adopts a pure funding system based on State resources. The funding will be provided by three fiscal measures, in addition to the existing State funding of RTVE, which amounts to approximately 500 million euros: a tax of 3% of the revenues of free-to-air commercial broadcasters and of 1.5% of pay-TV broadcasters; a tax of 0.9% of the revenues of operators of electronic communications;[7] and a share of 80% of the existing levy on radio spectrum use of up to 330 million euros.[8] However, despite the significant gains they received from the new law, commercial operators have already filed complaints to the EC regarding the new taxes. The results of the complaints will be discussed in the final sections of this chapter.

The new Zapatero 'counter reform' and its impact on RTVE.es

Chapter 7 has already explained how much RTVE online has expanded since the reform of 2005–2006 and has shown how the prominent reliance of RTVE on advertisements – approximately 65% of its financial resources[9] – has determined the strong entertainment and commercial vocation of RTVE.es' new portal. The abolition of advertisements might impinge on the development of RTVE online. On the positive side, its strong commercial orientation could be mitigated. On the negative side, as discussed in Chapter 7, if the revenues originated by advertising are not replaced by solid public investment, the recent progress achieved by RTVE online could be seriously compromised. Unfortunately, at the time of writing, the financial resources allocated by the government to RTVE seem to have returned to pre-reform levels.[10]

Commercial pressure on DR online: Complaints from the Danish newspaper association

Chapter 7 has demonstrated that DR's web platform is certainly one of the most advanced and most successful among European PSBs and that Denmark continues to stand in top spot for technological development in the world. Unlike in Spain, criticism towards DR online has arisen not from commercial television channels, but from Danish online news outlets. However, the overall impact of these complaints has been less invasive than in countries like the UK, where BBC Online has triggered numerous complaints from the commercial world.[11] DR seemed to enjoy strong support across the political spectrum and consequently the lobbying activities of the Danish newspaper association have been less effective in curbing the PSB online service, at least until the aftermath of Communication 2009.[12]

DR's strong political support is exemplified by the introduction in 2007 of the Public Value Test (PVT) by the current Service Contract. In fact, the Danish PVT is to be conducted at the discretion of DR and entails neither a market impact assessment, nor any assessment of 'distinctiveness' from the commercial offering. According to the test, the assessment of whether a new service meets cultural, democratic or social needs in the Danish society must be based on whether:

- the service provides added value to society and/or the individual by meeting cultural, democratic or social needs; and

- the service is generally accessible to the Danish public. (Public Service Contract, 2007)

Furthermore, the ultimate decision on the launch of the new service rests upon DR and not on an independent authority. More precisely, after conducting the test,

> DR shall present the value tests for the new services and their results to the Radio and Television Board for their opinion before the activities commence. DR must await the opinion of the Board before implementing the new activities, as the final decision on implementation will be made by DR's management. (Public Service Contract, 2007)

However, the pressure by commercial interests to limit DR's online activity intensified in 2009. The Association of the Danish Newspaper Publishers and the Association of the Danish Specialized Press kept filing complaints to the Government against parts of DR's web activities. In a document released on 16 January 2009, the Association of the Danish Press clearly states that:

> the Association is extremely critical about the extensive presence of DR on the internet, which is based on a broad political agreement that the internet is attached to radio and TV as a third public service obligation. (Danske Dagblades Forening, 2009)

Additionally, the Association of the Danish Press added that:

> DDF is thus very interested in the section of Communication 2009, which sets out the direction for how to carry out the market evaluation 'The Amsterdam Test' (ex-ante test). In relation to this, the Association particularly points to ENPA's comments about the need to specify the usage of the test. It should not just be compulsory in relation to the planning of new services but also in relation to major changes to existing services. (Danske Dagblades Forening, 2009)

Furthermore, the Danish Ministry of Culture has been addressed by other initiatives aimed at restricting DR's activities. One such initiative has come from the Confederation of Danish Industry, which, once again, called for a reduction of public funding to DR (Nordicom, 2007).

As a consequence, on 11 June 2009 the Minister of Culture, Carina Christensen, demanded a PVT for all new services of DR. In August 2009, the first two PVTs were conducted on two different services of DR, with positive outcomes. The first service to be tested was the successful health websites.[13] The Radio and Television Board[14] (Bibliotek Og Medier) confirmed the positive result of the test. It acknowledged that the aim of the health website was to support social and democratic objectives, and that the website's editorial process was capable of filtering the commercial interests of the medical and pharmaceutical companies.[15]

So far, since the political support for DR has not faded, the activities of DR online have not been reduced. Yet, the recent policy-making of the EC has reinvigorated the opposition of the commercial counterparts to DR online, as discussed in Chapter 7. In fact, the Commission now demands that countries such as Denmark should adopt a stricter policy towards online PSB. In September 2009, following the adoption of the EC Communication Act, Minister Carina Christensen announced that the introduction of a market impact assessment would be put on the agenda during the negotiations for the next media political agreement. For the first time a market-failure approach to PSB was taken into consideration as a new tool to be introduced in the policy framework of DR. Even though the final word on PSB regulation rests with Danish policy-makers,[16] Communication 2009 has certainly given private competitors more bargaining power in the reduction of the scope of DR in the online market. Hence, in the summer of 2010, during the negotiations for the renewal of the Media Agreement for 2011–2014,[17] a new market impact assessment was introduced for the first time for new media services of DR. From the draft of the Public Service Contract with DR,[18] we learn that:

> DR shall provide public service content on a technology-neutral basis and support the Danes' use of the internet. Thus, DR on the web shall offer content that contributes to DR's public service purposes and is editorially founded on an equal balance with the content offered by other platforms. DR's internet sites must include programme-related information, independent news and relevant content for children and young people, opportunities for user interaction and information about DR as well as productions with sound, image and text. (draft of the Public Service Contract with DR, 2010)

At the time of writing it seems unclear what the concept of 'editorially funded' would actually mean. Nevertheless, the phrasing could aim at excluding certain online activities not explicitly 'editorially funded'. Yet, as former director of the Radio and Television Board (Bibliotek Og medier), Erik Nordahl Svendsen, states, the argumentations of the online competitors of DR are not based on evidence:

> The complaints from DDF over DR's internet activities are however not well founded in data: dr.dk covers only 1% of the time spent by Danes on the internet (2010), and 15% of the time was on Danish media sites in 2008, while more time, 39%, was on American sites and dominated by Google. Advertising revenue is moving from print to the internet, in 2009 estimated to 3000 MDKr of which Google earns over 1000 MDKr. Denmark is thus No. 1 Google market in the whole world. This describes a serious challenge to Danish newspapers, but DR is hardly the explanation of it. (Svendsen, 2011)

Commercial pressure on policies on France Télévisions: Complaints lodged with the European Commission

The history of complaints about France Télévisions by its commercial counterparts dates back to the 1990s. Since then, the newly privatized TF1 has been the most active player in submitting complaints to the Commission concerning France Télévisions' funding (Mortensen, 2006; Llorens Maluquer, 2005). As already shown in the discussion of the Spanish case, the creation of Europe's single market during the 1990s gave commercial broadcasters new grounds for filing complaints to the EC on alleged competition law breaches. A thorough examination of the series of State Aid cases on Public Service Broadcasting shows an intensified mobilization of commercial broadcasters making new demands on community regulatory regimes as well as an accumulation of European Court of Justice decisions on State Aid to PSBs. This increased mobilization is particularly evident in Southern European Member States like France, Spain, Italy and Portugal (Llorens Maluquer, 2005). The subjects of the complaints were also quite homogeneous, as the system of funding of these countries' PSBs is relatively similar. More precisely, commercial broadcasters in the south of Europe were complaining about the allegedly unlawful mixed funding system – a combination of public funding and advertisements. As it has been already mentioned, the first case to be brought to the attention of the EC was the Gestevision Telecinco complaint in March 1992 (Court of First Instance, 1998). The second case dates back to 10 March 1993, and involved TF1 complaining against against the French State for the supposed infringement by

France 2 and France 3 of Articles 81, 86(1) and 87 of the Treaty (now Art. 106–107) (Court of First Instance, 1996).

Since its privatization, TF1 has been extremely active in demanding a clear intervention by the EC regarding the funding of the French PSB (Court of First Instance, 1996). In 2000 TF1 was joined in its case against France Télévisions by the Association of Commercial Television in Europe (ACT), which pursued not just the objectives of TF1 but also of the other commercial networks M6 and Canal +. However, the subsequent recognition of the legitimacy of the mixed funding system for PSBs led the EC to close the procedure against France Télévisions (EC, 2004b). Later on, the EC declared the aid to RTVE compatible with the common market regulations under Art. 86(2), now Art. 106 (2) of the Treaty (European Commission, 2005).[19] In a press release, the European Commission explained its decision thus:

> Towards the end of 2003, the Commission issued a preliminary request asking those Member States to implement appropriate measure in respect of their existing financing schemes for their national public broadcasters (see IP/03/1399 and IP/03/1686), measures which the Commission has today formally recommended. These measures reflect the Commission's general approach as laid down in its 2001 Communication on applying state aid rules to public service broadcasting (see IP/01/1429). In particular, the measures aim to ensure that public and private broadcasters compete on equal terms in commercial markets such as TV advertising. Moreover, financing of public broadcasters should not exceed the strict minimum necessary to ensure the proper execution of the public service mission should not unduly benefit commercial activities (cross-subsidies) and should be transparent. (European Commission, 2005)

Commercial pressure at the national level: How it shaped France Télévisions' policies

As this chapter has described, in Spain commercial broadcasters' demands have been more focused on obtaining the abolition of advertising from TVE than on reducing the scope of RTVE online. This fact can be explained by acknowledging that RTVE online is a relatively recent development in Spain and that it never constituted a significant threat to the profits of commercial broadcasters and online publishers. Likewise in France, commercial forces have seemed to be less concentrated on curbing the online expansion of France Télévisions than in

.obbying the government to limit advertisement funding to the French PSB (Regourd, 2008; Cayrol, 2009). Nevertheless, the pressure exerted by the commercial broadcasting sector has certainly had an important impact on the new reform of France Télévisions. Significantly, not only does the reform affect its organization and funding system, it also shapes its Internet policies.

On 8 January 2008 in a famous press conference at Elysée Palace President Sarkozy realized what has been defined as an extraordinary 'coup politique': he declared the end of advertisements on French Public Service Broadcasting. He declared:

> I propose that we accomplish a real cultural revolution in our Public service television. (...) I'd like that the *Cahier des charges* of our Public television will be reviewed and that we think about totally suppressing advertisement on our Public channels, that could be financed by a tax of the advertisement revenues of commercial chains and by one small tax on the revenues of electronic communications.[20]

By proposing to abolish advertisements, the French President achieved a reform that was strongly advocated by the Socialist party and, what's more, by French intellectuals (Musso, 2010). In 1989 a similar proposal was advanced by the Prime Minister, Michel Rocard (Regourd, 2008). As Roland Cayrol (2009) explains:

> It has been a political coup. In fact, the abolition of advertisements has always been an issue for traditional debates of the left: private funding for private institutions and public funding for public institutions. The whole spectrum of the leftist parties was against advertisements, while in the right, they were in favour. So Sarkozy was extremely excited to take ideas from the left and to actually claim to have achieved a reform that the left never managed to deliver. So of course, when the political advisor of Sarkozy, Alain Minc, came up with this idea of surprising the whole political world and effectively embarrassing the left party with this reform, Sarkozy made this idea his own very quickly. (Cayrol, 2009)

But Sarkozy had other motivations for totally revolutionizing the French PSB from that of taking a policy from the Left. Furthermore, Sarkozy's reform was undertaken with incredible urgency and haste. Suddenly announced in January 2008, it was transformed into law in March 2009.

Arguably, there were two important reasons for Sarkozy to pursue the reform. First was to facilitate the commercial competitors of FTV, and second was to be more in control of France Télévisions. Sarkozy was furious about the way that France 2 and France 3 had depicted him during the electoral campaign. So this was an opportunity to clip their wings and be sure to have no further problems with France Télévisions (Cayrol, 2009).

The reform cut by about 30% the total resources of France Télévisions collected through advertisement revenue. Unsurprisingly, it was overtly welcomed by the entire commercial broadcasting world. Moreover, in explaining the reasons for the urgency of the reform – contained in Act 258 of 5 March 2009 – the civil servants of the Department for Media Development of the government declared that 'the reform was needed so quickly because of the deep crisis of the French advertising market' (Barges, 2009; Croix, 2009; Levassor, 2009). Yet, this explanation hides one significant outcome and purpose of the reform: Sarkozy's new law is a strategy to ensure more revenues to commercial broadcasters in that it gives them the possibility to collect the resources that were once assigned to France Télévisions. The fact that the government faced intense lobbying of private television interests during the years before the reform proves this argument. Likewise, the close friendship between Sarkozy and Martin Bouygues – the owner of the most successful television channel in France, TF1 – is further evidence of the significant weight of commercial pressure on the policy devised by the government (Daugnaud, 2009; Cayrol, 2009; Sergeant, 2009).

During the work of the Copé Commission described in Chapter 7, a White Paper by TF1 (Livre Blanc du TF1, 2007) was made public (*Le Monde*, 2008; Les echos, 2008). It contained the demands of TF1 for a reform of the TV market in France (Regourd, 2008). The paper suggested the abolition of advertisements on France Télévisions in order to build a healthy TV market. Importantly, the White Paper was submitted to the government in 2007, that is, much earlier than Sarkozy's famous press conference. More specifically, the paper states that:

mixed funding system of FTV is indeed dangerous for the whole system of commercial broadcasters in France. In order to fix the financial structural arrangement of the television market, we should take the British model as example: a strong public service, with a clear mission and financed purely by public funds. In this way, we would stabilize the advertisement market in France, by submitting it just to the laws of supply and demand. (Livre Blanc TF1, 2007; my translation)[21]

The intense lobbying of commercial broadcasters to gain a favourable reform of France Télévisions was so evident that, in November 2007, Goldman Sachs released a document that stated:

> We are expecting in the following months a great change in the audio-visual market in France, a change that will certainly be a strongly positive factor for TF1 and M6. (Sénat, 2008: 37)[22]

Moreover, as we can learn from the speech given by Senator Jack Ralite during a Senate Session of 5 February 2008, the reform was strongly influenced by a study by Société Générale 'sur le secteur des medias' (on the media in France), which clearly advanced the interests of the market alone, without considering other public interest rationales:

> I have been incredibly struck by a study of Société Générale of 2 November 2007, according to which 'the legal framework of the French audiovisual market is one of the most restrictive in Europe, with strong investments obligations [...] and a lack of flexibility as regarding to advertisement'. This study has become a sort of a 'red book' of the audiovisual sector in French, as the same arguments of the study have been employed in a letter from the President to the Communication minister on the matter and in subsequent declarations by the Communication minister. That study has been carried out for TF1 and M6. (speech by Jack Ralite, Sénat, 2008: 37)[23]

As highlighted in Chapter 7, on 5 March 2009 the French Parliament promulgated a new law amending the Law on Communications of 1986. Law 258 of 2009 gradually banned advertisements on state television. It began in the same year with the abolition of advertisement after 8pm and established that a complete ban of advertisements would have been reached by the end of 2011.[24]

Given that advertisement revenue represented about 30% of France Télévisions' resources (EC, 2010a: 12; France Télévisions, 2008 and 2008a), the challenge for France Télévisions in terms of funding was indisputable. At the time of the reform, it was calculated that the total loss in advertisement revenue for France Télévisions amounted to 833 million euros a year (Copé Report, 2008). The revenues lost as a result of the reduction and discontinuance of advertising by 30 November 2011 in public TV channels would be compensated by:

- A state budgetary grant (of €450 million for 2009, €460 million in 2010, €500 million in 2011 and €650 million in 2012. (EC, 2010a: 15)

- The customary TV licence fee, which amounted to €1,945 million in 2008 and is indexed to inflation. (France Télévisions, 2008 and 2008a)
- A new system of taxes on advertising revenues of commercial broadcasters and electronic communication operators. (TV Law 2009: Art. 32)

In the first version of Law 258 of 2009 (TV Law 2009) and according to the EC (EC, 2010a), the tax was set at 3% of the advertisement revenues of commercial broadcasters. At the time the Copé Report calculated that the new tax would raise about 80 million euros.. Along with the tax on commercial broadcasters, the law introduced a tax of 0.9% on Internet mobile operators' revenues from subscribers (this was calculated to raise about 380 million euros).[25] Also, the government estimated that the total loss of advertisement revenue following the abolition of commercials after 8pm would amount to 450 million euros (Cope Report, 2008). Yet, the benefit for commercial broadcasters of the eventual elimination of advertising on France Télévisions is difficult to disprove. The EC itself, in the letter that opened the investigation on State Aid to France Télévisions (EC, 2010a: 18–19) affirmed that:

> private broadcasters, one of which is allegedly in a dominant position (TF1), benefit from the nearly total withdrawal of France Télévisions. France has not provided any clear assessment of those effects. (EC, 2010a: 10)

Not surprisingly, right after the announcement of the reform, the price of TF1 and M6s' shares on the French stock market increased by 15% and 7% (Esposito, 2008). Consistently, media agency Carat[26] called the reform 'an unparalleled gift for the two private broadcasters' (Carat, 2008), while the announcement was compared to the London 'Big Bang' (Carat, 2008). Moreover, the agency predicted that the reform 'Could allow TF1 and rival M6 to absorb at least half of the advertisement of France Télévisions' (Carat, 2008; my translation).[27] The agency OMG-Omnicom[28] shared the same view; it argued that the two channels would accede to 40% and 50% of the advertisement revenues of France Télévisions (OMG-Omnicom, 2008).

Commercial complaints against France Télévisions after the reform: The reduction of taxation on commercial broadcasters

Despite having won the battle to abolish advertisements on France Télévisions, a mobilization by commercial broadcasters against the new system of taxation started immediately after the work of the Copé Commission had begun. Thus, the three competitors, TF1, M6 and Canal+, joined forces in the ACP – Association of Private broadcasters (Association des Chaînes Privées). In a press release in June 2008, ACP harshly criticized the new system of taxation, claiming that it was introduced at a time 'when the audio-visual sector is in deep upheaval, facing technological and economic challenges, forcing us to strongly invest' (ACT, 2008).[29] Moreover, it added 'It is unacceptable that the private broadcasters have to finance the competition of a public sector' (ACT, 2008).[30]

Soon after the complaints began, subsequent amendments to the reform Act (TV Act 2009, 2009) started reducing the amount of taxation on commercial broadcasters' revenues. In fact, both the Copé Report (2008) and the first version of the reform Act (TV Act 2009, 2009) had considered a 3% tax on the revenues of the private channels. The outrage against the tax exploded immediately after, along with an intensive lobbying to obtain a reduction of the tax (L'Express, 2008; Renault, 2010). Two subsequent amendments have further reduced the taxations of private channels. First, in November 2008, Christian Kert from UMP – the majority party within the government – presented an amendment to reduce the tax from 3% to a figure between 1.5% and 3%. Yet, according to Jean-François Copé – the UMP chief whip in the Chamber – 'the modification of the text is not a gift for commercial televisions, but a fair way to handle the crisis' (L'Express, 2008).[31] Later, in October 2010, the rate was reduced to 0.5% by an amendment presented in the Finance Bill by Michèle Tabarot and Patrice Martin Lalande (Renault, 2010).

No cash, no reform: The total abolition of advertisement is postponed

According to the data released by *La Tribune* on 20 August 2010, instead of the prospective 80 million euros to be raised by the taxes on private broadcasters, the taxes on private channels realized just 28 million euros (La Tribune, 2010). More precisely, TF1 has paid 9.3 million euros into the state budget; M6, 3.9 million euros; and Canal +, 3.3 million euros. On top of this, the tax on telecoms only collected 186 million euros for 2009, very far from the 380 million euros expected by the government (Le Tribune, 2010). Moreover, the same tax is the object of an infringement procedure by the EC[32] for the alleged breach of the 2002 Electronic framework (European Union, 2002) and in particular of Art. 12 of the telecoms Authorisation Directive (European Union, 2002). According to Art. 12, 'charges can be levied on telecoms operators to cover only certain administrative and regulatory costs (mainly authorisations and regulatory functions) and should be objective, transparent and proportionate' (EC, 2010b).

Consequently, the government found itself in a difficult position. It had to face the global economic crisis, on the one hand, and, on the other, the intense lobbying of private broadcasters and telecom operators against taxation. Hence, from April 2010, the government started reconsidering the reform as whole. In particular, the total abolition of advertisements before 8pm that was due to start in November 2011 has been put on hold. Jean-François Copé claimed that the economic crisis did not allow for the full ban to commence in November 2011 (*Le Monde*, 2010; LePoint.fr, 2010). In fact, on 7 April 2010, he stated in front of the Cultural Affairs Commission of the Chamber that it was important 'to demonstrate political intellect more than the ability to adapt'.[33] He explained:

> We know the difficult situation of our public budget and I think that the ratio costs/benefits that come from the total suppression of advertisement before 8pm needs to be reassessed. (*Le Monde*, 2010; my translation)

Following this statement, two Senators from the UMP, Catherine Morin-Desailly and Claude Belot, presented the amendment to stop the abolition of advertisements before 8pm on France Télévisions (*Le Monde*, 2010; Le Point.fr 2010). In September 2010 Culture Minister Frédéric Mitterand placed a two-year 'moratorium' on the advertisement ban before 8 pm on France Télévisions (*Le Monde*, 2010a).[34] Immediately afterwards, TF1 made its position clear: maintaining advertising during the day would be 'very awkward' for the balance of the sector (Le Point.fr 2010). The CEO of the Bouygues subsidiary, Nonce Paolini, added that he was 'convinced' that this situation will be 'here to stay' and called again for the suppression of the tax on turnover that private channels have to pay to compensate for the lack of advertising income for the public group (Le Point.fr 2010).[35] Following the announcement, the leading trade union of the audiovisual group CGT welcomed what it called 'excellent news', both editorially and financially (*Le Monde*, 2010a):

> Double financing (from both licensing fee and advertising) is a long-term solution which we've been defending from the beginning. This gives us some relief until 2014. (Jean-François Téaldi, CGT spokesman, in *Le Monde*, 2010a)

Complaints lodged with the EC: Their effects on the reform of France Télévisions and RTVE

As discussed in Chapters 6 and 8, major reforms took place in both France and Spain in 2009. First, in March 2009, the French government put an end to paid advertising on France Télévisions. The reform triggered a very similar law in Spain. Adopted on 1 September 2009 (Law 8/2009), it has radically reshaped the financial arrangements of TVE. Similarly to what happened in France, the new law abolishes teleshopping, merchandising and pay-per-view services on TVE.[36] These two very similar reforms can be seen as an example of policy transfer between two European countries. Both of them have activated an incredible mobilization of forces within the telecom and TV industries.[37]

The EC investigated the two reforms with two distinct procedures. First, it ascertained whether the new mechanism of financing of France Télévisions and RTVE were compatible with State regimes and would not lead to overcompensation of the two Public Service Broadcasters. Second, it verified – in a separate procedure conducted by the Information Society Service – whether the taxes on telecom operators were not in breach of the rules of the EU framework on Electronic Communication (EU, 2009). The first positive decision for France Télévisions arrived on 1 September 2009, when the EC authorized payment of State Aid of 450 million euros[38] for France Télévisions in 2009 as complying with EC Treaty State Aid rules and, in particular, with the Commission Communication on State Aid for the Funding of Public Service Broadcasters (EC, 2009a: 1).

In justifying the decision, Competition Commissioner Neelie Kroes explained:

> The decision of France Télévisions to place greater emphasis on its general-interest mission as part of the reform of public service broadcasters is in line with the policy of media plurality which the European Union supports. The Commission has embarked today on a detailed review of this reform and it calls on stakeholders to submit their comments before a final decision is taken. In the meantime, continuity of funding for France Télévisions' public service is guaranteed. (EC, 2009a: 1)

In approving the first subsidy, the Commission opened another formal procedure 'to investigate certain aspects of the annual subsidy for subsequent years, which could add up to over 1.5 billion euros by 2012' (EC, 2010e: 1). As the Commission explained, the reform triggered worries about 'the possible use of the revenue from the new taxes to finance the annual subsidy and the danger of over-compensation for public service costs up to 2011–2012' (European Commission, 2010e: 1). On 20 July 2010, the Commission found the new funding system of France Télévisions compatible with State Aid rules. In elucidating the reasons for the decision, it explained that the annual subsidy would be calculated according to the public service costs incurred by France Télévisions and that the revenue from the taxes introduced by the reform would not be used for this aid measure and would not affect its amount (EC, 2010e: 1).[39]

On the same day, the Commission also approved the new funding system of RTVE, following an investigation started in December 2009, after the adopted reform. Similarly with the French case, the Commission found that 'the amount of the aid to be granted to RTVE does not depend on the revenue generated by these taxes, but is only determined by the net operation costs of the broadcaster' (EC, 2010f: 1). Nevertheless, as highlighted, these favourable decisions do not exempt the new funding systems from a compatibility check with other EU legislation and specifically the rules of the EU Framework on Electronic Communication (EU, 2009).

Hence, on 28 January 2009 and on 18 March 2010, the Commission opened two infringement procedures[40] against France and Spain respectively for breach of the EU Electronic Communication Framework and specifically Article 12 of the Licensing Directive, which details the rules on administrative charges that Member States can impose on telecom/ network providers (EU, 2002). As Member of the EC Viviane Reding – responsible for Information Society and Media – made clear:

> I have expressed doubts about the 'telecoms tax' on a number of occasions. Not only does this new tax on operators seem incompat- ible with the European rules, it also concerns a sector that is now one of the major drivers of economic growth. Moreover, there is a serious risk that it will be passed on to customers at a time when we are in fact trying to reduce their bills by cutting termination rates and the costs of mobile phone calls, data transfer and text message roaming. (EC, 2010c: 1)

On 30 September 2010, the Commission requested Spain and France to abolish the 'telecoms tax' as it found the scheme incompatible with the EU Electronic Communication Framework. In fact, the EU framework states that in order to be compatible the taxes 'need to be specifically and directly related to covering the costs of regulating the telecoms sector' (EC, 2010d: 1). This constitutes a victory for the telecom industry in Spain and France. However, at the time of writing, both the countries had failed to amend their reforms and were still imposing these charges on the turnover of telecoms operators in breach of EU law.[41]

Conclusion

This chapter has discussed the extent to which the commercial world has shaped and influenced the PSB policy framework in European Member States. A different type of mobilization of commercial forces emerges in the North and the South of Europe. Overall we can detect two different tendencies in the South of Europe. Firstly, the mobilization of commercial forces mostly concerns commercial broadcasters complaining about the advertising funding of each country's PSBs. Secondly, the new PSB reforms introduced both in France and Spain have for the first time seen the telecom world drumming up support to abolish the telecom taxes to fund RTVE and France Télévisions. The first trend has been in evidence since the inception of the European single market. The demands of commercial broadcasters – especially Tf1 in France and Telecinco and Antena 3 in Spain – have the same objectives: since the first complaint against TVE in 1993 (Court of First Instance, 1998), commercial broadcasters aimed to abolish advertisements on public television. In the Southern Member States at issue here, the commercial lobbies succeeded in obtaining two radical reforms of their PSB frameworks, which entailed the gradual abolition of advertisements. However, the reform also gave rise to complaints by telecom operators and, given the intervention of the EC, both France and Spain will have to revise their funding arrangements for their respective PSBs. Also, the pressures being exerted by the commercial world in the South of Europe were not directed specifically at their online activities, but rather at their funding arrangements. This situation can be explained by the fact that the online activities of the PSBs of both countries have never constituted a commercial threat and so there was no need to limit their growth. Importantly, the abolition of advertisements from the public channels will have a high impact on both PSBs' online activities; if political support and resources are wavering, then they will be significantly curtailed.

A very different picture emerges from the analysis of the situation in Denmark. In fact, in this Northern European country the bulk of complaints against the PSB DR concentrated on DR's online expansion (in a similar way to what happened in the UK). The disapproval shown by the commercial world of DR's online activities intensified in 2009. The Association of Danish Newspaper Publishers and the Association of the Danish Specialized Press kept filing complaints to the government against parts of DR's web activities. As a consequence, in the aftermath of the adoption of Communication 2009 by the EC (EC, 2009), the introduction of a market impact assessment of the new media services of DR was for the first time put on the agenda. Eventually, the new media agreement and public service contract with DR introduced the new market impact assessment test, in line with commercial rivals demands (Danske Dagblades Forening, 2009) and with Communication 2009.

The next chapter will provide a synthesis of the empirical findings of the study in light of the theoretical concepts elaborated in the theoretical framework.

9
Conclusion

This study has examined to what extent the principles traditionally enshrined in Public Service Broadcasting in Europe have translated into the new online environment. It has investigated the most significant policy initiatives carried out by PSBs in Europe on the new platforms, and analysed how the public service philosophy has been reinvented by policy-makers at the national and European level, by PSB institutions and by their competitors. It has explored how historical and nation-specific factors, the European framework and commercial pressures have moulded these policies and practices. Finally, it has established – and discussed – a normative framework for PSB online in Europe (PSB 2.0).

This final chapter elaborates on the findings and adds a further normative evaluation of the policy ambitions and concerns, the policy measures chosen and results of these policies and practices. Hence, it attempts to appraise how well PSB Internet policies comply with the normative criteria of PSB 2.0 and, therefore, to what extent the PSB ethos has been transferred online.

Path dependency: National peculiarities overcome convergence

The theoretical framework recognized that institutional factors impinge strongly on policy developments. From this starting point, the study has assessed the extent to which national, historical characteristics shaped the policies of PSB online in the States considered. The findings of the case studies strongly suggest that the online expansion of the PSBs follows a path-dependent model. The long-term established ethos of each PSB framework constrains policy trajectories regarding PSB development

145

online. There is a clear parallel between PSBs' online and offline activities, in which a typical broadcasting ethos rooted in historical, cultural, political and institutional factors is replicated online. For instance, in the case of Denmark, where traditionally the PSB framework has been strongly supportive of DR and has guaranteed a relevant place for DR in the television market, the same pattern is noticeable online. Since the official launch of DR online in 1996, it was already clear that 'DR online' constituted 'the third arm of DR', rather than being a complementary service to broadcasting. Also, the major drive towards innovation, originality and unviersality has enabled DR to transfer the same public service objectives to its online platform. For example, the news offering has been crucially important since the beginning, as well as the commitment to experiment with new participative platforms online.

Conversely, this study has explained how Spain has embodied a tradition within which its PSB, TVE, has enjoyed a secondary place in the market, with scarce public resources invested and high commercialization. Again, the same blueprint was noticeable in the online policies of RTVE; for example, a strong entertainment and commercial vocation was apparent in the new portal. However, the achievements of RTVE online since 2008 could lead to a stronger presence overall, therefore deflecting from its path dependency. In fact, in less than two years, RTVE outperformed the success of its commercial broadcasting competitors online and was able to invest more in its offering of online news and public affairs. Yet, the reform of 2009–2010 could constitute another twist for RTVE online policies that could bring RTVE back to its path-dependent policy trajectory. On the one hand, the abolition of advertisements could guarantee a less commercial output. But on the other, if the resources are not secured, the recent progress of RTVE.es could be jeopardized.

The case of France also confirms a path-dependency development. The policies on French PSB have been historically characterized by a strong government influence. The position of the two PSB channels, Antenne 2 and France 3 – now managed under the public company France Télévisions – have been overshadowed by TF1, once a public broadcaster, which was privatized in 1987. Since then, the two PSBs have been subjected to more competition to secure advertising and the pressure to aim for higher ratings. Given the *etatiste* characteristic of the French policies on PSB, it is not surprising that the development of France Télévisions online rested only on government decisions rather than on France Télévisions' ability to experiment and innovate. This explains the delay in its development, clearly owing to a lack of interest from French politicians, who were overtly more concerned about television outputs.

As a consequence, the Internet activities of France Télévisions have been considered a complementary means of broadcasting. Moreover, despite the recent restructuring of the public channels under France Télévisions, the difficulties of coordination persist. Each channel has its distinctive and separate online offering without a clear central organization. As a result, France Télévisions' online platforms are still placed 25th in the ranking of top most visited websites in France, far behind the strongest commercial competitor, TF1. Once again, the ethos of France Télévisions online coincides with the broadcasting offering, as it simply replicates each channel offering online. As with RTVE, the reform of 2009 could impact on the development of France Télévisions online, especially if the resources are not assured. For example, France Télévisions could face a funding crisis and therefore could lack the necessary support to embark on a strategy of innovation and harmonization of its online output.

The analysis has also benefited from the examination of the Italian and the UK cases. In fact, although historically RAI has always gained from a strong position in the Italian television market, since the 1980s, it has developed an extremely entertainment-oriented offering, quite similar to that of RTVE. In Italy, constant changes of government and, consequently, of management at RAI, have thwarted the expansion of PSB on the web. So far, investments have been minimal, with priority going to DTT implementation rather than online.

Indeed, while since its inception, 'BBC online' constituted 'the third arm of the BBC' rather than being a complementary service to broadcasting, the same conclusion cannot be drawn for RAI, where there is still no clear long-term strategy and where online merely complements the broadcasting offer.

Furthermore, the different funding models adopted by the five broadcasters studied are highly significant for the online offering. With its huge resources, the BBC has been able to offer wide-ranging outputs, from educational and cultural programmes for the web, to news, public affairs and interactive forums. Also DR, given its strong political support and public funding, has been able to seize new opportunities and innovate online. In contrast, the weaker positions of the three broadcasters in the South of Europe have thwarted their online expansion. Hence, as with broadcasting policy (Humphreys, 2007; Levy, 1997, 1999; Radaelli, 2004), national peculiarities strongly characterize public and institutional policies of PSBs online. Yet, as it will be described in the next section, commercial forces that are increasingly mobilizing against PSB online can lead to an increased convergence of the policies.

Marketization: Two distinct types

As detailed in Chapter 8, this study has identified different type of commercial forces mobilizing against PSB between the North and the South of Europe. In France and Spain, we have seen commercial broadcasters complaining about the advertising funding of their countries' PSBs, while in Denmark and in the UK, the mobilization of commercial opposition has specifically addressed the PSB online offering. Moreover, the new PSB reforms introduced both in France and Spain have for the first time seen the telecoms world drumming up support to abolish the new telecoms taxes, which were designed to fund RTVE and France Télévisions. The two different phenomena belong to two different aspects of marketization.

We can describe the first type of marketization as 'enabling marketization' as, in the two Southern European cases, this process has secured more corporate access to the advertising markets and reinforced the funding opportunities of commercial broadcasters. The fact that the commercial mobilization has not addressed the online activities in both countries is simply explained by the fact that RTVE and France Télévisions have never constituted a threat for either the commercial broadcasters or the online press, and so there was no need to limit their growth. However, the abolition of advertisement from the public channels will also have a high impact on both PSBs' online activities. For example, we have seen how much RTVE.es has improved its offering since 2008. These improvements could be jeopardized if the funding of RTVE becomes uncertain once again. The same is also true for France Télévisions, which needs resources to develop a long-term and centralized strategy online.

The second process of marketization can be defined as 'marketization through reduction of PSBs' scope'. In fact, in the case of Denmark, the intense mobilization of the online press aimed explicitly at reducing the online weight of DR. Therefore, certainly reinforced by the adoption of Communication 2009 by the EC (European Commission, 2009), when the negotiation for a new media agreement for 2011–2014 started, the introduction of a market impact assessment on the new media services of DR was put on the agenda for the first time.

'Marketization through reduction of PSBs' scope' coming from the EU

In reviewing and assessing the most important State Aid decisions taken by the Commission regarding PSBs' new media activities and discussions that led to the adoption of Communication 2009 (European Commission, 2009), Chapter 7 examined the progressively restrictive attitude of the EC towards PSB online. While, up until 2002, the Commission advocated the expansion of PSB online, its decisions regarding the BBC Digital Curriculum (European Commission, 2003) signalled a paradigmatic shift in EU PSB policy. This process culminated with the adoption of Communication 2009, which sets a higher barrier for PSBs' online activities. In fact, when venturing online, PSBs will have to demonstrate their 'added value' compared to the offering of their commercial rivals, thus forcing Member States to adopt a market-failure line when defining their remit online. This type of marketization is also pursued by the introduction of an *ex ante* market impact assessment on all new media services of PSBs.

For the first time, the tests require that 'Member States shall assess, based on the outcome of the open consultation, the overall impact of a new service on the market by comparing the situation in the presence and in the absence of the planned new service' (European Commission, 2009).

Europeanization as marketization

As this study demonstrates, the phenomenon of marketization in PSB policy frameworks is also noticeable at the national policy level, independently from the EU's influence. However, the role played by the Commission in fostering a pro-market approach is undeniable. As we have seen, the Commission has demanded that national authorities adopt a stricter policy towards online PSB in states such as Denmark that had previously presented an enabling framework towards PSB online. The case of Denmark is emblematic. In fact, the policy debate for the new agreement between DR, the Danish PSB, and the government was strongly influenced by Communication 2009.

Although the final decision rested on the Danish policy-makers, Communication 2009 certainly gave private competitors more leverage in their demands to reduce the scope of DR in the online market. Hence, in the summer of 2010, during the negotiations for the renewal of the Media Agreement for 2011–2014, a new market impact assessment was introduced for the first time for the new media services of DR.

Furthermore, this new European framework, spurred by Communication 2009, is impacting on other European States that had so far resisted the pressure of commercial operators. This outcome could certainly be seen as a process of Europeanization of PSB online policies. Hence, the study suggests that we are witnessing a process of Europeanization through marketization of the policies of PSB online. Spain has adopted the new *ex ante* mechanism through the Act that is part of the second reform of RTVE (Spanish TV Act, 2010). Art. 41(3) established the new *ex ante* control that entails a public consultation and the evaluation of the overall impact of each new service on the market, to be conducted by the Consejo Estatal de Medios Audiovisuales (Spanish TV Law, 2010).

Moreover, from the analysis of the BBC policy framework, this study inferred that this type of Europeanization cannot be seen as a 'top-down' mechanism, where European institutions mandate the form that national policy choices should take. On the contrary, the study detects Europeanization as 'bottom-up' process that occurs when specific policy schemes are then transferred to the European level.

Bottom-up Europeanization and the BBC policy transfer

The discussion of the UK case shows that the increasingly pro-market inclination of its national policy framework has led to stronger controls on BBC Online, even independent from the EC's influence. More importantly, it can be argued that Communication 2009 is in the end a 'BBC policy document' and that we are witnessing a policy transfer between the United Kingdom and Brussels, given that the *ex ante* test is substantially modelled on the BBC's PVT.

Despite acknowledging that the BBC has often been regarded as the most influential and functional model of PSB in Europe, it is difficult to argue that a 'BBC policy' adopted on a European scale through Communication 2009 could be beneficial to all PSBs in Europe. Although some authors argue that PVT is an effective instrument for the dimension and reach of the BBC, the same conclusion cannot be drawn for all PSBs in Europe. Rather, the test could have the detrimental effect of curtailing the possibilities for other PSBs in Europe to achieve their remits online. A compulsory *ex ante* test can be harmful for the smaller PSBs of smaller European States, which need continuous public funding to operate. Small Member States' PSBs operate under difficult conditions of small internal markets, and a shortage of resources (sales income, licence fee and public funds), while their dependency and vulnerability to media globalization and concentration is certainly higher than the BBC's. Furthermore, it could also impede the development of PSBs in the South, as in the Spanish and French cases, where their online activities are not yet consolidated.

Challenging the Hallin–Mancini model: Towards a generalization of the findings

The national peculiarities that characterized the development of PSBs' Internet policies in the cases considered corroborate the validity of Hallin and Mancini's model (2004), because the differences between the clusters considered – the Northern European model and the Mediterranean – are still clearly observable. Yet, as this study has described, a process of marketization could gradually bring more uniformity of PSB online policies around Europe. As a consequence, this result would represent a clear exception to the framework constructed by Hallin and Mancini in their 2004 study.

Moreover, the findings that concern PSBs online within the same Mediterranean cluster add to the Hallin and Mancini model significant details that have been overlooked by such a broad model. Because of the intense politicization that has ascribed them to the same group, described as a 'politics over broadcasting system' model (Hallin and Mancini, 2004: 106), France Télévisions, RAI and RTVE online have developed different responses to the Internet world.

It was highlighted in the discussion how Spain embodies a tradition within which its PSB has enjoyed a secondary place in the market, with scarce resources and high commercialization. In contrast, France Télévisions and RAI have benefited from a stronger position in the market even though they were both under strong competition for ratings. However, the recent determination to invest in RTVE online has pushed the Spanish case apart from its historical path dependency and from the less established online ventures of the French and Italian cases.

Since the first Zapatero reform, and especially after 2007, the development of RTVE has overshadowed both France Télévisions' and RAI's online output. RTVE has not only outperformed the success of its commercial broadcasting competitors online, but has been able to develop a stronger offering of online news and public affairs, which represents a remarkable achievement in two years of activity. Yet, the 'counter-reform' of Zapatero (Law 8/2009) that abolished advertisement on RTVE.es could bring the clock back to 2004 in Spain and, therefore bring the three countries' policy frameworks closer once again.

Normative aims

Throughout the study, it has been argued that PSB online has an essential democratic and cultural potential as long as it embodies the four key principles – of citizenship, universality, quality and trust – introduced earlier as the core components of the normative framework that I have called PSB 2.0. Here, I review the policies and practices of PSBs online in the three States considered and discuss how they relate to the overall normative criteria established for PSB 2.0.

Citizenship

The first criterion identified as one of the components of PSB ethos online is citizenship. Citizenship concerns and arguments were present in all the states considered when developing PSB online, but their prominence varied greatly among the countries, with Spain certainly showing the least engagement in enhancing citizenship values. As explained in the preceding chapters, variance from the normative model is due to the impact of the institutional variables employed in the study.

While the 'Council of the Wise men' that drafted the reform of RTVE (Informe, 2005) seemed committed to creating a citizen platform online by stressing that 'the internet of RTVE should [...] be strongly participative and democratic for the citizens according to a vision of public service', RTVE's strategy seemed on the contrary to be more focused on enhancing the 'business' (RTVE, Informe Anual, 2005) and catching up on its delayed online offering. This is also corroborated by the frequently stated necessity to be competitive in the market in order to avoid 'integrating in the information society with so many disadvantages in comparison to private competitors' (Diarios, 2004: 22). This clearly shows that market concerns – spurred by the need to secure advertising for its funding – were critical when RTVE online started its development. The drive of making RTVE.es a great business success was also clear, as the head of the online strategy in 2008 explained that 'the portal should also spur the online advertisement market that in Spain is still stagnant at 7%' (Lloret, 2008). Once again, the focus was more on the business imperative than citizenship imperatives. The practices of RTVE online also reflect the same ethos, as the offering was shown to be strongly entertainment-oriented, with RTVE.es being listed in the category of 'entertainment media' instead of 'news provider' by ODJ Interactiva. However, the abolition of advertisements will have a high impact not only on the budget of RTVE.es, but also on its content. The strong commercial orientation that has so far characterized RTVE on the web could diminish and more space could be given to news, public affairs and educational programmes. Although this outcome could be guaranteed by solid public investment allied to political will, at the time of writing, the finances of RTVE seem to have been returned to the realm of uncertainty, as in the pre-reform years.

The case of France is different, as the objective of enhancing citizens' participation seemed more evident in the policies of France Télévisions online. However, the most important principles of PSB ethos – the cultural enrichment of the citizens, pluralism of output, integration, solidarity and respect of civil rights – were clearly to be realized by France Télévisions as a broadcaster, rather than by its online arm. From the start in France, the role of the Internet was conceived as a tool to 'enrich and complement' the broadcasting offering of France Télévisions, which is why no investment in the interactivity possibility of internet as a means to enhance citizenship objectives was put in place. Also, after the reform of 2009 (TV Law, 2009), the policies did not show new commitment to increasing participative opportunities for citizens through the Net.

The situation of Denmark and the UK are radically dissimilar. From the earliest days, the Internet was considered as a new branch of the PSB, responsible for 'strengthen[ing] citizens' capacity efficiency in a democratic society; therefore, the policy framework supported DR and the BBC towards experimenting with the specific interactivity features of the Internet So, for example, the Danish Service Contract (2007) stressed that DR should pay attention to the use of the Internet to connect with young people and to increase the educational offering. Therefore, new services catering to the specific character of the Net have been offered since the beginning, from new online communities to forums, blogs and archives.

Universality

The concern with achieving universality, as conceived in normative terms, has been strongly present in DR and BBC online policies and strategies, but almost absent in the Spanish, Italian and French cases. In fact, since its beginning, the policies on DR online emphasized the objective of the social inclusiveness of the Danish public. Indeed, the Internet was immediately seen as a solution to the problem of reaching certain remote areas of the Danish territory in a country that in 2010 ranked top (at 80%) in broadband penetration in Europe (Eurostat, 2010). Moreover, universality also meant catering for minority groups defined by cultural differences or age-range, and making sure that DR online's offering addressed 'the many and the few' (Nissen, 2009). As DR online was conceived as a third arm of DR and not a complementary tool for broadcasting, the service contract had also given it a more specific universality purpose: to reach younger audiences. This objective has been reached by launching several successful youth platforms to share news, readings, discussion forums and finally the Mit-DR experiment. Much has also been accomplished for what concerns another component of universality: the access to content online. The online archive, Bonanza, has already made available to the public over 2,000 DR TV programmes without copyright restrictions.

On the contrary, the online policies of France Télévisions, RAI and RTVE did not seem to be focused specifically on enhancing universality through the new platform. As explained, RTVE.es developed slowly and, since the beginning, was focused on attracting the public through a commercially skewed offering. Yet, the wording of the new Mandato Marco (2007) indicated that the intention was to expand the content offering to 'diverse content for every type of public and genre' but without any specific mention of the opportunities offered by the medium. Still, RTVE.es – launched on 20 May 2008 – achieved an impressive reach in two years: the number of unique users rose from an average of fewer than 1 million a month in 2007 to an average of almost 2 million in 2008 and to 7 million in 2010 (OJD Interactiva, 2008, 2010).

Likewise, France Télévisions online and RAI online, which were conceived as services to complement the broadcasting offering, did not yet exploit the new opportunities of the Internet to achieve universality. Instead, they restated the universality aims of the broadcasting offer, expressly indicating that France Télévisions should relate 'not to an audience that is profitable, but to a socially legitimate audience' (COM: 6–7). Also, as regards one component of universality – *retrievablity* – France Télévisions shows its weakest point. It still presents a very fragmented online offering that lacks central harmonization, with each PSB channels in competition with the other. Finally, it should be noted that among the Southern European cases considered, the investment in broadband infrastructure – fundamental to achieve universality objectives of PSB 2.0 – has been remarkable in France. From just 30% of broadband penetration in 2006, it reached 67% in 2010.

Quality and trust

As discussed in Chapter 4, quality – with reference to the Internet – is a principle that entails a culture of avoiding deception; and it is the same culture that is needed to build trust. The struggle towards impartiality, accuracy, balance, fairness, objectivity, rigour, self-awareness, transparency and truth are components both of trust and of quality.

Certainly, the cases of Denmark and the UK demonstrated a strong drive towards quality, conceived also in terms of innovation and originality. Since 1996, DR online has constantly experimented with new services and new offerings beyond broadcasting, to the extent that its new channel 'Update' has been created for the web, and after its online success, it became a digital channel. Moreover, the forums, online communities and the vast Bonanza archive are all testaments to DR online's commitment to quality and innovation online. Moreover, DR.dk has always been at the frontline in the delivery of online news, therefore investing in achieving trust and creating an alternative to the commercial offering of its competitors.

Spain has achieved important results in terms of quality, given the drive towards experimentation that has characterized RTVE online since the reform. From being the lowest-ranking PSB online in 2006, it has rapidly launched new online news services – a similar platform to the BBC i Player, Television a la carta – and achieved an impressive audience increase. However, RTVE's online ethos struggles to build that online dialogue between citizens and their PSB that has been identified as a crucial component of trust online. In fact, RTVE.es is not yet considered a point of reference for impartial and accurate news online. It is more a competitor of the commercial broadcasters' online offering than of online news providers – like El Mundo or El Periodico – that enjoy an unchallenged monopoly of online news. Therefore, it certainly does not constitute a safe platform where Spanish citizens can find reliable online news.

As elucidated, France Télévisions has not developed yet a centrally organized online platform but its online offering is still divided among its different channels, thus making it very difficult to build a relationship with the viewers. Therefore, France Télévisions' policies are far from the realization of principles of trust and quality. Interestingly, the online news service has not been assigned the same relevance of broadcasting news according to the idea that the online branch should have an ancillary role in relation to France Télévisions. However, a first step in the direction of harmonization has been achieved since the launch of a news portal that retransmits all video news produced by france 2.fr, france 3.fr and rfo.fr. A last comment should be made on fr5.fr. Among France Télévisions channels, fr5.fr is certainly the one that has explored and innovated the most in terms of its Internet offering, being focused on providing excellence in educational content, and therefore delivering in terms of quality.

Final remarks

In conclusion, this investigation clearly demonstrates that the development of policies concerning the online expansion of PSBs is framed essentially by each national context. Owing to different national socio-political systems, markets and traditions, Public Service Broadcasting online continues to express national peculiarities. PSBs' expansion online follows primarily a path-dependent model in which PSBs simply replicate their offline content and approach.

In fact, the strong tradition of the public broadcasting ethos of DR, characterized by an extensive offering of PSB-characteristic outputs, such as news, public affairs, educational and cultural programmes, is reproduced in its online offering. Likewise, the BBC's inclination towards investing resources, energy and ideas in pioneering new activities and services for the public has led to its early and successful online venture. However, the commercial pressure that has clearly impinged on the most recent national policies on PSB in the United Kingdom and in Denmark and that has spread its influence in Brussels is clearly impacting on the online expansion of PSBs. This can be detrimental, especially for the South of Europe, where PSB online has not yet developed as an autonomous entity and is still in its infancy. With downsized PSBs online, the possibility of developing a public service broadcasting philosophy across the Internet will become less probable.

If we wish to develop the philosophies of empowered citizenship and public interest that are embodied by the original Public Service Broadcasting framework (PSB 1.0), we need a new policy framework and a new set of public service imperatives that can bring those ideals into the online world. We cannot rely on a restrictive approach designed primarily to placate commercial operators. We must design for public interest from the ground up.

This returns us to the four key principles of citizenship, universality, quality and trust: these are core components of a renewed online policy framework that I have called PSB 2.0. PSB 2.0, as envisaged here, would constitute a set of new policies to be supported legally and financially by Member States and implemented by PSBs, both alone and in conjunction with other relevant institutions. It would aspire to achieve universality and a stronger partnership with the publics it serves. It would aim for intimate involvement with civil society and would encourage partnerships with other players such as libraries, universities, museums, charities, sporting bodies, Parliaments and local government. Together these entities could build a public forum that would realize the massive public interest potential of the web rather than simply allow its inexorable commodification.

A starting point for the introduction of PSB 2.0 would be to reform existing institutions, which have so far shown little inclination to move beyond their historical legacies. It will, however, require an enabling and sympathetic framework to emerge from Brussels rather than the restrictive and hostile one that is currently beginning to materialize. If the online world is to be infused with the same public service ethos that characterized traditional broadcasting and served Europe well for over 50 years, European policy-makers and institutions need to be persuaded that a reconfiguration of public service values and principles – in other words, PSB 2.0 – is now becoming essential.

Notes

1 Introduction

1. Although, as explained in Chapter 6, the complete abolition of advertisements before 8.00 p.m., due to start in November 2011, has been postponed.
2. The new Communication on the Application of State Aid to PSBs adopted on 2 July requires stricter controls on PSBs' expansion in the new media, by introducing an '*ex ante* test'. The test will oblige Member States to assess the overall impact of new PSBs' services on the market and balance this effect against the public value of the services in question. The Commission launched a public consultation in January 2008 (which closed on 10 March 2008) concerning a review of the Communication on the Application of State Aid Rules to Public Service Broadcasting (2001/C320/04), OJ C 320, 15 November 2001.
3. The body of work developed by media scholars that embraces a 'social democratic approach to media policy', such as studies by Garnham (1990), Curran (1991) and Scannell (1989), ascribes a relevant role in a democratic society to PSB.
4. As will be explored in Chapter 4, Born and Prosser (2001) have identified the main common elements of a PSB as being 'citizenship, universality and quality' (Born and Prosser, 2001: 258).
5. Many rationales for regulation can be illustrated as 'market failures'. As Baldwin and Cave (1999) argue, regulation is 'justified because the uncontrolled market place will, for some reason, fail to produce behaviour or results in accordance with the public interest' (Baldwin and Cave, 1999: 10). Indeed, market failures represent a very common argument for encouraging the provision of PSB, even in the new digital environment. The principal causes of market failures in broadcasting derive from the concept of 'monopoly', 'public good', 'externalities' and 'merit good'.

    The notion of monopoly clashes with the idea of a competitive and efficient market. In fact, one of the most important policy questions is whether there is enough competition in a market to avoid the need of State intervention. In the broadcasting market, the economies of scope and scale are so elevated that the tendency is still towards concentration and private monopolies (McChesney, 2000), justifying the need for regulation.

    In economic terms 'public goods' are the opposite of private goods, for they are 'non-rival' and 'non-excludable'. Broadcasting is a public good since 'it is non-rival because the fact that one person watches a television programme does not impair another's consumption simultaneously' (Helm, 2005: 7). But it is also non-excludable since 'there is no obvious way to exclude people from watching a programme, unless some artificial barriers are created' (Helm, 2005: 7). Therefore, the market will tend to under-provide these types of goods.

    Externalities 'are the spill-over effects of television on social behaviour'. 'Good' broadcasting can encourage behaviour that is beneficial to society. If 'bad programmes' (e.g. ones that glamorize violence) are more profitable than good programmes (e.g. educational programmes), then the private sector will produce too many 'bad' and too few 'good' programmes (Robinson, Ravel and Low, 2005: 108).

Merit goods are 'goods the consumption of which is beneficial rather than enjoyable' (Robinson, Ravel and Low, 2005: 108). The value of certain programmes such as news and information is not always immediately appreciated by the public, hence the market, left to itself, would under-provide them.

6. See, for example, the studies conducted by Dieter Helm (2005), Damian Green (2005) and Andrew Graham (2005).
7. See, especially, studies by David Levy (1999), Maria Michalis (2007), Harrison and Woods (2001) and Irini Katsirea (2008).

2 The European and Global Policy Framework of Public Service Broadcasting

1. See the speech given by Vivian Reading, EU Commissioner responsible for Information Society and the Media, at the Joint EBU–MTV Conference 'From secret service to public service' held in Budapest on 3 November 2006.
2. As explained in Chapter 1, the Protocol on Public Service Broadcasting clearly states that 'the system of public broadcasting in the Member States is directly related to the democratic, social and cultural needs of each society and to the need to preserve media pluralism'.
3. Resolution of the Council and of the representative of the governments of the Member States, meeting within the Council of 22, 25 January 1999, concerning public service broadcasting(1999/C 30/01), http://eurlex.europa. eu/LexUriServ/site/en/oj/1999/c_030/c_03019990205en00010001.pdf.
4. Under the Treaty of Lisbon, the EU Charter of Fundamental Rights (EU Charter, 2000) is legally binding. The Charter explicitly recognizes and protects access to service of general economic interest (public services).
5. See European Commission (2001), *Communication on the Application of State Aid Rules to Public Service Broadcasting* (2001/C320/04), OJ C 320, 15/11/2001.
6. The numbering was changed after the new Lisbon Treaty of 1 December 2009 came into force. According to the old numbering of the Treaty establishing the European Community, these Articles were 86 and 87.
7. See Art. 107§1 EC.
8. See Art. 107§3 EC.
9. According to Art. 106§2 EC, 'Undertakings entrusted with the operation of services of general economic interest or having the character of a revenue-producing monopoly shall be subject to the rules contained in this Treaty, in particular to the rules on competition, in so far as the application of such rules does not obstruct the performance, in law or in fact, of the particular tasks assigned to them'.
10. See, among others, the Altmark Decision, Case C-280/00, Altmark, (2003) ECR I-7747, where the European Court of Justice defined the conditions under which public service compensation does not constitute State Aid.
11. See European Commission (2001), *Communication on the Application of State Aid Rules to Public Service Broadcasting*.

12. Prosser (2005) explains in details the conditions put by the Commission: first 'the service in question must be a service of general economic interest and clearly defined as such by the Member States' (Prosser, 2005: 217); second, 'The public service remit is entrusted to the broadcaster by means of an official act' (ibid.: 217); third, 'the funding of public service broadcasting must meet a proportionality test' (ibid.: 217).

13. Puppis (2008) notes two of the most important principles of GATT: non-discrimination and market access (GATT, Articles I–III and XI):

    '1. Non-discrimination. The most favoured nation (MFN) principle prohibits discrimination between a country's trading partners. Benefits granted to one trading partner have to be granted to all other World Trade Organization (WTO) member states as well. The principle of national treatment forbids the discrimination of imported goods compared to locally produced goods. However, national treatment only applies once a product has entered the market allowing for customs duties.

    2. Market access. For competition to take place at all, foreign goods first require market access. Hence, the WTO member states committed themselves to lowering trade barriers (customs duties or quotas that restrict quantities) (Puppis, 2008: 408)'.

14. The ITU, or International Telegraph Union, became part of the United Nations in 1947. As Costanza (2004) explains: 'the organization is responsible for the coordination of international agreements on technical standards, the management of cross-border spectrum use, and the allocation of satellite orbits' (Costanza, 2004: 5). The ITU is also the host organization for the World Summit on the Information Society.

3　Theorizing Public Service Broadcasting Online

1. The term 'new' is used to juxtapose it with the seminal work of classic political economists such as Max Weber.

2. The notion of institution refers to 'rules, informal constraints (norms of behavior and conventions) and their enforcement characteristics. Together they define the humanly devised constraints that shape human interaction' (North, 1990: 364).

3. The thesis refers mainly to the works of scholars such as Nicholas Garnham, Vincent Mosco, Peter Golding, Graham Murdock and Robert McChesney, who have contributed to a new version of political economy of the media that breaks with previous shortcomings of the approach, rejecting a rigid determinism and reductionism (Mosco, 1996).

4. According to Levy (1997), 'broadcasting policy making is highly politicized, both because policy changes are very visible (on the screen) and because of the intense interest that politicians take in the cultural, political and, increasingly, the economic impact of television'.

5. For a comprehensive discussion on the meanings of Europeanization, see Featherstone (2003), 'In the Name of Europe', in K. Featherstone and C.M. Radaelli (eds) *The Politics of Europeanization* (Oxford: Oxford University Press, 3–26).

4   A Normative Framework for PSB Online: The Idea of PSB 2.0

1. Certain common characteristics of PSBs as institutions can be traced. As Jacubowitz (1999) recalls, Blumer (1992) distinguished certain elements of PSB:

   - a comprehensive remit;
   - a generalized mandate (broadly worded obligations in legal documents);
   - diversity, pluralism and range (offering programming reflecting the concerns of all groups in society, covering all programme types and genres);
   - cultural role: generating and disseminating the linguistic, spiritual, aesthetic and ethnic wealth of the nation, playing a societally integrative role;
   - place in politics: news, current affairs and political programming serves as a political arena;
   - non-commercialism (Blumer, 1992, quoted in Jacubowitz, 1999).

2. The EC defines PSBs as 'broadcasters with a public service mandate. [...] Such a mandate would be consistent with the objective of fulfilling the democratic, social and cultural needs of a particular society and guaranteeing pluralism, including cultural and linguistic diversity. To fulfil this mandate, the public broadcaster benefits from licence fees or direct financial support from the State'. See the website of the European Union, http://europe.eu.int/comm/avpolicy/.

3. As Smith and Steemers (2007) point out, Web 2.0 can be defined as 'a second generation of internet services that focus on an active participatory world of online collaboration and sharing, where users actively fashion their own consumption, reusing material, making their own content and communicating with each other through social networking sites such as MySpace.com and YouTube' (Smith and Steemers, 2007: 49).

4. For a thorough discussion of the 'myths of cyberspace', see Mosco (2003), *The Digital Sublime: Myth, Power, and Cyberspace.*

5. As Bellamy (2008) explains: 'For Hobbes, human beings were apt to pursue their self-interest aggressively and distrust others [...] and were inclined to consent to any sovereign power capable of offering them security against the risks individuals posed to each other. By contrast, Locke had a much more benign view of the human nature and was inclined to believe that Hobbes underestimated the decree to which state power might be an even greater danger to individual liberty than other individuals' (Bellamy, 2008: 42).

6. John Stuart Mill (1806–1873) is considered a classical liberal philosopher. He assigned an essential role to freedom of speech in achieving democracy. Alexis de Tocqueville (1805–1859) underlined the importance of associational life in a democracy.

7. According to this view, people increasingly judge politics not by its effects on the 'common good' but by how it affects their individual lives and households. Moreover, 'experts' and technicians have the skills to respond to society problems, while 'markets' invisible hand determines which 'experts do the best job' (Baker, 2002: 131). As Scammell (2000) points out: 'Elite theory is often disliked because of its profound pessimism about democratic

possibilities and rejection of the grander liberal and socialist ideals of freedom, equality, popular sovereignty and the realization of human potential' (Scammell, 2000: 5).

8. This also has huge consequences for the role of the media: 'the press need not provide for nor promote people's intelligent political involvement or reflection' (Baker, 2002: 133). Therefore, exposure of government corruption or incompetence, the classic watch-dog role, becomes the most important task. Unfortunately, as Baker points out, for elitist theorists 'the media check on private corruption or incompetence is less a priority than the check on public misconducts' (Baker, 2002: 133).

9. Here I am referring mainly to the work of Dahl (1965).

10. Jurgen Habermas's theory has been pervasive in media studies, partly through his notion of 'public sphere'. The public sphere designates 'an institutional mechanism for rationalizing political domination by rendering states accountable to (some of) the citizenry. At another level, it designated a specific kind of discursive interaction [...] The result of such discussion would be public opinion in the strong sense of a consensus about the common good' (Fraser, 1992: 112).

11. Mouffe (1999) explains that the model of 'agonistic pluralism' she is advocating asserts 'that the prime task of democratic politics is not to eliminate passions nor to relegate them to the private sphere in order to render rational consensus possible, but to mobilize those passions towards the promotion of democratic designs' (Mouffe, 1999: 753).

12. For a detailed account of Marshall and his critiques, see Turner (1990) and Turner (1997).

13. For the 2003 WSIS Geneva Declaration on Principle, see http://www.itu.int/wsis/docs/geneva/official/dop.html. For an analysis of the results of the Summit, see Andrew Calabrese (2006), 'The Symbolism of International Summits and Declarations: Reflections on the World Summit on the Information Society'.

14. The Peacock Committee was set up by the government of Margaret Thatcher on 27 March 1985, and issued its report on 29 May 1986. The objective of the Committee was to report on the BBC and the financing of PSB in the UK.

15. Digital Rights management concerns the technical measures that allow the protection of digital copyright.

16. For a detailed explanation of the different vocabularies, see Costera Meijer (2005).

17. See the paragraph on democracy and citizenship.

5   Comparing Histories of PSB in Denmark, France, UK, Spain and Italy

1. Interestingly, in January 2010 the market share of TVE1 surpassed that of Telecinco, reaching 18.6% compared to Telecinco's 14.8% (Uteca, 2010).

2. Until 2004, TV2 received a share of the licence fee, which was then suspended. Yet, the regional stations distributed on TV2 and produced independently from TV2 receive part of the licence fee revenues. The Danish public authorities decided to privatize TV2 in May 2003, but implementation of this decision was delayed after questions were raised concerning the financing of the

broadcaster. In May 2004, the European Commission concluded that TV2 had received illegal public funding and demanded that it pay back 84.4 million euros to the Danish authorities. An appeal was lodged against the recapitalization plan, and the Court of First Instance of the European Communities set aside the Commission's decision in its judgment of 22 October 2008.

3. Even though the Danish government had decided to privatize TV2 back in 2000, a series of complaints for alleged unlawful State Aid prevented implementation of the decision. In May 2004, the EC found that the Danish government had overcompensated TV2 by 84.3 millions euros (Mortensens, 2006a). After that different cases have been brought to the Court of First Instance that have further delayed the sale of TV2. In the media agreement of 2011–2014 the government again repeated its intention to pursue the privatization of TV2 (Danish Media Agreement, 2010).

4. It should be noted that this data refers to the year pre-reforms of RTVE and France Télévisions.

5. Although it is important to note that TV2's share is included in the overall PSB share.

6. While the Internet access rate in Italy rose from 40% in 2006 to 59% in 2010, the broadband connection by household reached just 49% in 2010, from 16% in 2006.

7. Nicolai Federik Severin Grundtvig was a Lutheran pastor, philosopher and social commentator who lived between 1783 and 1872. He is the founder of the *Folkehøjskole* movement (folk high school), which provided education for people from all backgrounds, an idea that developed much earlier from the Protestant ideal that everybody should be able to read the Bible. On Grundtvig, see A.M. Allchin, D. Jasper, J.H. Schjørring and K. Stevenson (eds) (1993) *Heritage and Prophecy*.

8. He introduced the concept of *folkelig* (popular) in a series of lectures at Borch's College in Copenhagen in 1838.

9. I discuss the current legal and policy framework of DR in Chapter 7.

10. Law No. 82–652 of 29 July 1982 on Audiovisual Communication, *Official Gazette*, 30 July 1982, p. 2431 (hereafter, Law on Audiovisual Communication, 1982).

11. As a result this is seen as the beginning of the constitutional model of 'cohabitation' between a Socialist president (Mitterand) and a Gaullist prime minister (Chirac).

12. The new authority's main responsibilities were:

    - granting licences to private television and radio stations;
    - monitoring television and radio programming;
    - issuing opinions on government broadcasting bills.

13. The CSA previously had responsibility for appointing the director of PSB, but this was changed in the law of 5 March 2009 (TV Law, 2009). Today, it is the President of the Republic who nominates the General Director of France Télévisions.

14. The White Paper sets out the government's policy on the BBC for the next Charter period. These policies are implemented through the new Royal Charter and Agreement.

15. For more details on service licences, see the Agreement (2007).
16. The White Paper confirms that the BBC has six public purposes: 'sustaining citizenship and civil society; promoting education and learning; stimulating creativity and cultural excellence – including film; reflecting the UK's Nations, regions and communities; bringing the world to the UK and the UK to the world; and Building Digital Britain' (DCMSa, 2006: 6).
17. The administrative board 'was made up of twelve people, six named by the House of Commons (Congreso de Diputados) and six by the Senate, by means of a qualified vote of two-thirds in favour. [...] In practice, this arrangement was interpreted as meaning political representation within the Administrative Board, each member being chosen proportionally on party political grounds to reflect the typical make up of the Parliament' (Escobar, 1992: 245).
18. See Art. 1 of Act 4/1980 (Spanish TV Act, 1980).
19. It should be noted that before the arrival of private broadcasters in Spain, autonomous television channels were already operating at a regional level through a mixed system of funding. In fact, the Spanish Constitution (Art. 143–148) recognizes the possibility of each autonomous community being assigned the direct management of a state television channel for the territory of the community.
20. As Escobar (1992) explains, 'It was evident that the economic health of public television would depend on its ability to attract as large an audience as possible, and that it could only manage this by showing a popular range or programmes which could compete with the commercial channels, that is, by fighting on their own ground' (Lopez-Escobar, 1992: 251).
21. It is worth noting that the law did not completely follow the recommendations of the *Informe*, which has meant the problem of political influence on TVE has not been fully resolved.
22. The Committee of experts that produced the *Informe* was established by Royal Decree (Royal Decree 744/2004, 23/04/2004); it was composed of Enrique Bustamante Ramirez, Victoria Camps Cervera, Emilio Lledo Iñigo, Fernando Vázquez Savater and Fernando Gonzalez. The report was finalized in February 2005.
23. For more information, see *Informe para la reforma de los medios de comunicación de titularidad del Estrado, Elaborado por el Consejo creado al efecto, según Real Decreto 744/2004, de 23 de abril.*

6 The Impact of Historical, Political and Cultural Legacies on PSB Online in Europe

1. As will be discussed in detail in Chapter 8, on 1 September 2009 (Spanish Law, 2009) the financial arrangements of RTVE were once again altered. If the Act of 2006 reaffirmed a mixed funding system based on State funding for one-third of the budget and advertisements for two-thirds, the new law bans advertising and adopts a pure funding system based on State resources. The funding will be provided by two new fiscal measures and one existing measure, in addition to the existing State funding of RTVE. However, on 30 September 2010, the Commission requested Spain to abolish the

'telecom tax' as it found the scheme incompatible with the EU Electronic Communications Framework.

2. The first Mandato Marco can be compared to the Royal Charter of the BBC (with the difference of emanating from Parliament), and was signed on18 December 2007. The 'Contrato Programa', which will better define the type of activities, the organization and the budget for RTVE has yet to be produced by the government.
3. Acuerdo para la costitucion de la Corporacion RTVE, 12 July 2006 (Acuerdo RTVE, 2006).
4. As noted above, at the time of writing, the Contrato Programa has not been approved and adoption of the new reform of 2009–2010 has been delayed.
5. See the speech of Luis Fernandez, former President of RTVE (Diarios, 2006).
6. In 2007 the total budget of RTVE was 1.189 million euros, while public funding reached 435 million euros.
7. The document *Danmarks Radio* 1995–2005 indicated that radio and television were a 'service for the people'. The values behind DR are clearly expressed by this statement from the Document: 'In order to reinforce citizens' capacity to act in a democratic society DR must be a broadcasting organisation that, dependent on the wishes and needs of the entire population but independent of economic and political interests, increases the options available compared to market-determined radio (and TV), with special emphasis on what is Danish' (*Danmarks Radio, 1995–2005*).
8. A cogent summary of the principles contained in the document can be found at http://www.nordicmedia.info/nmn/Engelsk/94-3e.htm.
9. Interview with Christian Nissen, Copenhagen, March 2009.
10. Interview with Henrik Søndergaard, Copenhagen, March 2009.
11. See Danish Broadcasting Act 2007, on the Danish Ministry of Culture website: http://www.kum.dk/graphics/kum/English%20website/Legislation/Bekendtg%F8relse%20af%20lov%20om%20radio_EN.pdf.
12. The Media Policy Agreement 2010–11 was signed with a wide consensus among the parties. In fact it was approved by the Government made up of Liberals and the Conservative People's Party and the opposition comprising the Socialist, Danish People's Party, the Radical Left and the Socialist People's Party. A new agreement was discussed in the summer of 2010 and introduced changes that will be discussed in detail in Chapter 8.
13. See Broadcasting Act, 2000.
14. According to the Public Service Contract 2007, DR is to reflect the Danes' use of the media by delivering its programmes and services to the Danes on the various platforms. Therefore, the necessary resources must be made available to DR for democratic, social and cultural reasons, as well as the right and the duty to offer public service content on all relevant platforms to the general public (Public Service Contract, 2007).
15. 'In the programmes and services offered, DR shall
Strengthen citizens' capacity efficiency in a democratic society

- DR shall provide access to important information on society and debate.
- DR shall through programme content and services encourage participation in the public debate and the democratic process.

- DR shall contribute to popularisation of the new digital media by creating new programmes and information services likely to make viewers, listeners and users familiar with the technology, thereby inspiring them to use it.

Reflect Denmark and the Danes

- DR shall provide a broad social coverage of Denmark, thereby reflecting the diversity of culture, philosophy of life and living conditions in different regions of the country.
- DR shall place particular emphasis on Danish language and Danish culture.
- DR shall contribute to preserving and developing the Danish language through an active language policy, so that the Danish language heard, seen and experienced by listeners, viewers and users is correct and understandable.
- DR shall contribute to promoting integration.

Stimulate creativity and culture

- DR shall place particular emphasis on its role as initiator and provider of Danish art and culture, including the Danish cultural heritage.
- DR shall enrich Danish culture with original content.

Promote knowledge and understanding

- DR shall stimulate Danish interest in and knowledge of a wide range of subjects and areas through easily accessible and well-presented content.
- DR shall increase Danish knowledge and understanding of the surrounding world, international affairs and other cultures and viewpoints, including providing a general presentation of European culture and history'. See *Global Information Technology Report 2008–2009* released by the World Economic Forum in March 2009.

16. See http://www.dr.dk/skum.
17. See http://www.dr.dk/t/.
18. http://www.dr.dk/Oline/.
19. http://www.dr.dk/skole/.
20. http://www.dr.dk/Bonanza/index.htm.
21. Loi 1067 du 30 Septembre 1986 relative à la liberté de communication (Freedom of Communication Law, 1986).
22. For a description of the role of CSA, see Chapter 5.
23. Chapter 8 will examine in depth the financial arrangements introduced by the new reform (Communication Act of 2009).
24. A committee was established under the chairmanship of Jean Françoi Copé, the leader of the governing party's parliamentary group, to make recommendations on the future of public television. The committee, composed of both parliamentarians from across the party spectrum and media professionals, published its report in June 2008 (Copé Report, 2008).

25. See Copé Report 2008: 24–5.
26. As detailed in Chapter 5, France 2 is the main provider of news; France 3 is for local news and culture; France 4 is dedicated to younger audiences and France 5 to educational aims.
27. The service contract or 'contratto di servizio' between the Ministry of Communication and RAI indicates the objectives to be achieved by the PSB provider.
28. Art. 26 on 'multimedia services' stated that 'RAI *will* ensure new opportunities and know-how for experimental forms of multimedia productions and new audiovisual languages, also to be sold abroad (for example, it *will* develop new internet services)' (RAI, 1997). Art. 25 of Service Contract 2000–2002 reaffirms the same aims. (RAI, 2000). Art. 23 (1) of the Service Contract 2003 declares: 'In order to promote the industrial development of the country and the introduction of new techniques of transmission, RAI is obliged to foster the conversion of programmes and services to the digital terrestrial modality' (RAI, 2003).
29. Whereas in the previous service contracts the development of multimedia services, including 'internet services', was listed among the new obligations of RAI, Art. 25 of the 2003 Services Contract listed a series of services that RAI *can* develop, placing investment in the multimedia offer within the realm of possibility. The words 'RAI will develop internet services' of the 1997 and 2000 Contract of Service are replaced in the 2003 Contract by the words 'RAI can develop internet services' (RAI, 2003). Moreover, in the official version of the Service Contract, the figure of 7% indicated in the draft has been substituted for 'RAI will allocate increasing resources to the acquisition of the copyrights of the programmes' (RAI, 2007a, Art. 6).
30. For more information, see http://creativecommons.org/about/.
31. RAI Educational is the directorate in charge of the educational programmes of RAI dealing with arts, history, culture and science. See http://www.educational.rai.it/programmi.asp.
32. RAI International broadcasts throughout the world the programmes of RAI Radio Televisione Italiana, as well as original programmes made for Italians living abroad.

7 European Union Influence on PSB Online

1. See Chapter 2 for a detailed discussion of the different resolutions by European institutions in support of PSB online.
2. In its 1999 Resolution, the Council declared that 'Public Service Broadcasting has an important role in bringing to the public the benefits of the new audiovisual and information services and the new technologies', emphasizing that the 'fulfilment of Public Service Broadcasting's mission must continue to benefit from technological progress' (Council, 1999), and 'it is legitimate for Public Service Broadcasting to seek to reach wide audiences' (ibid.).
3. Having established that BBC Digital Curriculum did not constitute an 'ancillary service' of the traditional BBC's educational provision, the Commission approved the service under Art. 106§2 derogation. However, as note 29 in this chapter will explain, BBC Jam (the actual name of the service launched

following the approval) was suspended by the BBC Trust in 2007. Evidently, the Trust's decision can be explained as a precautionary one, given that it had not conducted a market impact assessment on the service before its launch. Therefore, the Trust decided to avoid the risk that the service could have been subsequently found to be in conflict with European Commission rules.

4. 'The provision of educational material over the internet may be considered to be within the "existing aid" nature of the scheme to the extent that it remains closely associated with the BBC's television and radio services' (European Commission, 2003: Para. 36).

5. Para. 43 of the Decision explains that 'The Commission understands that "the commissioning plan" ("the Plan"), which is required to be published at least fifteen months before the launch of the Digital Curriculum service, will set out the subjects to be covered during the first five years of the service' (European Commission, 2003), thus guaranteeing competitors the opportunity to plan their strategies accordingly. Michalis (2007: 234) notes that this requirement was put forward for the first time by the Commission in the Decision regarding the BBC's nine digital channels, where it stated that the details are important 'for non public-service operators so that they can plan their activities'. (European Commission, 2003: Para. 36).

6. That is, the BBC 24 hours' news service (European Commission, 2009).

7. It should be noted that the Commission initiated a procedure against NOB on 3 February 2004 after receiving complaints on different aspects of the financing regime of NOB. It subsequently divided the assessment into two different parts. The first concerned a 'new aid', which came to an end on 22 June 2006, 'on the *ad hoc* financing of Dutch public service broadcasters' (C 2/2004/, ex NN 170/2003). The second procedure – an existing aid procedure – concerned the financing of the Public Service Broadcasters through annual State payments and the Stimulation Fund (E-5/2005). This second decision was announced on 26 January 2006 (IP/10/52).

8. The European Commission thus closed the procedure as 'The Dutch authorities will ensure that the prior evaluation process will take place in a transparent way. As part of this prior evaluation process interested parties will be consulted and the market effects of new audiovisual services will be assessed and balanced against the benefits of the new service for the Dutch society' (European Commission, 2010).

9. It should be noted that in this case the Danish Act already considered chatrooms and games to be outside the remit of PSB, so here there was actually no need for the Commission to examine further. Widermann (2004) rightly observes that 'the fact that the Commission nonetheless examined the question suggests that it was determined to make general observations about "commercial internet activities" with a view to consider other pending state aid cases' (Widermann, 2004: 13).

10. See European Commission, 2007, Para. 240: 'the Commission does not consider that the determination of a "manifest error" can be based on the mere use of new delivery platforms, where the content is distributed over new platforms under conditions which are identical or similar to those for traditional television broadcasting'.

11. In this case, Belgium was requested to clarify 'the definition of the public service remit, especially in relation to new media services, the effective supervision

and control of VRT's fulfilment of its public service obligations, as well as the prevention of overcompensation for public service activities' (Tosic et al., 2008: 82).

12. In the Irish case, 'the Commission considered that the funding system which dated from before Ireland's accession to the EU could be considered as existing aid. At the same time, the Commission raised concerns regarding the compatibility of the scheme. The Commission considered that the definition of the public service remit in particular in fields other than broadcasting was not sufficiently clear. Furthermore, it expressed concern that there were no satisfactory *ex-post* controls to verify whether State funding exceeded the net public service costs (overcompensation), whether commercial activities had unduly benefited from licence fee revenues (cross-subsidization) or whether the public service broadcasters' commercial activities were in line with market principles' (Tosic et al., 2008: 83).

13. http://ec.europa.eu/competition/state_aid/reform/archive.html#broadcasting.

14. Ibid.

15. http://ec.europa.eu/competition/consultations/2009_broadcasting_review/index.html.

16. Furthermore, Art. 89 clarifies that 'Such an assessment would only be objective if carried out by a body which is effectively independent from the management of the public service broadcaster, both with regard to the appointment and removal of its members, and has sufficient capacity and resources to exercise its duties which are effectively independent from the management of the public service broadcaster, also with regard to the appointment and removal of its members, and has sufficient capacity and resources to exercise its duties' (European Commission, 2009).

17. See the common position paper of 24 September 2008: 'Main principles for a revision of the Broadcasting Communication of the European Commission', available at http://www.ebu.ch/CMSimages/en/Position%20paper%20BC%20annex%20letter%20to%20Commissioner%20Kroes_tcm6-63803.pdf.

18. See the first draft of the Communication (European Commission, 2008) and specifically Art. 59–62.

19. According to the explanations given by the Republic of Austria, there is a connection with broadcast programmes in the case of services that 'accompany' and 'supplement' programmes (European Commission, 2009, Para. 29).

20. Art. 36 of the EU Charter of Fundamental Rights affirms that: 'The Union recognizes and respects access to services of general economic interest as provided for in national laws and practices, in accordance with the Treaty establishing the European Community, in order to promote the social and territorial cohesion of the Union'.

21. The case of Denmark will be discussed in detail in Chapter 8, as the Danish domestic policy debate has been highly influenced by Communication 2009. In fact, in September 2009 Carina Christensen (Minister of Culture of the time) announced that the introduction of a market impact assessment would be put on the agenda during negotiations for the next media political agreement.

22. For further information, see http://www.bbc.co.uk/bbctrust/framework/charter.html.

23. The Secretary of State's approval was required by the previous Royal Charter in the case of the launch of new services under Art. 3(b) of the Royal Charter.

24. For more details, see Graf (2004).
25. The independent review of BBC Online (the Graf Report) set out by the Secretary of State in April 2003 aimed to:

    - Consider whether, in providing its online service known as BBC Online, the BBC is acting in accordance with the facts and assurances on the basis of which approval to proceed with the service was given;
    - Produce an assessment of the market impact of BBC Online;
    - Consider, in the context of the approaching review of the BBC's Charter, what the role of BBC Online should be within the BBC's overall service (Graf, 2004: 3).

26. The Public Value Test was introduced by the last Royal Charter. This test consists of a public value assessment carried out by the BBC Trust of the consumer-citizen benefits of the proposals and a market impact assessment carried out by Ofcom.
27. The BBC's main activities should be the promotion of its Public Purposes through the provision of output, which consists of information, education and entertainment, supplied by means of (a) television, radio and online services (Royal Charter 3). The Public Purposes of the BBC are as follows (a) sustaining citizenship and civil society; (b) promoting education and learning; (c) stimulating creativity and cultural excellence; (d) representing the UK, its nations, regions and communities; (e) bringing the UK to the world and the world to the UK; (f) in promoting its other purposes, helping to deliver to the public the benefit of emerging communications technologies and services and, in addition, taking a leading role in the switchover to digital television. 'A service licence must define the scope of the service, its aims and objectives, its headline budget and, where appropriate, other important features, having regard to the needs of licence fee payers and others who may be affected. In particular, a licence must describe the key characteristics of the service' (Agreement, Art. 17).
28. It should be noted that in 2006–2007 the BBC spent £116 million on bbc.co.uk and£37.7 on BBC Jam, the now suspended service, for an overall cost of £153.7 million. In 2007–2008, £3.9 million was spent on I player (BBC, 2007, 2008).
29. As note 3 clarified, BBC Jam was a free interactive online learning service for 5 to 16 year olds, reflecting UK school curricula. For more details, see David Puttnam, 'No Jam tomorrow' *Guardian*, 26 March 2007, available at http://media.guardian.co.uk/mediaguardian/story/0,,2042548,00.html; Jason Deans, 'Jobs at risk as BBC Jam scrapped', *Guardian*, 14 March 2007, available at http://media.guardian.co.uk/newmedia/story/0,,2033642,00.html; Andrew Scott, 'Puttnam weighs in on BBC Jam', available at http://lsemediapal. blogspot.com/search?q=jam.
30. Ibid.
31. See the decision taken by BBC Trust on 21 November 2008 at: www.bbc. co.uk/bbctrust/news/press_releases/2008/local_video_prov.html.
32. According to Thompson (2006), the PVT 'will contribute to increasing the BBC's transparency and accountability that will be of benefit to both licence fee payers and the commercial organisations that operate within the same markets'.

33. It is the *contrato-programa* – not yet signed – that will establish what is a new service. However, the draft of the *contrato-programa* indicates that new service will be clearly different from services already in place (Spanish Law, 2010).

8 Commercial Pressure from Rival Competitors: The Impact on PSB Online

1. As explained in Chapter 2, with its Communication, the Commission clarified the conditions under which State Aid for public service broadcasters is legitimate, and stressed once again that Member States should be free to decide the way in which PSB is financed and organized. The conditions posed by the Commission were clear: first, that the public service remit must be a service of general economic interest and defined as such by the Member State; second, that the public service remit is entrusted to the broadcaster by means of an official act; third, that the funding meets a proportionality test; and fourth, that Member States establish an authority monitoring PSB objectives.
2. See Chapter 5 for an analysis of the historical causes of the RTVE crisis.
3. See Chapter 7 for details on the Zapatero reform of 2006.
4. See the speech of the president of Uteca, Alejandro Echevarría, given at the 'Uteca day' on 12 November 2009 (Uteca, 2009).
5. Spanish Telecommunication Law (2009) relaxed media concentrations and cross-media ownership rules. Whereas before the law took effect, every company could own 100% of one channel and 5% of another television channel, the new rules introduced a limit of 27% of the total audience. Therefore, mergers between companies in the Spanish market are allowed until they reach 27% of the total audience and eight digital channels.
6. It is worth noting that the previous law on pluralism, adopted by the same Zapatero government (Law 10/2005, 14 June 2005, *medidas urgentes para el impulso de la TDT, de liberalización de la televisión por cable y de fomento del pluralismo*), was clearly demanding an increase in the number of channels in the Spanish audiovisual market, which led to the launch of Cuatro (Canal +) and la Sexta. In just a few years, the government had overseen a reversion to a situation that was even worse than the previous one. On 18 December 2009, PRISA and its subsidiary Sogecable reached an agreement with Telecinco to merge their free-to-air TV operations, Telecinco (Mediaset) and Cuatro (sogecable/Prisa). Mediaset, owned by Silvio Berlusconi, is the main stakeholder of the new entity. At the same time, Telecinco acquired a significant stake in the pay TV operations of Digital+, which was majority-controlled by Sogecable and had Telecinco as its leading stakeholder.
7. However, taxes are not to exceed 15% of the total budget of commercial channels, 20% of the total budget of pay TV and 25% of the total budget of telecommunications operators.
8. At the same time, new limits have been introduced for the acquisition of rights for sport events that cannot exceed 10% of its annual budget, with the exception of the Olympic Games. Moreover, the obligation for RTVE to invest in Spanish cinema has been increased from 12% to 20%.

9. This is consistent with RTVE online strategy that saw the portal as a means to 'spur the online advertisement market that in Spain is still stagnant at 7%' (Lloret, 2008).
10. As discussed in Chapter 7, RTVE online registered a significant increase in its active audience. In April 2010, RTVE reached 7 million unique users and surpassed the success of its commercial competitors online by 1 million unique users (ODJ Interactiva, 2010). According to ODJ Interactiva, the number of unique users of Antena 3 and Telecinco were both about 6 million (ibid.).
11. See Chapter 7 for a thorough discussion of these developments.
12. As Svendsen explains 'In 2008 the Danish Publishers' Association, Danske Dagblades Forening, published a pamphlet "Competing with the state" (*I konkurrence med staten*, in Danish only) with the subtitle: DR threatens the newspapers on the internet. DDF criticised that Denmark only used the PVA and not the MIA, and DDF argued that a rollback of DR on the internet and a negative-list like in Germany was necessary' (Svendsen, 2010).
13. As Svendsen (2010) explains, 'The three tests dealt with services using the internet in different ways. The first was about *distribution* of news and other programmes by the internet to private screens in public places like commercial centres, trains etc. where DR's content would be shown among other pieces including advertisements (which are not allowed on DRs own channels). It was accepted as public service when it was clear that DR was in full editorial control of its contributions, otherwise it could have been commercial activities (which DR can have besides its public service activities). The public value of the service was that News from DR through the screens in public places reached more and other audiences than through its own channels. The second and third tests were about *new portals* on the web (www.dr.dk). One about health was open for all parties with messages and advice about health (except the medical or pharmaceutical industry), and DR had the ultimate editorial control. Some private web portals about health protested publicly about the service, but since the test was only about PVA not MIA, the health portal was judged by RTB to be excellent public service. The last test was about a portal with advice for youth. Again it was open for all types of advisory bodies and the RTB thought this would meet clear social needs among Danish youth. Nobody protested about this service, on the contrary half the initial budget was covered by a private foundation (which is allowed under the Broadcasting Act), and after RTB had a promise from DR, that the portal was expected to be permanent, RTB had no objections'.
14. The Radio and Television Board is the independent regulatory authority in charge of supervising the implementation of the Danish broadcasting legislation.
15. The second service to be tested concerned a new service offered by DR on public screens in public and commercial locations such as train stations and airports with topical information from DR.
16. It should be mentioned that there was a significant change at the Department of Culture with the February 2010 appointment of Per Stig Møller, a former DR executive, as the new Minister of Culture.
17. The Media Agreement for 2011–2014 includes several norms concerning Danish media. For example, it states once again the intention to privatize

TV 2, and it includes the establishment of a new public service radio station, privately owned and financed by licence funds and therefore requires DR to give up its radio stations.

18. The new Public Service Contract for 2011–2014 was published in January 2011 and is available at http://www.bibliotekogmedier.dk/medieomraadet/tv/medieaftalen-for-2011–2014/.

19. Decision C (2003) 4407 of the EC was later appealed to the Court of First Instance on 13 April 2004. Under Order of the Court of First Instance of 19 May 2008, the case was dismissed.

20. Press conference of President Nicolas Sarkozy at Palais de Elysée Palace on 8January 2008: 'Je propose aussi que nous accomplissions une véritable révolution culturelle dans le service public de la television [...] Je souhaite donc que le cahier des charges de la télévision publique soit revu profondément, et que l'on réfléchisse à la suppression totale de la publicité sur les chaînes publiques, qui pourraient être financées par une taxe sur les recettes publicitaires accrues des chaînes privées, et par une taxe infinitésimale sur le chiffre d'affaires de nouveaux moyens de communication, comme l'accès à l'Internet ou la téléphonie mobile' (Sarkozy, 2008).

21. 'Ce mode de financement mixte se révèle donc dangereux pour l'ensemble des acteurs commerciaux de la télévision. Afin de remédier au sous-financement structurel de la télévision, il conviendrait de prendre exemple sur le modèle britannique: celui d'un service public de l'audiovisuel fort, dont les missions sont clairement identifiées et qui est financé exclusivement par des fonds publics. Cette approche aurait le mérite d'assainir le marché publicitaire français soumis enfin aux seules lois de l'offre et de la demande' (Livre blanc TF1, 2007).

22. 'Nous attendons à ce que le secteur audiovisuel français connaisse des changements importants dans les mois qui viennent, ce qui devrait être un facteur positif pour TF1 et M6' (Sénat, 2008: 37).

23. 'Mais j'ai surtout été frappé par une étude dela Société Générale, datée du 2 novembre 2007, selon laquelle la télévision publique française a *"le cadre réglementaire le plus contraignant en Europe, caractérisé par des obligations d'investissement pesantes [...] et une flexibilité publicitaire limitée."* Cette étude constitue un petit livre rouge de l'audiovisuel, qui n'hésite pas à s'appuyer sur la lettre du Présidentde la République à sa ministre et sur les déclarations de cette dernière [...] Cette étude de la Société Générale a été réalisée pour TF1 et pour M6' (Sénat, 2008: 37).

24. However, as it will be explained later in the chapter, on 7 September 2010 the then Culture Minister, Frédéric Mitterand, froze for two years the advertisement ban on the country's public networks until 2014.

25. It should be noted that the advertisement revenues will be taxed only for amounts that exceed 11 million euros, while electronic communication revenues will be taxed above 5 million euros (EC, 2010a: 18–19). As I will describe later in the chapter, the tax on commercial broadcasters has been subsequently reduced, first to a percentage between 3 and 1.5, and finally to a percentage of 0.5, thus further decreasing the funding collected for France Télévisions.

26. See http://www.carat.com/carat/index.jsp.

27. 'Cette annonce est une aubaine sans précédent pour ces deux chaînes privées ... pourrait permettre aux deux chaînes d'absorber près de la moitié du chiffre d'affaires de France Télévision' (Carat, 2008).

28. For more details, see http://www.omnicomgroup.com/ourcompanies/mediaservices.

29. 'A un moment où le secteur audiovisuel vit de profonds bouleversements, à la fois technologiques et économiques, face auxquels les chaînes sont déjà contraintes d'investir fortement' (ACP, 2008).

30. 'Inacceptable que les chaînes privés soient appelées à financer la concurrence d'un secteur public' (ACP, 2008).

31. 'Cette modification du texte du gouvernement "n'est pas un cadeau" aux chaînes privées "mais un élément de justice en raison de la crise qui affecte les recettes publicitaires"' (L'Express, 2008).

32. The important role of the European Commission investigation on the reform, both in Spain and in France, will be described in the final section of the chapter.

33. It is important to 'preuve d' intelligence politique que de savoir s'adapter' (*Le Monde*, 2010a).

34. Although this study examines the policies developed up until December 2010, the recent framework was once again changed. The moratorium on the ban is still in place, but it has been decided that France Télévisions will adopt a full ban on advertisement from 2016 (*Le Monde*, 2010).

35. TF1 has also called for the suppression of sponsorship after 8pm, which generates revenue of more than 70 million euros per year for France Télévisions, and for a limitation on advertising time during the day, accusing the public group of 'dumping' (*Le Monde*, 2010).

36. As explained at the beginning of the chapter, the funding will then be provided by 'A tax on the revenues of free to air commercial broadcasters (3%) and pay TV broadcasters (1.5%); 0.9% tax on the revenues of electronic communications operators; a share of 80% of the already existing levy on radio spectrum use, up to a maximum amount of €330 million' (EC, 2010f).

37. The time frame of the two reforms strongly suggests a policy transfer between France and Spain, as the policy idea behind the French reform has been exported to Spain. At the same time, the convergence of these policy frameworks could be framed as 'enabling marketization', as the concluding chapter will suggest.

38. As already mentioned, 450 million euros is the amount deemed necessary for France Télévisions to compensate for the loss of advertisements.

39. Another interesting point concerns the newly established long-term funding mechanism for France Télévisions. In its decision, the Commission highlighted that it had to verify whether the newly created taxes formed an integral part of the aid scheme. If that were the case, the compatibility of the aid would have been affected by the legality of these taxes (an investigation on the matter has been carried out by the Information Society service of the Commission). However, the Commission has clearly found that 'The revenue from these taxes will go to state funds, without being formally earmarked' (EC, 2010e: 1), and therefore it concluded that the aid was compatible with the State Aid regime. Yet, this acknowledgement raises serious concerns about the fragility of the funding scheme for France Télévisions.

If the resources coming from taxes are not 'formally earmarked', this could mean that they could be diverted and that no protection is in place for the funding of France Télévisions.
40. As the guardian of the EC Treaty, under Art. 226 of the EC Treaty, the Commission can start infringement proceedings against a Member State for alleged infringement of Community law. For more information, see: http://ec.europa.eu/information_society/policy/ecomm/implementation_enforcement/infringement/index_en.htm.
41. On 14 March 2011, the EC referred France and Spain to the EU's Court of Justice because they had failed to amend the tax system (EC, 2011).

Bibliography

Aberbach, J. and Christensen, T. (2005) 'Citizens and Consumers', *Public Management Review* 2 (7): 225–245.

ACP (2008) *Association des Chaînes Privées Rencontre Christine Albanel*. Press release, 23rd of June.

Acuerdo RTVE (2006) Acuerdo para la Constitución de la Corporación RTVE, 12th of July.

AGCOM (2009) Annual Report, 2009 <http://www.agcom.it/Default.aspx?message=viewrelazioneannuale&idRelazione=18>.

Agreement (2007) An Agreement Between Her Majesty's Secretary of State for Culture, Media and Sport and the British Broadcasting Corporation, 2007.

Albers, R. (1996) 'Quality in Programming from the Perspective of the Professional Programme Maker'. In S. Ishikawa (ed.), *Quality Assessment in Programming*. Luton, UK: University of Luton Press, pp. 101–144.

Allchin, A. M. et al. (eds) (1993) *Heritage and Prophecy: Grundtvig and the English-Speaking World*. Aarhus, Denmark: Aarhus University Press.

Aristotle (1995) *Politics*. Oxford, UK: Clarendon Press.

Arriaza Ibarra, K. (2009) 'The Promotion of Public Interest through New Policy Initiatives for Public Television: The Cases of France and Spain', *Interactions: Studies in Communication & Culture* 1 (2): 267–282.

Arthur, W. B. (1989) 'Competing Technologies, Increasing Returns, and Lock-In by Historical Events', *Economic Journal* 97: 642–665.

AUC (2009a) 'La Asociación de Usuarios de la Comunicación ve Confirmadas sus Sospechas de Que la Verdadera "Hoja de Ruta" de las Privadas lleva a la Desaparición de la Televisión Pública'. Press release, 17th of April.

AUC (2009b) 'La Asociación de Usuarios de la Comunicación Desconfía de la Voluntad de las Televisiones Privadas para Financiar la Televisión Pública'. Press release, 8th of May.

Audiweb-Nielsen Online (2008) Top Web Parent Companies, Italy.

Azurmendi, A. et al. (2007) *La Reforma de la Television Publica Española*. Valencia, Spain: Prosopopea.

Baker, E. (2002) *Media, Market and Democracy*. Cambridge, UK: Cambridge University Press.

Bakker, P. (2006) 'Public Broadcasters and the Internet. Webcasting in a Commercial Environment'. Paper prepared for the RIPE conference on Public Service Broadcasting in a Multichannel Environment: Programmes and Platforms, Amsterdam, Hilversum, 16–18 November.

Baldi, P. and Hasebrink, U. (2007) *Broadcasters and Citizens in Europe: Trends in Media Accountability and Viewer Participation*. Bristol, UK and Chicago, USA: Intellect.

Baldwin, R. and Cave, M. (1999) *Understanding Regulation: Theory, Strategy, and Practice*. New York: Oxford University Press.

Bangemann, M. (1994) Europe and the Global Information Society: Recommendations to the European Council. Bangemann Report. Brussels: European

Commission <http://www.ispo.cec.be/infosoc/backg/bangemann.html> [accessed on 10th November 2008].

Barges, E. (2009) Interview with Elisabeth Barges, Ministry of Culture and Communication, April.

Barnett, S. (2006) 'Public Service Broadcasting: A Manifesto for Survival in the Multimedia Age (A Case Study of the BBC's New Charter)'. Paper delivered to the RIPE conference in Amsterdam, November.

Barnett, S. and Michalis, M. (2010) 'Engagement and Public Value Tests: The German and United Kingdom Cases Compared', *Interactions: Studies in Communication and Culture*. 1 (2): 171–184.

BBC (2000) BBC Annual Report and Accounts 2000/2001.

BBC (2008) Annual Report and Accounts 2007–2008 <http://downloads.bbc.co.uk/annualreport/pdf/2007-08/bbc_ara_2008_exec.pdf>.

BBC Trust (2007a) bbc.co.uk, Service Licence, issued 30 April 2007 <http://www.bbc.co.uk/bbctrust/assets/files/pdf/regulatory_framework/service_licences/online/online_servicelicences/bbc_co_uk_servicelicence_30apr2007.pdf>.

BBC Trust (2007b) BBC On-Demand Proposals: Public Value Test Final Conclusions on Demand, April 2007 <http://www.bbc.co.uk/bbctrust/assets/files/pdf/consult/decisions/on_demand/decision.pdf>.

Beaud, P., Sauvage, P. and Flichy, M. (1984) 'La Télévision comme Industrie Culturelle', *Réseaux* 9: 3–21.

Beckett, C. (2008) Can We Trust the Internet? <http://www.charliebeckett.org/?p=887> [accessed on 10th November 2008].

Bellamy, R. (2008) *Citizenship: A Very Short Introduction*. Oxford, UK: Oxford University Press.

Belsey, A. and Chadwick, R. (1995) 'Ethics as a Vehicle for Media Quality', *European Journal of Communication* 10 (4): 461–473.

Benkler, Y. (2006) *The Wealth of Networks: How Social Production Transforms Markets and Freedom*. New Haven, CT and London: Yale University Press.

Benilde, M. (2006) 'M. Sarkozy déjà Couronné par les Oligarques des Médias?' In Le Monde Diplomatique <http://www.monde-diplomatique.fr/2006/09/BENILDE/13928> [accessed on 19th September 2009].

Bennett, C. (1991) 'What is Policy Convergence and What Causes It?' *British Journal of Political Science* 21: 215–233.

Bennett, C. J. (1988) 'Different processes, one result: the convergence of data protection policy in Europe and the United States', Governance, vol. 1.

Berg, C. E. and Lund, A. B. (2012) 'Financing Public Service Broadcasting: A Comparative Perspective', *Journal of Media Business Studies* 9 (1): 7–22.

Betzel, M. (2008) Public Service Broadcasting in Europe: Distinctiveness, Remit and Programme Content Obligations. In E. de Bens, C. Hamelink, K. Jakubowicz & K. Nordenstrengit (eds), *Media between Culture and Commerce: An Introduction*. London: Intellect.

Blaug, R. (1997) 'Between Fear and Disappointment: Critical, Empirical and Political Uses of Habermas', *Political Studies* 45 (1): 100–117.

Blumler, J. (1992) *Television and the Public Interest*. London: Sage.

Blumler, J. G., Brylin, M. and Nossiter, T. J. (1986) 'Broadcasting Finance and Programme Quality: An International Review', *European Journal of Communication* 1: 343–64.

Blumer, J. (1992) *Television and the public interest*. London: Sage.

Bonanza (2008) Kultur arv Projekt <http://www.dr.dk/Kulturarv/Bonanza.htm> [accessed on 1st July 2009].

Bondebjerg, I. (1996) 'Modern Danish Television after the Monopoly Era'. In I. Bondebjerg and F. Bono (eds), *Television in Scandinavia: History, Politics and Aesthetics*. Luton, UK: John Libbey Media.

Bondebjerg, I. and Bono, F. (eds) (1994) *Television in Scandinavia: History, Politics and Aesthetics*. Luton, UK: John Libbey Media.

Born, G. (2006) 'Digitising Democracy', *The Political Quarterly*, 76: 102–123.

Born, G. and Prosser, T. (2001) 'Culture and Consumerism: Citizenship, Public Service Broadcasting and the BBC's Fair Trading Obligations', *Modern Law Review* 64 (5): 657–687.

Börzel, T. (1999) 'Towards convergence in Europe? Institutional adaptation to Europeanisation in Germany and Spain', *Journal of Common Market Studies* 37 (4): 573–96.

Börzel, T. A. (2002) 'Pace-Setting, Foot-Dragging, and Fence-Sitting: Member State Responses to Europeanization', *Journal of Common Market Studies* 40 (2): 193–214.

Botbol, D. (2009) Interview with David Botbol, France Television, Paris.

Bourdieu, P. (1996) *Sur la Television, Suivi de L'Emprise du Journalisme* (On Television, Followed by the Influence of Journalism). Paris: Liber.

Brevini, B. (2008) 'European Public Service Ethos and the Internet: The Idea of PSB 2.0'. Paper presented at the Ecrea conference in Barcelona, 25th–29th November.

Brevini, B. (2010a) 'Towards PSB 2.0? Applying the PSB Ethos to Online Media in Europe: A Comparative Study of PSBs' Internet Policies in Spain, Italy and Britain', *European Journal of Communication* 25 (4): 348–365.

Brevini, B. (2010b) 'Under Siege by Commercial Interests? BBC and DR Online between the National and European Policy Frameworks', *Interactions: Studies in Communication & Culture* 1 (2): 203–215.

Brevini, B. (2012) 'Ex Ante Assessments for Public Broadcasters in Southern Europe: Delayed Europeanization?' In K. Donders and H. Moe (eds), *Exporting the Public Value Test: The Regulation of Public Broadcasters' New Media Services across Europe*. Göteborg, Sweden: Nordicom.

Brink, A., Lund, A. B. and Berg, C. E. (2009) 'Television Diversity by Duopolistic Competition and Co-Regulation', *The International Communication Gazette* 71 (1–2): 19–37.

Broadcasting Research Unit (1985) *The Public Service Idea in British Broadcasting: Main Principles*. Luton: John Libby.

Broadcasting Research Unit (1989) *Quality in Television: Programmes, Programme Makers, System*. London: John Libbey.

Brügger, N. (2009) Interview with Niels Brugger, Aarhus University, March 2009, Aahrus, Denmark.

Brügger, N. (ed.) (2010) *Web History*. New York: Peter Lang.

Brun-Buisson, F. (2001) 'Le Reflet d'une Culture Etatique', *Dossier de l'Audiovisuel*, 100: 20–23.

Bulmer, S. and Radaelli, C. M. (2004, forthcoming) 'The Europeanisation of public policy' in C. Lequesne and S. Bulmer (eds), *Members States and the European Union*. Oxford: Oxford University Press.

Burri, M. (2010) 'Cultural Diversity As a Concept of Global Law: Origins, Evolution and Prospects', *Diversity* 2: 1059–1084.

Busck Porsbo, N. (2009) Interview with Nicolai Busck Porsbo, Head of DR Online, Copenhagen, March.

Bustamante, E. (1989) 'TV and Public Service in Spain: A Difficult Encounter', *Media Culture and Society* 11 (1): 67–87.

Bustamante, E. (2006) *Radio y Televisión en España: Historia de una Asignatura Pendiente de la Democracia*. Barcelona: Gedisa editorial.

Bustamante, E. (2007) *Storia della Radio e della Televisione in Spagna*. Roma: Rai Eri.

Bustamante, E. (2008a) Interview with Enrique Bustamante, Madrid, July 2008.

Bustamante, E. (2008b) 'Public Service in the Digital Age: Opportunities and Threats in a Diverse Europe'. In Isabel Fernandez Alonso and Miquel de Moragas I Spa (eds), *Communication and Cultural Policies in Europe*, Barcelona: Generalitat de Catalunya. Department de la Presidència, 2008. Collecció Lexikon, vol. 4, pp. 151–182.

Bustamante, E. (2010) 'La Contrarreforma Audiovisual Socialista', *Le Monde Diplomatique en Español*, February, pp. 1 and 4–5.

Cahier de Charge (2002) *Cahier de Missions et Charges de France 2 et France 3*.

Cahier de Charge (2009) *Cahier de Missions et Charges de France Televisions*.

Calabrese, A. (2004) 'The Promise of Civil Society: A Global Movement for Communication Rights', *Continuum: Journal of Media and Cultural Studies*, 18 (3): 317–329.

Calabrese, A. and Burgelman, J. C. (1999) (eds) *Communication, Citizenship, and Social Policy: Rethinking the Limits of the Welfare State*. Lanham, MD: Rowman & Littlefield.

Carat (2008) TF1 et M6 Capteront de 40 à 50% des Pubs de France TV <http://www. easybourse.com/bourse/communication/article/5158/tf1-et-m6-capteront-de-40-a-50-des-pubs-de-france-tv.html> [accessed on 19th September 2009].

Castells, M. (1996) *The Information Age: Economy, Society, and Culture: The Rise of the Network Society, Volume 1*. Oxford: Blackwell.

Cave, M. Collins, R. and Crowther, P. (2004) Regulating the BBC. Telecommunications Policy, 28: 249–272.

Cayrol, R. (2009) Interview with Professor Roland Cayrol, April 2009.

Chan-Olmsted, S. and Ha, L. (2003) 'Internet Business Models for Broadcasters: How Television Stations Perceive and Integrate the Internet', *Journal of Broadcasting and Electronic Media* 47 (4): 597–617.

Chauveau, A. (1997) *L'Audiovisuel en Liberté: Histoire de la Haute Autorité*. Paris: Presses de Sciences-Po.

Christiansen, N. F., Petersen, K., Edling, N. and Haave, P. (2005) *The Nordic Model of Welfare: A Historical Reappraisal*. Copenhagen: Museum Tusculanum Press.

Civil Society Declaration to the WSIS (2003) Shaping Information Societies for Human Needs: Civil Society Declaration to the World Summit on the Information Society, Geneva, December 8 <http://www.itu.int/wsis/docs/geneva/civil-society-declaration.pdf>.

Clarke, J., Newman, J., Smith, N., Westmarland, L. and Vidler, E. (2007) *Creating Citizen-Consumers: Changing Publics and Changing Public Services*. London: Sage.

CNMV (2010) Report of Comisión Nacional del Mercado de Valores, First Quarter.

Colebatch, H. K. (2002) *Policy (Second Edition)*. Buckingham, UK: Open University Press.

Collins, R. (2003) 'The BBC: Too Big, Too Small or Just Right?' *Political Quarterly* 74 (2): 164–173.

Collins, R. (2007) Public Value and the BBC. A report prepared for The Work Foundation's public value consortium, The Work Foundation, March 2007.

Collins, R. and Sujon, Z. (2007) 'UK Broadcasting Policy: The "Long Wave" Shift in Conceptions of Accountability'. In P. Baldi and U. Hasebrink (eds), *Broadcasters and Citizens in Europe: Trends in Media Accountability and Viewer Participation*. Bristol, UK and Chicago, USA: Intellect.

Com (2001) 'Contrat d'Objectifs et de Moyens 2001–2005 entre France Télévision et l'Etat'.

Com (2005) 'Contrat d'Objectifs et de Moyens 2001–2005 entre France Télévision et l'Etat'.

Communication Act (2003) Act of Uk Parliament <http://www.legislation.gov.uk/ukpga/2003/21>.

Communication Act (2009) Act on French audiovisual and new PSB act, 5th of March.

Consolidated Broadcasting Law (2005) Law No. 117/2005 on Consolidated Broadcasting.

Constitutional Court (1988) 'Sentenza 826/1988', *Giur. Cost.* 1: 3894.

Constitutional Court (1994) 'Sentenza 420/1994', *Giur. Cost.* 5: 3751.

Contri, A. (2009) Interview with Alberto Contri, CEO RAI Net, June 2009.

Contri, A. (2010) Interview with Alberto Contri, CEO RAI Net, June 2010.

Copé Report (2008) Report of the Commission Copé for the reform of public television in France.

Costanza-Chock, S. (2005) 'The Globalization of Media Policy'. In R. McChesney, R. Newman and B. Scott (eds), *The Future of Media: Resistance and Reform in the 21st Century*. New York, London, Toronto, Melbourne: Seven Stories Press, pp. 259–275.

Costera Meijer, I. (2005) 'Impact or Content? Ratings vs. Quality in Public Broadcasting', *The European Journal of Communication* 20 (1): 27–53.

Council (1999) Resolution of the Council and Representatives of the Governments of the Member States Concerning PSB, OJ C 30/1.

Council (2000) 'Presidency Conclusion'. Lisbon European Council, 23rd and 24th March 2000.

Council of Europe (1994) Resolution n. 1 on the Future of Public Service Broadcasting, adopted at the 4th European Ministerial Conference on Mass Media Policy (Prague, December 1994).

Council of Europe (1996) Recommendation of the Committee of Ministers to Member States on the Guarantee of Independence of Public Service Broadcasting, R (96) 10.

Council of Europe (1999) 'Recommendation No. R (99) 1 of the Committee of Ministers to Member States on Measures to promote Media Pluralism'. Adopted by the Committee of Ministers on 19 January 1999.

Council of Europe (2007) Recommendation of the Committee of Ministers to Member States on the Remit of Public Service Media in the Information Society, 31st of January.

Council of Europe (2009) Recommendation 1878 (2009) of the Parliamentary Assembly on Funding of Public Service Broadcasting.

Court of First Instance (1996) Third Chamber, Extended Composition, Judgment of 3rd June 1999, Case T-17/96, *Télévision Française 1 SA (TF1) v. Commission of the European Communities*.

Court of First Instance (1998) Third Chamber, Judgment of 15th September 1998, Case T-95/96, *Gestevision Telecinco SA v. Commission of the European Communities*.

Court of First Instance (2008) Judgment of the Court of First Instance in Joined Cases T-309/04, T-317/04, T-329/04 and T-336/04, 22 October 2008.

Cowles, M. G., Caporaso, J. and Risse, T. (eds) (2001) *Transforming Europe: Europeanisation and Domestic Change*. Ithaca and London: Cornell University Press.

Craufurd Smith, R. (2001) 'State Support for Public Service Broadcasting: The Position under European Community Law', *Legal Issues of Economic Integration* 28 (1): 3–22.

CRIS Campaign (2005) *Assessing Communication Rights: A Handbook*, CRIS Campaign.

Croix, S. (2009) Interview with Sebastien Croix, Ministry of Culture and Communication, April 2009.

Curran, J. (1991) 'Mass Media and Democracy: A Reappraisal'. In J. Curran and M. Gurevitch (eds), *Mass Media and Society*, London: Edward Arnold, 82–117.

Curran, J. and Witschge, T. (2009) 'Liberal Dreams and the Internet'. In N. Fenton (ed.), *New Media, Old News: Journalism and Democracy in the Digital Age*. London: Sage.

Dagnaud, M. (2000) *L'Etat et les Médias: Fin de Partie* (The State and the Media: Endgame). Paris, Editions Odile Jacob.

Dagnaud, M. (2008) Télévision Publique: Le Retour de l'Etat Culturel <http://www.teloseu.com/fr/article/television_publique_le_retour_de_l_etat_culturel> [accessed on 1st September 2009].

Dagnaud, M. (2009) Interview with Monique Dagnaud, April 2009.

Dahl, R. (1965) *Preface to Democratic Theory*. Chicago: University of Chicago Press, 1.

Dahlgren, P. (2008) 'Internet and Civic Potential'. In Dahlgren (ed.), *Media and Political Engagement: Citizens, Communication and Democracy*. New York: Cambridge University Press.

Danish Broadcasting Act (2002) Act 1052 on the Danish radio and television broadcasting act, 17the of December.

Danish Broadcasting Act (2007) Act 338 of 2007 <http://www.kum.dk/graphics/kum/English%20website/Legislation/Bekendtg%F8relse%20af%20lov%20om%20radio_EN.pdf> [accessed on 10th April 2009].

Danish Media Agreement (2006) Danish Media Policy Agreement for 2007–2010, 6th of June.

Danish Media Agreement (2010) Danish Media Policy Agreement for 2011–2014, 1st of January.

Danmarks Radio (1995) Danmarks Radio 1995–2005.

Danmarks Radio (2008) Annual Report.

Danske Dagblades Forening (2009) Contribution to the Communication 2009 by the Danish Newspapers Association Danske Dagblades Forening, 16th of January 2009.

Davies, N. (2008) *Flat earth news*. London: Chatto and Windus.

DCMS (Department for Culture, Media and Sport) (2006) Royal Charter for the continuance of the British Broadcasting Corporation, October 2006.

DCMS (Department for Culture, Media and Sport) (2006a) *White Paper A Public Service for All: The BBC in the Digital Age*. London: HMSO.

Deacon, D., Pickering, M., Golding, P. and Murdock, G. (1999) *Researching Communications: A Practical Guide to Methods in Media and Cultural Analysis*. London: Arnold.

Depypere, S. and Tigchelaar, N. (2004) 'The Commission's State Aid Policy on Activities of Public Service Broadcasters in Neighboring Markets', *Competition Policy Newsletter* 2: 19–22.

Diarios (2004) Congreso de los Diputados, Año 2004 VIII Legislatura Num, 172.

Diarios (2006) Congresos de los Diputados, VIII Legislatura, Num. 155.

Digital Britain (2009) Digital Britain. The Final Report, 16th of June 2009.

Dolowitz, D. and Marsh, D. (1996) 'Who Learns What from Whom: A Review of the Policy Transfer Literature', *Political Studies* 44 (2): 343–357.

Dolowitz, D. and Marsh, D. (2000) 'Learning from Abroad: The Role of Policy Transfer in Contemporary Policy-Making', *Governance* 13 (1): 5–24.

Donders, K. and Pauwels, C. (2008) 'Does EU Policy Challenge the Digital Future of Public Service Broadcasting?' *Convergence: The International Journal of Research into New Media Technologies* 14 (3): 295–311.

Draft of the Public Service contract with DR (2010) Draft of the Public Service Contract with DR for the Period 2011–2014, November.

Draft of Public Service contract (2011) Public Service Contract between DR and the Danish Minister for Culture for the Period 1 January 2011–31 December 2014.

Dworkin, R. (1985) *A Matter of Principle*. Cambridge, MA and London: Harvard University Press.

Dye, T. (1976) Policy analysis: what governments do, why they do it, and what difference it makes. Alabama: University of Alabama Press.

EBU (2002) 'Media with a Purpose: Public Service Broadcasting in the Digital Age', Report of the EBU Digital Strategy Group, November.

EBU and BBC (2007) *Broadcasting and the Internet*, November.

Elliott, P. (1982) 'Intellectuals, the "Information Society" and the Disappearance of the Public Sphere', *Media, Culture & Society* 3 (4): 243–253.

Elstein, D. (2008) 'How to Fund Public Service Content in the Digital Age'. In T. Gardam and D. A. Levy (eds), *The Price of Plurality: Choice, Diversity and Broadcasting Institutions in the Digital Age*. Oxford: Reuters Institute for the Study of Journalism, in association with Ofcom, pp. 86–94.

EMB (2009) 'European Media Business Welcomes Clarification of Rules Applying to State Aid to Public Broadcasters', published on the 2nd of July, <http://pr.euractiv.com/files/Joint%20Press%20Release%20-%20European%20Media%20Business%20on%20State%20Aid%20to%20Public%20Broadcasters%20-%202%20July%202009.pdf> [accessed on 19th September 2009].

Enli, S. (2006) 'Redefining Public Service Broadcasting: Enlightenment, Entertainment and Participation'. Paper presented at the Fourth Annual Conference of RIPE on Public Service Media in the 21st Century: Participation, Partnership and Media Development, hosted by the Zweites Deutsches Fernsehen and the two universities of Mainz, Germany <http://yle.fi/ripe/Papers/Enli.pdf> [accessed on 9th September 2009].

Esping Andersen G. (1990) *The Three Worlds of Welfare Capitalism*. Cambridge, UK: Polity Press.

Esping Andersen. G. (1996) 'Welfare States without Work: Achievements, Crisis and Prospects'. In E. Andersen (ed.), *Welfare States in Transition: National Adaptations in Global Economics*. London: Sage.

Esposito, M. (2008) 'No Ads on French Public TV by 2009', *The Guardian*, Monday, 14th of January.

EU Charter (2000) Charter of Fundamental Rights, as signed and proclaimed by the presidents of the European Parliament, the Council and the Commission at the European Council meeting in Nice on 7th of December 2000.

European Audiovisual Observatory (2008) Europe: Public service television daily audience market shares 1999–2007.

European Commission (1999) Case NN 88/98 on Financing of a 24-Hour Advertising-Free News Channel Out of the Licence Fee by the BBC, OJ C 78/6, 2000s.

European Commission (2001) Communication 2001 on State Aid to PSB, OJ C 320, pp. 5–11.

European Commission (2002) Case N631/2001 on Nine Digital Services, OJ C 98/1, 2002.

European Commission (2003) Case N37/2003 on BBC Digital Curriculum, OJ C 271/47, 2003.

European Commission (2004a) Case C 2/03 (ex NN 22/02), State Financing of TV2/Danmark, OJ L 85/1, 2006.

European Commission (2004b) Decision C (2003) 4497 final of the Commission of the European Communities of 10 December 2003 on State aid implemented by France for the benefit of 'France 2' and 'France 3', OJ L 361, p. 21–39, 2004.

European Commission (2004) 'Ad-Hoc Measures to Dutch Public Broadcasters and NOB Invitation to Submit Comments Pursuant to Article 88(2) of the EC Treaty', OJ C 61/8, 2004.

European Commission (2005) 'State Aid: Commission Closes Inquiries into French, Italian and Spanish Public Broadcasters Following Commitments to Amend Funding Systems', 20th of April, IP/05/458.

European Commission (2006) Case C 2/2004/ (ex NN 170/2003) on the Ad-Hoc Financing of Dutch Public Service Broadcasters.

European Commission (2007) Case E 3/2005 (ex CP 2/2003, CP 232/2002, CP 43/2003, CP 243/200 and CP 195/2004) on Financing of Public Service Broadcasters in Germany.

European Commission (2008a) Case E8/2006 on the Public Financing of Public Service Broadcaster VRT.

European Commission (2008b) Case E 4/2005 (ex NN 99/1999) on Ireland State Financing of *Radio Teilifís Éireann* (RTÉ) and *Teilifís na Gaeilge* (TG4).

European Commission (2008c) Speech given by European Commissioner for Competition Policy Neelie Kroes 'The Way Ahead for the Broadcasting Communication Broadcasting', Strasbourg, 17th of July 2008, SPEECH/08/396.

European Commission (2008) 'First Draft for a Revised Communication on the Application of State Aid Rules to Public Service Broadcasting' <http://ec.europa.eu/competition/state_aid/reform/archive.html#broadcasting> [accessed on 19th September 2009].

European Commission (2009a) State Aid: Commission Approves Immediate Payment of Subsidy to France Télévisions and Opens In-Depth Investigation into Long-Term Funding Mechanisms. Brussels, 1st September 2009, case N 34/2009, IP/09/1264.

European Commission (2009a) Case E 2/2008 (ex CP 163/2004 and CP 227/2005) on Financing of ORF.

European Commission (2009) 'Communication from the Commission on the Application of State Aid Rules to Public Service Broadcasting', adopted on the 2nd of July 2009, 27th of October, OJ C 257.

European Commission (2010a) Case 27/09 (ex N 34/A/09 & N 34/B/09) on Subvention Budgétaire France Télévisions (2010–2012) Invitation to Submit Comments Pursuant to Article 88(2) of the EC Treaty, OJ L C 237/9, 2010.

European Commission (2010b) 'Telecoms: Commission Requests Information from Spain on New Charge on Operators; Closes Infringement Case on Universal Service'. Brussels, 18th of March 2010, IP/10/322.

European Commission (2010c) 'Telecommunications: Commission Takes Action against France over "Telecoms Tax"'. Brussels, 28th of January 2010, IP/10/67.

European Commission (2010d) 'Digital Agenda: Commission Requests France and Spain to End "Telecoms Taxes"'. Brussels, 30th of September 2010, IP/10/1211.

European Commission (2010e), 'State Aid: Commission Approves Long-Term Funding Mechanism for France Télévisions'. Brussels, 20th of July 2010, case C 27/2009, IP/10/979.

European Commission (2010f) 'State Aid: Commission Approves New Tax-Based Funding System for Spanish Public Broadcaster RTVE'. Brussels, 20th of July 2010, case C 38/2009, IP/10/978.

European Commission (2010) 'State Aid: Commission Clears Annual Financing Regime for Dutch Public Service Broadcasters after Amendments', 26th of January 2010, IP/10/52.

European Commission (2011) 'Digital Agenda: Commission Refers France and Spain to Court over "Telecoms Taxes"'. Brussels, 14th of March 2011, IP/11/309.

European Council (1999) 'Resolution of the Council and Representatives of the Governments of the Member States Concerning PSB', OJ C 30/1.

European Parliament (1996a) 'Motion for a Resolution on the Future of Public Service Television in a Multi-Channel Digital Age', Committee on Culture, Youth, Education and the Media, 11th of July, A4-0243/96.

European Parliament (1996b) 'Resolution on the Role of Public Service Television in a Multi-Media Society', 19th of September, A4-0243/96.

European Parliament (2004) 'European Parliament Resolution on the Risks of Violation, in the EU and Especially in Italy, of Freedom of Expression and Information' (Article 11(2) of the Charter of Fundamental Rights) (2003/2237(INI)), adopted on 22nd of April 2004.

European Union (2002) Directives 2002/21/EC '... on a common regulatory framework for electronic communications networks and services, 2002/19/EC on access to, and interconnection of, electronic communications networks and associated facilities, and 2002/20/EC on the authorisation of electronic communications networks and services', OJ L 337/37, 2009.

Eurostat (2010) Broadband access in EU27 and per country 2002–2010 (share of households).

Featherstone, K. (2003) 'In the Name of Europe'. In K. Featherstone and C. M. Radaelli (eds), *The Politics of Europeanization*. Oxford: Oxford University Press, pp. 3–26.

Flew, T. (2006) 'The Social Contract and Beyond in Broadcast Media Policy', *Television and New Media* 7 (3): 282–305.

Foreningen af Danske Interaktive Medier (FDIM) (2009) Ranking of top Danish Internet sites, March 2009.

France Télévisions (2008) Rapport Annuel, 2008.

France Télévisions (2008a) Rapport Financier, 2008.

France Télévisions (2009) Rapport Annuel, 2009.

France Télévisions (2009a) Rapport Financier, 2009.

Fraser, N. (1992) 'Rethinking the Public Sphere: A Contribution to the Critique of Actually Existing Democracy'. In C. Calhoun (ed.), *Habermas and the Public Sphere*. Cambridge, MA and London: The MIT Press, pp. 109–143.

Fraser, N. (2007) 'Transnationalizing the Public Sphere: On the Legitimacy and Efficacy of Public Opinion in a Post-Westphalian World', *Theory, Culture & Society* 24 (4): 7–30.

Freedman, D. (2002) 'A "Technological Idiot"? Raymond Williams and Communications Technology', *Information, Communication and Society* 5 (3): 425–442.

Freedman, D. (2008) *The Politics of Media Policy*. Cambridge, UK: Polity Press.

Freedom of Communication Law (1986) Act 1067/86 on freedom of communication, 30th of September, 1986.

Frendreis, J. P. (1983) 'Explanation of Variation and Detection of Covariation: The Purpose of and Logic of Comparative Analysis'. In *Comparative political studies*. London: Sage.

Fukuyama, F. (1999) The Great Disruption: Human Nature and the Reconstitution of Social Order. New York: Touchstone.

Galperin, H. (2004) 'Beyond Interests, Ideas and Technology: An Institutional Approach to Communication and Information Policy', *The Information Society* 20: 159–168.

Garnham, N. (1983) 'Public Service versus the Market', *Screen* 24 (1): 6–27.

Garnham, N. (1990) 'The Media and the Public Sphere', *Capitalism and Communication Global Culture and the Economics of Information*. London: Sage.

Garnham, N. (1992) 'The Media and the Public Sphere'. In C. Calhoun (ed.), *Habermas and the Public Sphere*. Cambridge, MA & London: The MIT Press, pp. 359–77.

Gaskell, G. et al. (2000) *Qualitative Researching with Text, Image and Sound: A Practical Handbook for Social Research*. London: Sage.

Gasparri Law (2004) Law No. 66 of 20 March 2001.

Giddens, A. (1995) *Central Problems in Social Theory: Action, Structure and Contradiction in Social Analysis*. London: The Macmillan Press.

Gilder, G. (2000) *Telecosm: How Infinite Bandwidth will Revolutionize Our World*. New York: The Free Press.

Goetz, K. (2002) 'Four worlds of Europeanisation', Paper prepared for the ECPR Joint Sessions of Workshops, Turin, Italy, 22–27 March 2002.

Golding, G. M. and Schlesinger, P. (1986) (eds) *Communicating Politics: Mass Communication and the Political Process*. Leicester, UK: Leicester University Press.

Golding, P. and Murdock, G. (2001) 'Digital divide :communications policy and its contradictions', *New economy* 8 (2): 110–115.

Gore, A. (1994) Remarks to the International Telecommunications Union, Buenos Aires, 13th of October, 1994.

Graf, P. (2004) Report of the Independent Review of BBC Online <http://news.bbc.co.uk/nol/shared/bsp/hi/pdfs/05_07_04_graf.pdf> [accessed on 10th March 2010].

Graham, A. (2005) 'It's the Ecology, Stupid'. In D. Helm et al. (eds) *Can the Market Deliver? Funding Public Service Television in the Digital Era*. Eastleigh, UK: John Libbey, pp. 78–99.

Gramsci, A. (1996) 'Quaderni dal Carcere'. In A. Rosa (ed.), *Letteratura Italiana Einaudi, Le Opere*. Torino, Italy: Einaudi.

Green, D. (2005) 'The Public Realm in Broadcasting'. In D. Helm et al. (eds) *Can the Market Deliver? Funding Public Service Television in the Digital Era*. Eastleigh, UK: John Libbey, pp. 101–128.

Gunter, B. (2000) *Media Research Methods*. Thousand Oaks, CA: Sage.

Gunter, B. and Wober, M. (1992) *The Reactive Viewer*. London: John Libbey.

Habermas, J. (1974) 'The Public Sphere: An Encyclopedia Article', *New German Critique* 1 (3): 49–55.

Habermas, J. (1996) 'Three Normative Models of Democracy'. In S. Benhabib (ed.), *Democracy and Difference: Contesting the Boundaries of the Political*. Princeton, NJ: Princeton University Press.

Habermas, J. (2006) 'Political Communication in Media Society: Does Democracy Still Enjoy an Epistemic Dimension? The Impact of Normative Theory on Empirical Research', *Communication Theory* 16 (4): 411–426.

Hall, P. A. (1986) *Governing the Economy: The Politics of State Intervention in Britain and France*. Oxford and New York: Oxford University Press.

Hallin, D. C. and Mancini, P. (2004) *Comparing Media Systems: Three Models of Media and Politics*. Cambridge, UK: Cambridge University Press.

Harcourt, A. (2002) 'Engineering Europeanisation: The Role of the European Institutions in Shaping National Broadcasting Regulation', *Journal of European Public Policy* 9 (5): 736–755.

Harcourt, A. (2005) *The European Union and the Regulation of Media Markets*. Manchester, UK: Manchester University Press.

Harrison, J. and Wessels, B. (2005) 'A New Public Service Communication Environment? Public Service Broadcasting Values in the Reconfiguring Media', *New Media and Society* 7 (6): 834–853.

Harrison, J. and Woods, L. M. (2001) 'Defining European Public Service Broadcasting', *European Journal of Communication* 16 (4): 477–504.

Ham, C. and Hill, M. (1993) *The Policy Process in the Modern Capitalist State*. London: Harvester Wheatsheaf.

Heclo, H. (1974) *Modern Social Politics in Britain and Sweden*. New Haven, CT: Yale University Press.

Hedstrom, P. and Swedborg, R. (1998) 'Social Mechanisms: An Introductory Essay'. In P. Hedstrom and R. Swedborg (eds), *Social Mechanisms: An Analytic Approach to Social Theory*. Cambridge, UK: Cambridge University Press, pp. 3–24.

Helm, D. (2005) 'Consumers, Citizens and Members: Public Service Broadcasting and the BBC'. In D. Helm et al. (eds), *Can the Market Deliver? Funding Public Service Television in the Digital Era*, pp 1–21. Eastleigh, UK: John Libbey.

Hibberd, M. (2001) 'The Reform of Public Service Broadcasting in Italy', *Media Culture and Society* 23 (2): 233–252.

Hill, K. A. and Hughes, J. E. (1998) *Cyberpolitics: Citizen Activism in the Age of Internet*. Lanham, MA: Rowman and Littlefield.

Hills, J. and Michalis, M. (2000) 'The Internet: A Challenge to Public Service Broadcasting?' *Gazette: The International Journal for Communication Studies* 62 (7): 477–493.

Hilson, M. (2008) *The Nordic Model: Scandinavia since 1945*. London: Reaktion.

Hogwood, B. W. and Gunn, L. A. (1984) *Policy Analysis for the Real World*. Oxford: Oxford University Press.

Howlett, M. and Ramesh, M. (2003) *Studying Public Policy: Policy Cycles and Policy Subsystems*. Oxford: Oxford University Press.

Humphreys, P. (1994) *Media and Media Policy in Germany: The Press and Broadcasting since 1945*. Oxford, UK and Providence, RI: Berg.

Humphreys, P. (1996) *Mass Media and Media Policy in Western Europe*. Manchester, UK: Manchester University Press.

Humphreys, P. (2006) 'Globalization, Regulatory Competition, and EU Policy Transfer in the Telecoms and Broadcasting Sectors', *International Journal of Public Administration* 29 (4): 305–334 (30).

Humphreys, P. (2007) 'The EU, Communications Liberalisation and the Future of Public Service Broadcasting'. In S. Katharine (ed.), *Media and Cultural Policy in the European Union, European Studies Series 25*. Amsterdam/New York: Rodopi, pp. 91–112.

Humphreys, P. (2008) 'Redefining Public Service Media: A Comparative Study of France, Germany and the UK'. Paper presented at the Fourth Annual Conference of RIPE on Public Service Media in the 21st Century: Participation, Partnership and Media Development, hosted by the Zweites Deutsches Fernsehen and the two universities of Mainz, Germany <http://www.uta.fi/jour/ripe/papers/Humphreys_P.pdf> [accessed on 9th September 2009].

Humphreys, P. (2009) 'EU Competition Policy and Public Service Broadcasting'. Paper presented at CAMRI and ECREA joint symposium on Is the Public Interest under Threat? Media Policy Responses to the Private Sector Recession in Europe. London.

Informe (2005) Informe Para la Reforma de los Medios de Comunicación de Titularidad del Estado, Elaborado por el Consejo Creado al Efecto, según Real Decreto 744/2004, 23 of April.

Introna, L. D. and Nissenbaum, H. (2000) 'Shaping the Web: Why the Politics of Search Engines Matters', *The Information Society* 16 (1): 169–185.

Iosifidis, P. (2011) *Global Media and Communication Policy*. London and New York: Palgrave Macmillan.

Ishikawa, S. (ed.) (1996) *Quality Assessment of Television*. Luton, UK: John Libbey Media.

Jacka, E. (2003) '"Democracy as Defeat": The Impotence of Arguments for Public Service Broadcasting', *Television & New Media* 4 (2): 177–191.

Jacubowicz, K. (2007) 'Public Service Broadcasting: A Pawn on an Ideological Chessboard'. In E. de Bens, C. Hamelink and K. Jakubowicz (eds), *Media between Culture and Commerce*. Bristol, UK: Intellect.

Jakubowicz, K. (2008) 'Public Service Broadcasting in the 21st Century: What Chance for a New Beginning?' In G. F. Lowe and J. Bardoel (eds), *From Public Service Broadcasting to Public Service Media. RIPE@2007*. Göteborg, Sweden: Nordicom, pp. 29–51.

Jérame, B. (1994) *Haute-Fidélité: Télévision et Pouvoir 1935–1994*. (High-Fidelity. Television and Power 1935–1994). Paris: Le Seuil.

Jespersen, K. (2004) *A History of Denmark*. London: Palgrave Mcmillan.

Jessop, B. (1978) 'Capitalism and Democracy'. In Littlejohn et al. (eds), *Power and the State*. New York: St Martin's Press.

Joint Declaration (2007) Joint declaration on the diversity of broadcasting by rapporteurs of the UN, the OSCE, the OAS and the ACHPR <http://www.osce. org/fom/29825>.

Joint Declaration (2010) Joint declaration on key challenges to media freedom by rapporteurs of the UN, the OSCE, the OAS and the ACHPR <http://www. osce.org/fom/41439>.

Karagiannis, C. and Radaelli, C. M. (2007) 'Policy Making' <http://socialsciences. exeter.ac.uk/politics/research/.../radaelliPolicyMaking.doc>.

Katsirea, I. (2008) *Public Broadcasting and European Law: A Comparative Examination of Public Service Obligations in Six Member States.* New York: Wolters Kluwer International.

Kettle, D. (2000) *The Global Public Management Revolution: A Report on the Transformation of Governance.* Washington, DC: Brookings.

Krugman, P. (1991) 'Increasing Returns and Economic Geography', *Journal of Political Economy* 99: 483–499.

Kuhn, R. (1983) 'Broadcasting and Politics in France', *Parliamentary Affairs* 36 (1): 67–83.

Kuhn, R. (1995) *The Media in France*, London: Routledge.

La Tribune (2010) 'La Taxe pour Financer France Télévisions Ne Rapporte Pas Assez', 20th of August.

Law on Audiovisual Communication (1982) Law No. 82–652 of 29 July 1982 on Audiovisual Communication, *Official Gazette*, 30th of July.

Lawrence, S. and Giles, C. L. (1999) 'Accessibility and Distribution of Information on the Web', *Nature* 400: 107–109.

Legér, N. (2009) Interview with Natalie Legér, France Télévisions, April.

Leggatt, T. (1996) 'Quality in Television: The Views from Professionals'. In S. Ishikawa (ed.), *Quality Assessment in Programming.* Luton: John Libbey Media, pp.145–168.

Le Monde (2008) TF1 Avait Demandé à l'Elysée la Suppression de la Publicité sur les Chaînes Publiques Fin 2007, 7th of March <http://www.lemonde.fr/actualite-medias/article/2008/03/07/tf1-avait-demande-a-l-elysee-la-suppression-de-la-publicite-sur-les-chaines-publiques-fin-2007_1019874_3236.html> [accessed on 19th September 2009].

Le Monde (2010a) Vers la Suppression de la Publicité Diurne sur France Télévisions, 14th of December <http://www.lemonde.fr/actualite-medias/article/2010/12/14/suppression-de-la-publicite-diurne-sur-france televisions_1452996_3236.html#ens_id=1271929> [accessed on 14th December 2010].

Le Monde (2010b) Deux Ans et Demi de Débats sur la Publicité à France Télévisions, 21st of September <http://www.lemonde.fr/actualite-medias/article/2010/09/21/deux-ans-et-demi-de-debats-sur-la-publicite-a-france-televisions_1413855_3236.html> [accessed on 16th September 2010].

Le Point.fr (2010) *France Télévisions: Sursis pour la Publicité Diurne sur les Chaînes du Service Public*, 17th of September <http://www.lepoint.fr/chroniqueurs-du-point/emmanuel-berretta/france-televisions-sursis-pour-la-publicite-diurne-sur-les-chaines-du-service-public-17-09-2010-1237746_52.php> [accessed on 18th September 2010].

Lequesne, C. and Bulmer, S. (eds) (2004) *Members States and the European Union.* Oxford: Oxford University Press.

Les Echos (2008) TF1 se Prévoit un Avenir Difficile dans un Document Adressé au Gouvernement, 7th of March <http://archives.lesechos.fr/archives/2008/LesEchos/20126-114-ECH.htm> [accessed on 18th September 2010].

Lessig, L. (2001) *The Future of Ideas: The Fate of the Commons in a Connected World*. New York: Random House.

Levassor, J. F. (2009) Interview with Jean-Christophe Levassor, Ministry of Culture and Communication, April.

Levy, D. (1997) 'Regulating Digital Bradcasting in Europe: The Limits of Policy Convergence', *West European Politics* 20 (4): 24–42.

Levy, D. (1999) *Europe's Digital Revolution: Broadcasting Regulation, the EU and the Nation State*. London: Routledge.

Lewis, J. (2003) 'Citizens and Consumers'. In M. Hilmes (ed.), *The Television History Book*. London: BFI.

L'Express (2008) Taxe sur la Pub: Les Députés UMP Soulagent les Télés Privées <http://www.lexpress.fr/actualite/media-people/media/taxe-sur-la-pub-les-deputes-ump-soulagent-les-teles-privees_706276.html> [accessed on 19th September 2009].

Lindolf, T. R. (1995) *Qualitative Communication Research Methods*. Thousand Oaks, CA: Sage.

Livre blanc du TF1 (2007) Livre Blanc du TF 1 <http://television.telerama.fr/television/extraits-du-livre-blanc-de-tf1-qui-demandait-la-fin-de-la-pub-sur-france-televisions,36954.php> [accessed on 15th November 2009].

Llorens Marruquer, C. (2005) 'La Política Audiovisual de la Unión Europea y Su Influencia en el Sistema Televisivo Español: La Televisión Pública y la Televisión Digital', *Sphera Pública* 5: 133–150.

Llorens, Maluquer, C. (2009) 'Escenaris de Futur per a la Radiotelevisió Pública a Europa'. In Isabel Fernandez Alonso & Miquel de Moragas I Spa (eds), *Communication and Cultural Policies in Europe*. Barcelona: Generalitat de Catalunya. Department de la Presidència, 2008. Collecció Lexikon, vol. 4, pp. 151–182.

Lloret, R. (2008) Interview with Rosalia Lloret, Director of Interactive Media at RTVE, July.

López-Escobar, E. (1992) 'Spanish Media Law: Changes in the Landscapes', *European Journal of Communication* 7: 241.

Lund, A. B. and Berg, C. E. (2009) 'Denmark, Sweden and Norway: Television Diversity by Duopolistic Competition and Co-Regulation', *The International Communication Gazette* 71 (1–2): 19–37.

Lund, A. B. (2007) 'Media Markets in Scandinavia: Political Economy Aspects of Convergence and Divergence', *Nordicom Review* 28 (1) 121–134.

Mandato Marco (2007) Aprobación por los Plenos del Congreso de los Diputados y del Senado794/000003 (S) del mandato-marco a la Corporación RTVE, 18 de diciembre de 2007 Núm. 470.

Mangen, S. (1999) 'Qualitative Research Methods in Cross-National Settings', *Journal of Social Research Methodology* 2 (2): 109–124.

Mansell, R. (2004) 'Political Economy, Power and New Media', *New Media & Society* 6 (1): 96–105.

Mansell, R. and Javary, M. (2004) 'New Media and the Forces of Capitalism'. In A. Calabrese & C. Sparks (eds), *Towards a Political Economy of Culture: Capitalism and Communication in the 21st Century*. Lanham, MD: Rowan & Littlefield.

March, J. and Olsen, J. (1984) 'The New Institutionalism: Organizational Factors in Political Life', *American Political Science Review* 78 (September): 734–49.

Marshall, T. H. (1950) *Citizenship and Social Class and Other Essays*. Cambridge: Cambridge University Press.

Marshall, T. H. (1964) *Class, Citizenship, and Social Development: Essays*. New York: Anchor Books, pp. 71–133.

Mason, J. (1996) *Qualitative Researching*. London: Sage.

Mazzoleni, G. and Vigevani, G. E. (2005) 'TV across Europe: Regulation, Policies and Independence: Italy'. In *TV across Europe: Regulation, Policies and Independence*, Budapest: Open Society Institute – EU Monitoring and Advocacy Program.

McChesney, R. (2000) *Rich Media, Poor Democracy: Communications Politics in Dubious Times*. New York: New Press.

McChesney, R. W. (2008) *The political economy of Media: Enduring Issues, Emerging Dilemmas*. New York: Monthly Review.

Mediametrie (2009) August Internet Ranking of Top Web Company in France.

Mepham, J. (1990) 'The Ethics of Quality in Television'. In G. Mulgan (ed.), *The Question of Quality*. London: British Film Institute, pp. 56–72.

Michalis, M. (2007) *Governing European Communications*. Lanham, MD: Lexington Books.

Mill, S. J. (1965) *On Liberty: Preface to Democratic Theory*. Chicago, IL: University of Chicago Press.

Miller, K. E. (1991) *Denmark: A Troubled Welfare State*. Boulder, CO: Westview Press.

Moe, H. (2008) 'Public Service Media Online? Regulating Public Broadcasters' Internet Services – A Comparative Analysis', *Television & New Media* 9 (3): 220–238.

Montalvo, J. (2010) Nueva Financiación de TVE: A las Cadenas Privadas les Salen la Cuentas, *Expansion* <http://www.expansion.com/2010/04/12/opinion/llaveonline/1271105328.html> [accessed on 20th September 2010].

Monteleone, F. (2001) *Storia Della Radio e Televisione in Italia*, Venezia: Marsilio.

Morin-Desailly, C. (2010) 'Vers la Suppression de la Publicité Diurne sur France Télévisions', *Le Monde* <http://www.lemonde.fr/actualite-medias/article/2010/12/14/suppression-de-la-publicite-diurne-sur-france-televisions_1452996_3236.html> [accessed on 19th September 2010].

Morley, D. (1980) *The Nationwide Audience: Structure and Decoding*. London: British Film Institute.

Morley, D. (1986) *Family Television: Cultural Power and Domestic Leisure*. London: Routledge.

Mortensen, F. (2006) 'Catch 22: The Privatization of Danish TV 2 vs. EU Rules of State Aid', *Politik* 2 (9): 74–82.

Mortensen, F. (2006) The European Commission and State Aid to Public Service Broadcasting <http://pure.au.dk/portal/en/persons/frands-mortensen%28d45b0768-74bf-442b-8fca-668cc12b71bd%29.html> [accessed on 10th July 2009].

Mosco, V. (1996) *The Political Economy of Communication: Rethinking and Renewal*. London: Sage.

Mosco, V. (2004) *The Digital Sublime: Myth, Power, and Cyberspace*. Cambridge, MA: The MIT Press.

Mouffe, C. (1993) *The Return of the Political*. New York: Verso.

Mouffe, C. (1999) 'Deliberative Democracy or Agonistic Pluralism?' *Social Research* 66 (3): 745–755.

Mulgan, G. (1990) 'Television's Holy Grail: Seven Types of Quality'. In G. Mulgan (ed.), *The Question of Quality*. London: British Film Institute, pp. 4–32.

Mundoplus (2009) UTECA Pide Garantías De Que TVE No Será un 'Competidor Desleal' <http://www.mundoplus.tv/noticias/?seccion=tv_digital&id=5398> [accessed on 19th September 2009].

Murdock, G. and Golding, P. (1999) 'Common markets: corporate ambitions and communications trends in the UK and Europe', *Journal of Media Economics* 12 (2): 117–132.

Murdock, G (2004) *Building the Digital Commons: Public Broadcasting in the Age of the Internet*. Vancouver: The 2004 Spry Memorial Lecture.

Murroni, C. and Irvine, N. (1997) *Quality in Broadcasting*. London: Institute for Public Policy Research.

Musso, P. (2010) *Télé-Politique: Le Sarkoberlusconisme à l'Ecran*. La Tour-d'Aigue: Ed. de l'Aube.

Negroponte, N. (1995) *Bing Digital*. New York: Alfred A. Knopf.

Negroponte, N. (1998) 'Beyond Digital', Wired, 6 December.

Nielsen NetRatings (2008a) 'Report on the Usage of the Internet in Italian Households and Offices'.

Nielsen NetRatings (2008b) Top Web Parent Companies, UK.

Nissen, C. S. (2006) *Making a Difference: Public Service Broadcasting in the European Media Landscape*. London: John Libbey.

Nissen, C. S. (2009) Interview with Christian Nissen, Copenhagen, March.

Nordic Media Market (2009) 'The Nordic Media Market 2009: Media Companies and Business Activities', Media Trends 11, Gothenburg: Nordicom.

Nordicom (2007) Nordic Media Policy, a Newsletter from Nordicom, Issue 2, 6th of June.

Nordicom (2009) Audience data Nordic PSBs.

North, D. C. (1990) *Institutions, Institutional Change, and Economic Performance*. New York: Cambridge University Press.

Ofcom (2007a) *New News, Future News*. London: Ofcom.

Ofcom (2007b) *Annexes to New News, Future News: Research and Evidence Base*. London: Ofcom.

Ofcom (2008) *Citizens, Communication and Convergence*, 11th of July 2008 <http://stakeholders.ofcom.org.uk/consultations/citizens/>.

Ofcom (2009) *Second Public Service Broadcasting Review Putting Viewers First*, 21st of January 2009 <http://stakeholders.ofcom.org.uk/binaries/consultations/psb2_phase2/statement/psb2statement.pdf>.

Ofcom (2010) *International Communications Market Report 2010*, 2nd of December <http://stakeholders.ofcom.org.uk/binaries/research/cmr/753567/icmr/ICMR_2010.pdf>.

OMG-Omnicom (2008) TF1 et M6 Capteront de 40 à 50% des Pubs de France TV <http://Easybourse.com> [accessed on 14th January 2008].

OJD Interactiva (2008) Ranking of Web Companies in Spain.

OJD Interactiva (2010) Ranking of Web Companies in Spain.

O'Neill, O. (2002) Reith Lecture 2002, 'Questions of Trust' <http://www.bbc.co.uk/radio4/reith2002/lectures.shtml> [accessed on 6th June 2008].

Ó Siochrú, S. (2004) 'Social Consequences of Globalization of the Media and Communication Sector: Some Strategic Considerations', Working Paper No. 36, May, Geneva.

O' Siochru, S. and Costanza-Chock, S. (2004) *Global Governance of Information and Communication Technologies: Implications for Transnational Civil Society Networking*. New York: Social Science Research Council Program on Information Technology and International Cooperation.

Padovani, C. (2006) 'Digital Expansion and the Public Service Remit: The Case of the Italian Public Service Broadcaster'. Paper prepared for the Ripe@2006 Conference, Amsterdam and Halverson, Netherlands, 16–18 November.

Peacock, P. (1986) *Financing the BBC, the Peacock Report*, 20th of November.

Peters, J. P. and Desmond S. K. (2005) 'The Politics of Path Dependency: Political Conflict in Historical Institutionalism', *The Journal of Politics* 67 (4): 1275–1300.

Petersen, V. G. (1984) 'The Challenge of New Technology: Impact on the Danish Broadcasting Monopoly', *International Political Science Review* 5 (2): 209.

Petersen, V. G., Prehn, O. and Svendsen & Svendsen (1992) Breaking 60 years of broadcasting monopoly. In Jankowski et al. (eds), *The People's Voice*. London: John Libbey & Comp. Ltd, pp. 45–61.

Petros, I. (2007) *Public Television in the Digital Era: Technological Challenges and New Strategies for Europe*. Houndmills, Basingstoke: Palgrave, Macmillan.

Pocock, J. (1930) 'The Ideal of Citizenship since Classical Times', *The Citizenship Debates* 31: 31–41.

Prehn, O. Svendsen. E. N. and Peterson, V. (1992) 'Denmark: Breaking 60 years of Broadcasting Monopoly'. In Jankowsky, Prehn & Stappers (eds), *The People's Voice: Local Radio and Television in Europe*. London: John Libbey.

Prisa (2010) *Cuatro and Telecinco Will Merge their Operations: Telecinco Will Buy a 22% Stake of Digital+ to Sogecable*. Press release, 18th of December.

Prosser, T. (2005) *The Limits of Competition Law: Markets and Public Services*. Oxford: Oxford University Press.

Protocol on PSB (1997) 'Protocol on the System of Public Broadcasting in the Member States', OJ C 340, 10 November.

Protocol on SGI (2007) 'Protocol on Services of General Interest Annexed to the Treaty of Lisbon', 13th December 2007.

Psychogiopoulou (2006) 'EC State Aid Control and Cultural Justifications', *Legal Issues of Economic Integration* 33 (1): 3–28.

Public Service Contract (2007) 'Public Service Contract between DR and the Danish Minister for Culture' for the period from 1 January 2007–31 December 2010.

Puppis, M. (2008) 'National Media Regulation in the Era of Free Trade: The Role of Global Media Governance', *European Journal of Communication* 23 (4): 405–424.

Raboy, M. (1996) *Public Broadcasting for the 21st Century*. Luton: John Libbey Media/University of Luton Press.

Raboy, M. (2003) 'Media and Democratization in the Information Society'. In S. O. Siochru & B. Girard (eds), Communicating in the Information Society. Geneva: United Nations Research Institute for Social Development, pp. 103–121.

Raboy, M. (2004) 'The World Summit on the Information Society and Its Legacy for Global Governance', *International Communication Gazette* 66 (3–4): 225–232.

Radaelli, C. M. (2000) 'Whither Europeanization? Concept Stretching and Substantive Change', *European Integration Online Papers (EIOP)* 4 (8) <http://eiop.or.at/eiop/texte/2000-008a.htm> [accessed on 19th September 2009].

Radaelli, C. M. (2003) 'The Europeanization of Public Policy'. In K. Featherstone & C. Radaelli (eds), *The Politics of Europeanization*. Oxford: Oxford University Press, pp. 27–56.

Radaelli, C. M. (2004) 'Europeanization: Solution or Problem', *European Integration Online Papers (EIOP)* 16 (8) <http://eiop.or.at/eiop/texte/2004-016a.htm> [accessed on 19th September 2009].

RAI (1997) Service Contract between the Minister of Communications and RAI, 1997–1999.

RAI (2000) Service Contract between the Minister of Communications and RAI, 2000–2002.

RAI (2003) Service Contract between the Minister of Communications and RAI, 2003–2005.

RAI (2007a) Final Draft of the Service Contract between the Minister of Communications and RAI, 2007–2009.

RAI (2007b) Service Contract between the Minister of Communications and RAI, 2007–2009.

Regourd, S. (2008) *Vers la fin de la Télévision Publique?* Toulouse: Editions de l'attribut.

Reich, R. B. (2008) *Supercapitalism: The Transformation of Business, Democracy, and Eeveryday Life*, New York: Knopf.

Reith, J. (1924) *Broadcast over Britain*. London: Hodder and Stoughton.

Reith, J. (1949) *Into the Wind*. London: Hodder and Stoughton.

ReMEC (2009) *Alegaciones al Ateproyecto de Ley General de la Comunicación Audiovisual*. Press release, 11th of August.

Renault, E. (2010) 'Les Députés Ont Adopté l'Amendement Réduisant la Taxe sur les Chaînes Privées à 0,5%', Le Figaro, 2nd of October <http://www.lefigaro.fr/medias/2010/10/22/04002-20101022ARTFIG00506-baisse-de-la-taxe-sur-les-televisions-privees.php> [accessed on 5th October 2010].

Repa, L., Tosics, N. and Dias, P. (2009) 'The 2009 Broadcasting Communication', *Competition Policy Newsletter*, 3-2009.

Ridinger, M. (2009) 'The Public Service Remit and the New Media', *Iris, Legal Observations of the European Audiovisual Observatory*, 6-2009.

Robinson, B., Raven, J. and Low, L. P. (2005) 'Paying for Public Service Television in the Digital Age'. In D. Helm et al. (contr.) *Can the Market Deliver? Funding Public Service Television in the Digital Era*. Eastleigh: John Libbey, pp. 101–128.

Rodriguez-Pardo, J. (2006) 'Facing Challenges through a New Legal Framework for DTT: Towards Are Definition of the Role of TVE in the Spanish Market?'. Paper delivered to the RIPE Conference in Amsterdam, November 2006.

Rosengren, K. E. with Carlsson, M. and Tagerud, Y. (1996) 'Quality in Programming: Views from the North'. In S. Ishikawa (ed.), *Quality Assessment of Television*. Luton: John Libbey Media, pp. 3–48.

RTVE (2000) Informe Anual 2000.

RTVE (2005) Informe Anual 2005.

Sarkozy, N. (2008) Press Conference on the 8th of January at the Palais de l'Elysée <http://www.sarkozynicolas.com/nicolas-sarkozy-conference-de-presse-8-janvier-2008-texte-integral/> [accessed on 1st September 2009].

Scammell M. (2000) 'The Internet and Civic Engagement: The Age of the Citizen Consumer', *Political Communication* 4 (17): 351–355.

Scammell, M. (2005) *Rethinking the Media's Duties to Democracy: Watchdog, Information and Representation* <http://www.media-politics.com/Scammell Media & Democ new version.pdf> [accessed on 19th September 2009].

Scannell, P. (1989) 'Public Service Broadcasting and Modern Public Life', *Media Culture and Society* 11 (2): 135–166.

Scharpf, F. (1999) Governing in Europe: Effective and Democratic? Oxford: Oxford University Press.

Schlosberg, D. (1998) 'Resurrecting the Pluralist Universe', *Political Research Quarterly* September, 51 (3): 583–616.

Schudson, M. (1995) 'Was There Ever a Public Sphere?' In M. Schudson (ed.), *The Power of News*. Boston: Harvard University Press.

Schudson, M. (2003) 'Click Here for Democracy: A History and Critique of an Information-Based Model of Citizenship'. In H. Jenkins, D. Thorburn & B. Seawell (eds), *Democracy and New Media*. Cambridge: MIT Press, pp. 49–60.

Schulz, W. (2008) *Some Suggestions on the Implementation of the Three-Step Test to Make the Remit of Public Service Broadcasters in Germany More Precise*. Berlin: Friedrich-Ebert-Stiftung.

Schumpeter, J. (1942) *Capitalism, Socialism and Democracy*. New York: Harper and Row.

Scriven, M. and Lecomte, M. (1999) *Television Broadcasting in Contemporary France and Britain*. New York: Berghahn Books.

Scirpo, B. (2009) Interview with Bertrand Scirpo, Head of Institutional Relations France Televisions, April 2009.

Selwyn, N. (2002) 'Establishing an Inclusive Society? Technology, Social Exclusion and UK Government Policy Making', *Journal of Social Policy* 31 (1): 1–20.

Sénat (2008) 'Table ronde: quelle reforme pour le secteur de l'audiovisuel?'. Sénat 231.

Sergeant, J. (1999) 'Cable Television'. In M. Scriven & M. Lecomte (eds), *Television Broadcasting in Contemporary France and Britain*, New York: Berghahn Books.

Sergeant, J. (2009) Interview with Jean-Claude Sergeant. Paris, April.

Shamir, J. (2007) 'Quality Assessment of Television Programs in Israel: Can Viewers Recognize Production Value?', *Journal of Applied Communication Research* 35 (3): 320–341.

Siebert, F., Patterson, T. and Schramm, W. (1956) *Four Theories of the Press*. Urbana, IL: Illinois University Press.

Smith, P. and Steemers, J. (2007) 'BBC to the Rescue! Digital Switchover and the Reinvention of Public Service Broadcasting in Britain', *Javnost The Public* 14 (1): 39–56.

Søndergaard, H. (1996) 'Fundamentals in the History of Danish Television'. In I. Bondebjerg & F. Bono (eds), *Television in Scandinavia. History, Politics and Aesthetics*. Luton: John Libbey Media.

Søndergaard, H. (2009) Interview with Henrik Sondergaard, Copenhagen, March.

Souloumiac, L. (2002) Interview with Laurent Souloumiac, *Le Journal du Net*, 21st June.

Spanish Telecommunication Law (2009) Act 7/2009 on urgent reforms in the telecommunications sector, 3rd of July.

Spanish TV Law (1980) Act 4/1980 on statute of radio and television, 10th of January.

Spanish TV Law (2006) Act 17/2006 on radio and television entitled to the State, 5th of June.

Spanish TV law (2009) Act 8/2009 on the financing of RTVE, 1st of September.

Spanish TV Law (2010) Act 7/2010 on General Law of Audiovisual Communications, 31st of March.

Steemers, J. (1999) 'Between Culture and Commerce – The Problem of Redefining Public Service Broadcasting for the Digital Age'. *Convergence: The Journal of Research into New Media Technologies* 5 (3): 44–67.

Stewart, D. W. and Kamins, M. A. (1993) Secondary Research. London: Sage.

Storsul, T. and Syvertsen, T. (2007) 'The Impact of Convergence on European Television Policy', *Convergence: The International Journal of Research into New Media Technologies* 13 (3): 275–291.

Sustein, C. (2007) *Republic.com 2.0*, Princeton, NJ: Princeton University Press.

Svendsen, E. N. (2002) 'The Regulation of Public Service Broadcasting, an EPRA Inquiry'. Paper presented at 16th EPRA meeting, Ljubljana, 24–25 October.

Svendsen, E. N. (2009) Interview with, Erik Nordahl Svendsen, Bibliotek Og medier, Copenhagen, March.

Svendsen, E. N. (2010) Interview with, Erik Nordahl Svendsen, Bibliotek Og medier, London, November.

Svendsen, E. N. (2011) 'Two steps towards a public value test: Danish public service broadcasting between two lines of control'. In K. Donders & H. Moe (eds), *Exporting the public value test: the regulation of public broadcasters' new media services across europe*. Nordicom, Göteborgs universitet, Göteborg, pp. 117–125.

Syvertsen, T. (2003) 'Challenges to Public Television in the Era of Convergence and Commercialization', *Television and New Media* 4 (2): 135–175.

Tambini, D. and Cowling, J. (2004) *From Public Service Broadcasting to Public Service Communications*, London: Institute for Public Policy Research, 2003.

Telecinco (2010) *Telecinco incrementa un 101% su beneficio neto del primer trimestre con 58,86 millones de euros*. Press relsease, 6th of May.

Thomson, C. (2006) *Speech at Oxford Media Convention, 19th of January* <http://webcast.oii.ox.ac.uk/?view=Webcast&ID=20060119_118 [accessed on 19th September 2009].

Thompson, M. (2008) The Trouble With Trust: Building Confidence In Institutions. Speech given at QEII Centre, London Tuesday 15 January 2008.

Tocqueville, A. (2003) *Democracy in America*. London: Penguin Books.

Tosic, N., Van De Ven, R. and Riedl, A. (2008) 'Funding of Public Service Broadcasting and State Aid Rules – Two Recent Cases in Belgium and Ireland', *Competition Policy Newsletter* 3.

Tracey, M. (1998) *Decline and Fall of Public Service Broadcasting*. New York: Oxford University Press.

Treaty of Lisbon (2007) Treaty of Lisbon Amending the Treaty on European Union and the Treaty Establishing the European Community, signed at Lisbon, 13th of December.

Tufte, B. and Tufte, T. (1996) 'Parental Control of Broadcasting, Film, Audiovisual and On-Line Services in Denmark'. In *Report Parental Control of Broadcasting, Film, Audiovisual and On-Line Services in the European Union*. Denmark: Country Report <http://www.nordicom.gu.se/common/publ_pdf/37_tufte&tufte.pdf>.

Turner, B. (1990) 'Outline of a Theory of Citizenship', *Sociology* 24: 189–217.

Turner, B. (1997) 'Citizenship Studies: A General Theory', *Citizenship Studies* 1 (1): 5–17.

Turner, B. (2001) 'The Erosion of Citizenship', *British Journal of Sociology* 2 (52): 189–209.

TV Law 2009 (2009) Loi No 2009-258 du 5 Mars 2009 Relative à la Communication Audiovisuelle et au Nouveau Service Public de la Télévision, March 5th 2009.

Uteca (2009) Speech of the President of Uteca, Alejandro Echevarría <http://www.uteca.com/uteca_contenidos/documentos/DISCURSO_ALECHU_2009.doc> [accessed on 10th January 2010].

Valentiner, C. (2009) Interview with Christian Valentiner, Copenhagen, March.

Van Cuilenburg, J. and McQuail (2003) 'Towards a New Communications Policy ParadigmD', *European Journal of Communication* 18 (2): 181–207.

Vaughan, L. and Thelwall, M. (2004) 'Search Engine Coverage Bias: Evidence and Possible Causes', *Information Processing & Management* 40 (4): 693–707.

Vedel, T. (2005) 'France', In *Open Society Institute – EU Monitoring and Advocacy Program, TV across Europe: Regulation, Policies and Independence.* Budapest: Open Society Institute.

Venturelli, S. (1998) *Liberalizing European Media Politics, Regulation and the Public Sphere.* Oxford: Oxford University Press.

Ward, D. (2006) 'Can the Market Provide? Public Service Media Market Failure and Public Goods'. In C. S. Nissen (ed.), *Making a Difference: Public Service Broadcasting in the European Media Landscape.* Eastleigh: John Libbey Publishing, pp. 51–63.

Westman-Herz, K. (2009) Interview with Karen Westman Herz, Former Head of DR Online, Copenhagen, March.

Widermann, V. (2004) 'Public Service Broadcasting, State Aid and the Internet: Emerging EU Law', *Diffusion Online* 47.

Williams, R. (1981) 'Communication Technologies and Social Institutions'. In R. Williams (ed.), *Contact: Human Communication and its History.* London: Thames & Hudson.

Williams, R. (1974) *Television: Technology and Cultural Form.* London: Fontana.

Williams, R. (1985) *Towards 2000.* Harmondsworth: Penguin.

World Economic Forum (2009) 'Global Information Technology Report 2008–2009', 26th of March.

World Summit on the Information Society (2003a) *Geneva Declaration on Principle* <http://www.itu.int/wsis/docs/geneva/official/dop.html> [accessed on 5th April 2008].

World Summit on the Information Society (2003b) *Plan of Action.* Document, WSIS-03/GENEVA/DOC/5-E <http://www.itu.int/wsis/docs/geneva/official/poa.html> [accessed on 5th April 2008].

Zela, M. (2009) Interview with Marco Zela, Rai Educational, 5th June 2009.

Index